WHO
MADE
CAPTAIN
JAMES
COOK?

(1728 - 1771)

Jean Eccleston asks the question.

First published 2018

An imprint of Moorleys Print & Publishing
23 Park Road, Ilkeston, DE7 5DA
www.moorleys.co.uk

ISBN 978-0-86071-765-2

CONTENTS

PART I TO BE A SAILOR

PART II EXPANDING WORLD

PART III ENDEAVOUR VOYAGE 1768-1771

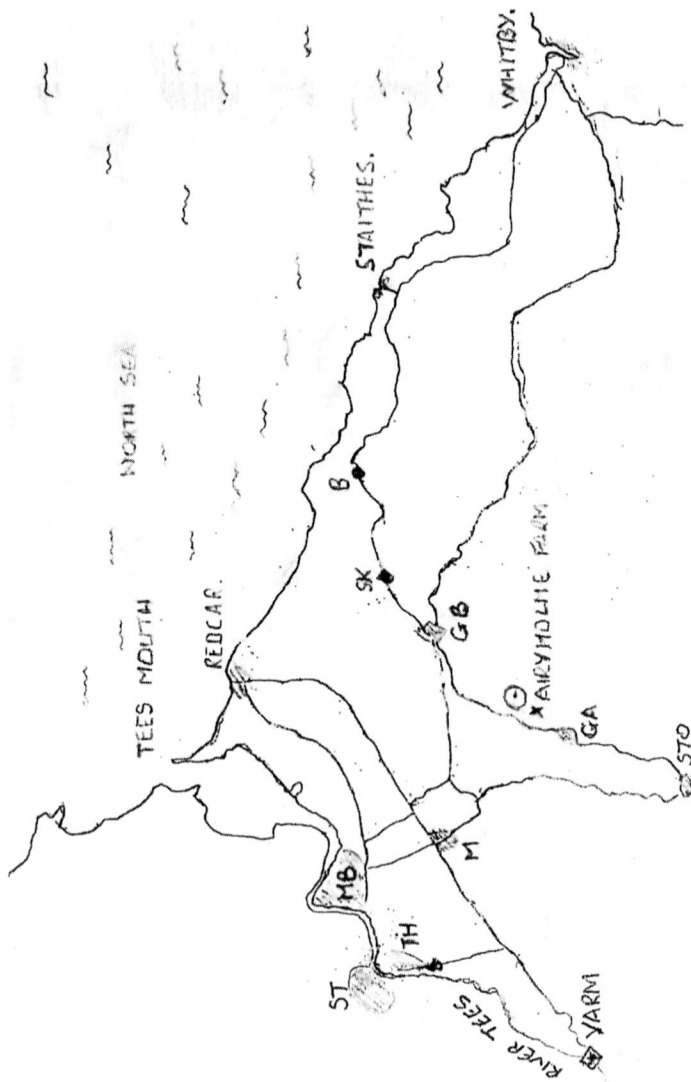

B Brotton GA Great Ayton GB Guisborough M Marton MB Middlesbrough
SK Skelton ST Stockton STO Stokesley T Thornaby ⊖ Roseberry Topping

iii

WARD AND JACKSON FAMILY TREES.

(simple version)

William Ward, dyer of Guisborough   m   Mary Reed.

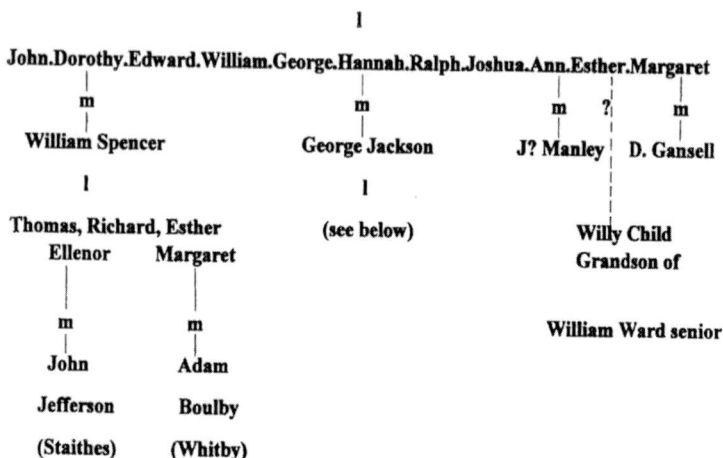

|

John.Dorothy.Edward.William.George.Hannah.Ralph.Joshua.Ann.Esther.Margaret

m	m	m	?	m
William Spencer	**George Jackson**	**J? Manley**		**D. Gansell**
Thomas, Richard, Esther	**(see below)**		**Willy Child**	
Ellenor Margaret			**Grandson of**	
m m			**William Ward senior**	
John Adam				
Jefferson Boulby				
(Staithes) (Whitby)				

Hannah and George Jackson

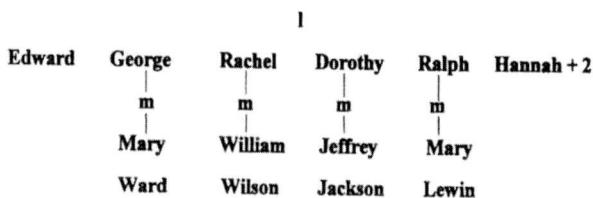

|

Edward	**George**	**Rachel**	**Dorothy**	**Ralph**	**Hannah + 2**
	m	m	m	m	
	Mary	**William**	**Jeffrey**	**Mary**	
	Ward	**Wilson**	**Jackson**	**Lewin**	

PART I

TO BE A SAILOR

1

WHO WAS HE?

Captain James Cook is rightly famous. In three great ocean voyages, he filled in the map of one third of the globe. Fame came to him late. It was only in the last ten years of his life, he was given the chance to excel.

Ten years of discoveries, which exploded in the minds of Europe, have obscured his early years, and the people who knew him. Those who set him on the path to fame, lie in the churchyards of England, near forgotten. The whole truth about him has not been told.

James Cook was born a Yorkshire farmboy. At 14 he worked for a grocer in the fishing village of Staithes, before going to sea in the Whitby coal trade. At age 26, with the coming of war, and the press gangs fearfully active, he volunteered for the Royal Navy, rising to be master of a modest surveying ship after the peace. He was nearly 40, not even an officer, when he was chosen to take the 368 ton *Endeavour*, on a great voyage around the world.

The main question about him has never been answered. Why was he chosen? In an age of rampant patronage, when the Royal Navy placed men on ships by personal favour, can we say, truly, he was a self-made man?

The answer lies in the Cleveland district of north Yorkshire, in the circles of his youth, and an influential family, who appear to have shaped him and promoted him from boyhood, and helped to appoint him to the *Endeavour.* How does a farm boy become a great man, without being helped a little?

Captain Cook was born in the village of Marton in Cleveland, under the pale sky of farmland south of the River Tees, in 1728.

To step back to that time, we need a leap of imagination, an eye for colour, and a deep forgetfulness. Forget, for instance, nine out of ten people. The population of England was just over 5 millions, thinly spread in a quiet green landscape. Forget our big northern towns, they did not exist, Middlesbrough was a muddy village of just twenty families.

Picture instead, a river. A flat unspoilt green valley where the grey River Tees winds to the sea. John Price, a joiner James Cook would know, is floating a raft of timber downriver on the current. The tide is out, he eases it past sloping mudbanks, by silvery willow, and salty flood meadows tufted with pinks. The quiet is broken only by birds. The tide turns, he anchors the raft on a sandbank, giving way to small flapping sloops, with tan sails, and two-man crews, calling out to him, as they pass upriver on the incoming tide, to the market town of Yarm. James Cook is a child raised among landsmen, who use the River Tees to move corn and butter, timber and sheep.

The joiner, John Price[1], knows nearly every tree on the farms of Cleveland. He fells them for buildings, for furniture and coffins. He values them for the heirs when the owners die. He bends saplings, to grow into shapes to build ships. He is a family man. His son is apprenticed to a boat-builder at Staithes, a job which may have been arranged by Mr. Ralph Ward, the landlord of John Price's farm at Yarm. And now meet the man who links together, those who promoted Captain Cook. It is the same, Mr. Ralph Ward, a shrewd old bachelor living in Guisborough.

3

South of the Tees, the old market town of Guisborough lies in an elegant bowl of farmland, held between two pleasant hills and the high, dark ridge of the North York Moors. At one end of the town's long puddled street, is a market cross, a parish church and an ancient ruined priory, emptily framing a changing blue sky. White clouds race by. The ruins enhance the formal gardens of the mansion house of Sir William Chalenor. Its fountains and forecourt lie gravelled and quiet; the family are away.

Next door, the Cock Inn is busy, the blacksmith Alex Pulman is attending a horse, the Court is in session and the stables are full. Dining at the Cock Inn is a circle of older men, who will put James Cook forward in life, to the point he is capable of fame. Two are Justices of the Peace: Squire Thomas Skottowe of Great Ayton, the employer of James Cook's father, and Mr. Ralph Ward, whose business links, friends, and large family circle, provide the true background of the future Captain Cook's career.

Mr. Ward is of the same generation as James Cook's parents. He is in a position to help their son from the beginning. If he chooses to. He is austere, financially tough, at times cantankerous, but can be merry with his gaggle of old friends, generous to the young and, in old age, will give his sister £15, in a testy way, her over-spending irritates him. He is the solid central figure, in his widely-scattered but large affectionate family, a family with influence in the Army, the Royal Navy, Parliament, the coal trade, the East India Company.

By observing Mr. Ward, and three of his nephews, the track of Captain Cook's early life comes clear.

So, let us meet these real people.

~~~

RALPH WARD Gentleman
1680 - 1759

Looking back, we see Mr. Ralph Ward as a gentleman who could have lived off his rents. It may not have occurred to him. He worked to the end of his life.

Apart from property in Guisborough, he was a managing partner in Boulby Alum Works, on the cliffs above Staithes. He owned Old Boulby farm, Loftus Grainge farm, houses in Yarm, more farms and land along the Tees valley. He had a lease on a Durham colliery, and shares in seven old ships working out of Whitby and nine more sailing out of Scarborough. He lent money at interest, acting as a banker, for there were no local banks. As a Justice of the Peace, he heard court cases with Squire Thomas Skottowe. The two men knew each other for years. By the age of 8, the future Captain Cook had moved to live under their influence.

In those days, it was known as acceptable patronage, a form of private charity. Money was crucial. Boys took their chance when it came to education. Progress was stopped by lack of it. For daily life did not include equality, or fairness, or health. It included an appalling death rate of children, surges of disease like diphtheria, or smallpox. People weighed adventure against the high risk of their life at home. All the adults we will meet, including James Cook, were already the lucky survivors.

How nice that Mr. Ward kept a diary. It begins in 1754, when he was 74. He records his daily transactions, notes his appointments, the weather, his crops. He gives pet names such as Looby and Fox, to his prize oxen at Loftus Grainge farm. And he enters his frequent journeys down the coast to Boulby and Staithes. For at Staithes lived his niece Elinnor, married to a rich ship-owner called John Jefferson, and there Mr. Ward was always welcome. Elinnor was sharp, her husband was jolly, Mr. Ward was amusing and combative. They gossiped, they laughed, they played cards, all to a tune on the fiddle.

Dignified Mr. Ward, had been the 6th child in a family of 12. He remained living in his mother's house at Guisborough, and acted as trustee for the Ward family money. There had been long-ago-but-not-forgotten family scandal. His eldest brother was a bankrupt disgraced Member of Parliament. Mr. Ward had proved a wily opponent; the family money was safe. Their patronage was ready by 1740, to help the next generation.

Mr. Ralph Ward had dozens of nieces and nephews. One worked at a high level for the Royal Navy, one had taken his ship by a new route into the Pacific, and the youngest, Ralph Jackson, of whom we can grow quite fond, was an alert but bashful boy, who kept a lifetime of diaries. He sewed some of their pages together himself.

RALPH JACKSON, Gentleman
1736/7 - 1791

Mr. Ward's boyish nephew, Ralph Jackson, grew up to be an earnest, kind-hearted young man, with a sense of propriety which kept him out of trouble. He suffered from a delight in gadgets, making a spike for the office bills, and searching out whalebone busks for his sisters' corsets. His brother George gave him a perambulating wheel to measure miles, and Mr. Allen, a neighbour, gave him a German flute, an early type of clarinet with one key, on which Ralph learned to play sonatas; he was always musical.

He went greyhound coursing, with his two dogs called Cato and Bean; he had a spaniel called Sankoe, and showed the same interest in horses as today's young men do in cars.

'Saturday 12th March, 1757. I set forward early upon
the great horse, called by some Rumbermash, to Boulby.'
Rumbermash seems to have had exhaust trouble.

The unmarried Ralph Ward decided to make this youngest nephew his heir. So he sent him, at the age of 13, to be bound an apprentice to Mr. William Jefferson, a wealthy coal 'fitter' of the city of Newcastle upon Tyne. Ralph Jackson was trained up to be a gentleman, a hard-headed businessman, a Hoastman of the Tyne, a man of influence and sophistication, who could take his solemn place among the leading men of the north.

Despite that, young Ralph's shy liveliness breaks through.

Aged 15 in Newcastle he writes happily:

'At night I went to the Play of King Richard the 3rd &
the farce was Trick upon Trick or the Vinter in the suds.'

Ralph Jackson's diaries begin in 1749 when his father Mr. George Jackson of Richmond, took him to Newcastle to start work. On Thursday 16th November, 1749, aged 13, he writes:

'Got bound apprentice at Peacock's. My Father, Master, Cousin Jefferson, John Campion [both of Staithes], Mr. Simpson and Mr. French being present.' Mr. Simpson had been his master's master in the Hoastmen Company of Newcastle freemen. Ralph was bound to his own Master, William Jefferson, for seven years. The new apprentice had to keep accounts of his pocket money, and the first volume ends delightfully with his father arriving, inspecting them, and deliberately losing at cards to put his son back in funds.

Through young Ralph Jackson's eyes we see the Whitby ships arriving for Tyne coal, meet their captains, learn their loading routines, tonnages, insurance and risks, during the very years James Cook was a seaman in the same Tyne trade. A coal 'fitter' arranged the buying of coal from the collieries and the loading of collier ships. James Cook's shipmaster, John Walker of Whitby, sometimes loaded with William Jefferson; in July 1753, Ralph was working to load Walker's ship *Freelove.*

On 26th December, 1756 when nearly 21, Ralph Jackson's apprenticeship was complete, and he came to live at Guisborough with his old Uncle Ralph Ward. Through their words we meet the real people James Cook knew. We see them at work, making business deals, playing card games, dining out, gardening, arguing, sea bathing, going to the races.

Years later, on the afternoon of 26th December 1771, Ralph then aged 35, writes that he was at his sister's house at Great Ayton, to meet Captain James Cook and his wife. Captain Cook had returned from his first circular voyage on the *Endeavour,* and was preparing to join the bark *Resolution* on a second great voyage around the world. While intrigued and impressed, Ralph does not detail what they talked of that day. Surely, there was just one topic?

In the family and connections of Ralph Jackson, and his Guisborough uncle Ralph Ward, lies the answer to the question: Why was James Cook chosen to command the *Endeavour*? The truth appears to be, they were perfectly placed to influence the choice. He was one of a number of men their patronage placed on *Endeavour.* And they had helped him since boyhood.

Patronage happened at all levels. Family groups promoted their own. James Cook's family not being related, had to be useful, reliable, of good character. And Mr. Ward would certainly know. In Cleveland family pedigrees are part of conversation.

2

FAMILY CIRCLES

The Parish Registers of Stainton in Cleveland, which contain Captain Cook's family, are like old memories, faded, blotched and blurred. By a piece of luck, most entries for his family are clean and neat.

> '1695. Dec. the 29th then married together
> John Pace & Deborah Butler

Captain Cook's grandparents, his mother's family, lived at Thornaby on Tees, in an open landscape of wide skies, rolling fields, scattered farms. Thornaby village was a tiny street of a few houses, with a long narrow green, and a 600 year old chapel. By ancient custom, a service was held there two Sunday afternoons a month, by the curate of the central parish church at Stainton. The whole parish, of five villages, was longsettled farmland where families intermarried.

Thornaby families were noted for producing twins, the wider parish even records triplets twice –'as God can do,' the amazed vicar wrote in the register. The Butlers were linked to this genetic trait. Deborah Butler was born in 1671, and Elizabeth Butler, or Mary, may have been her twin.

Elizabeth Butler married Thomas Harrison of Thornaby in 1693, producing twins, Thomas and John, born in 1697. Mary Butler was married the same week as Deborah, to an Edward Bainbridge also of

Thornaby, her sons also being Thomas and John but not twins. The name Pace does not appear in the parish registers until 1695. Deborah had not married a local man, and her daughter Grace would do the same.

James Cook's grandparents, John and Deborah Pace, produced their first set of twins, Thomas and John, for baptism on 5th June 1698. Sadly, baby John died. Two years later Deborah Pace had twin girls, Mary and Martha, baptised in 1701. Grace was born in 1702. Deborah appears in 1705. They were living in a part of the parish alongside the river.

Living at Thornaby, meant living with and on the river.

Thornaby village lay by the straight dirt road, which led to the horse-ferry to cross the river Tees, to Stockton. The first bridge was then miles upstream at Yarm. The slow tidal river curved around Thornaby, and looped back* upon itself. It was full of sand islands called batts. Ships sailed tediously around the loops upriver to Yarm port, the clean water was full of salmon. There were fish and eel traps staked out along the river banks, and the land on the bends was dyked to control flooding; the riverside marshy fields, called falls - which means crumbling - went underwater in winter. Working on the river was part of Thornaby life. The curate at Stainton received salmon from Thornaby, as part of his salary. The pulse of trade and tidal flow of the river was a living, or a route in and out, for many.

The loops of the river were later straightened by a cut.

~~~

CAPTAIN COOK'S PARENTS

In 1725 at the age of 23 Grace Pace married a Scotsman, aged 30, the ceremony, at Stainton parish church on its small hill, probably in the early morning, with two witnesses the only congregation, as was the custom then.

'Dec.10th marryed together James Cook and Grace Pace'.

This marriage of James Cook's parents makes us curious. Why did she not follow her sisters, and marry a local man? How did she meet a Scot? Why did he come south to England?

Captain Cook's father, James Cook, came from Ednam, near Kelso, just over Scotland's border with Northumberland, in the deeply agricultural valley of the River Tweed. There were still people alive who had known Captain Cook's father when, in 1817, the Rev. George Young wrote the following in his popular *History of Whitby*:

'His father, whose name was also James,

and is supposed from his dialect to have been

a Northumbrian, was a day-labourer, employed

chiefly by Mr. Mewburn, a farmer at Marton.'

James Cook senior was baptised in the church at Ednam on 4th March 1694, son of John and Jean Cook, a couple of modest means, who had more children born elsewhere, as they moved on.

The speech at Ednam today, is more Scots than Northumbrian. Their son James' speech may show that he was raised south of the border. Northumbrian is a soft, lilting dialect. Rs are pronounced as Ws, with an intake of breath, Berwick-on-Tweed for instance, Cwaster kipperws. He probably called his wife Gwace.

It is possible that Captain Cook's own voice ranged widely, from a soft lilt learned from his father, to a necessary bellow through a master's speaking trumpet on deck, the range of an actor with a quiet fall-back position giving an impression of rectitude; he is described that way.

Why did Captain Cook's father, travel down to England?

Were the Cook family respectable cattle drovers?

By the 1700s, the ancient Roman road out of Scotland, called Watling Street, formed part of a system of green tracks, one of which ran near Ednam. Down these drove roads, cattle were driven south into England. Some were destined for Cleveland as cattle to be fattened, many walked on to London to feed that expanding city. Sheep can be ferried across a river, but there were only two ways to bring large numbers of cattle across the river Tees into Cleveland. There was the narrow bridge at Yarm, or the swim at low tide across the sandbanks and channels between Stockton and Middlesbrough. Either way could put the waiting animals into the farmland of Thornaby and Stainton.

If Captain Cook's father was a young cattle drover, it is easy to see how he met a Thornaby/Stainton girl. Animals walked, and slowly, there would be time for romance.

In 1817, people remembered that Captain Cook's father had worked at Marton, chiefly for a Mr. Mewburn. There were many people called Mewburn scattered through the villages south of the Tees. One set of Mewburns were cattle dealers; their connections were spread as far as London, moving cattle long distances along the drove roads. If the Cook family were cattle drovers, it is possible that Mr. Cook had been known by the Mewburns for years.

After their marriage in 1725 the Scotland born James Cook, and his new wife, Grace, started their life together on a farm at Morton, a flat, reedy part of the parish of Ormesby, overlooked from the south by the switchback Cleveland Hills, the ridge dominated by the height of Roseberry Topping. The three farms at Morton were fertile, set on the last dry arable fields before the soggy flat land, called carrs. Cut by large ditches called stells, the carrs and stells drained into the river Leven.

The big river Tees flows thickly tidally east, its valley is shallow, open and wide. To the south, the thin little river Leven flows west, through an orderly flat landscape, of sheep in pastures and quiet fields with trim thickset hedges. Yellow rapeseed, blue flax, blunt golden corn, turnips, follow the seasons.

The innocent river Leven flows gently west without momentum, to join the tidal Tees upstream, near Yarm. But when it rains too much in the high moors above the Cleveland hills, hiccupping streams pour on the flat valley floor, the swelling little Leven backs-up to flood the fields and the villages like Great Ayton. Generations of farmers have drained it, dug stells, cursed and prayed. The endless back-breaking task of farm labourers on the Leven valley floor was to cut and clear the stells, and one way was to pole a punt boat along the narrow water. There were eels and small fish to be got in the stells, and rheumatism, and skill on water. It is near certain Mr. Cook would be adept at handling a boat.

There is an uncanny thing about Morton-in-Ormesby. It is almost an identical landscape to Ednam, Mr. Cook's birthplace. There is the same flat valley, the same line of switchback hills, the same landscape of fields, farms and river. Is that why he, a traveling man, stayed put?

Mr and Mrs Cook's first son, John, was baptised at Ormesby, on 10th January 1726/7. They soon moved to Marton, the next parish to the west where, on 27th October 1728 James the future Captain Cook was born, and baptised as the son of a 'day labourer'. By the Old Calendar, the new year began in March so John was baptised in modern style 1727, and there were less than two years between him and James.

Who did the Cooks work for at Ormesby? There is one entry in the local Pennyman accounts for him, but that may have been for the statutory days, for which all landowners had to provide men to mend the roads. The Pennymans owned Ormesby Hall.

Why did the Cooks move on to Marton? We do not know.
But we are allowed to speculate.
A clue may lie in the names they chose for their children. While

John and James were named in Scottish tradition - after grandfathers and father - the other children were not given family names. Their third child was not christened in Marton, as we might expect, but at Ormesby, on Sunday 31st January 1731 and named Christiana.

There is only one other girl named Christian in the Ormesby parish register, and she too was christened on 31st January, but in 1724. Thomas Scarfe, a farmer, had three daughters born at Ormesby: Christian, Dinah, Mary. Two sons followed, born at Marton, Thomas in 1728 and William in 1730. Two younger girls, Jane in 1732 and Lettice were again christened at Ormesby, implying the Scarfes had moved back there. Mr. Cook and his wife Grace gave their girls the same names in the same order: Christia[ah] being Christian and Dinah combined, then Mary, then Jane. The little Scarfe girls were 7, 6 or 9 when their namesake Cook baby girls were bom. They even shared similar birth months.

The arrangement of names reeks of affection, for another family, and it is possible Grace Cook was their nurse. Even in 1744, when William Scarfe was 14, Mrs. Cook called her last baby William.

The birthplaces of the children, both Cooks and Scarfes, match so well, we must ask was Thomas Scarfe the Cooks' employer? Did they move with him from Ormesby, to Marton for three years, and back to Ormesby? Farm leases were usually for 21 years, with a three year get-out clause. Three years gave young farmers the chance to build credibility to buy a longer lease. Mr. Ward often lent money for leases, to farmers he approved of. Did Thomas Scarfe take only a three-year lease at Marton? It looks like it. Both families had moved back to Ormesby by 1731.

Thomas Scarfe was a tenant farmer. On 16th Nov. 1722, the owner of his Ormesby farm had mortgaged it, showing the rent as £64-2-6d a year, a medium sized farm. By 1727, when the security was assigned, Thomas Scarfe's name does not appear on the deeds, his family had moved to Marton, but just for the three years during which James Cook was born. Did the Cooks then move back with the

Scarfes to Ormesby, only to help establish them there? This would account for Christiana's birth there. Thomas Scarfe's new farm had to support one growing family, not two. The Cooks had returned to Marton when their fourth child Mary was born in 1733.

~~~

Marton village lay on the first slope up from the river Tees flood plain. From their humble cottage they looked north, across the damp flat Tees valley with its tidal river, the flicker of passing sailing ships, the horizon a low dull ridge. The Tees valley was bleak in winter, hazy in summer. On a calm day, grey mist rolled up the valley from the sea. Marton on the hill stood above the dampness above the marshes which brought malaria from a fresh water mosquito, better for the children, not to get the 'ague'. Even so, the cottages were clay and thatched 'biggins' with tiny windows, and mud floors; though a good mud floor is not sticky, it can be smooth like concrete, it depends what is mixed with the mud. Thankfully, farming people live mostly outside.

We can imagine the two small boys, John and James playing in the fields, gleaning corn at harvest, helping to herd the cows. The drove cattle were Galloways, dark, hairy, lumbering, docile, not likely to bolt off. The local cows were shorthorns, not at that date developed by Mr. Culley's breeding methods, their horns sometimes bad tempered. Sheep were scraggy in modern terms, the corn very tall, stooked, the children played stooked finger games, 'Here is the church, here is the steeple, open the door and see the people ... .' and at the end of Haymaking, after everyone's hard work raking and drying by laycock, hipple, haycock, the master performed a mock 'Trial' in the field, before the last load was taken to the stack, followed by beer and fun. Mr. Ward always performed this country play himself in his fields at Guisborough.

As a day labourer, Mr. Cook was paid by the day, not by the job but, with a good master, it could be regular and secure for a hard worker, and family man. The pay was about 6 old pence a day which, with winter lay-off, would amount to about £6 a year. Winter was difficult. Good parishes helped, by ordering work on the roads. Good landlords employed men ditching and repairing buildings. Mr. Cook's father had worked as a mason and, as years later he built his own cottage, Mr. Cook may have stayed in work in winter as a builder.

The only map which could indicate the farms at Marton, is a copy of Thomas Foster's map of 1764. It shows George Mewburn's farm of 197 acres as a long block of land, between the drive up to the present Captain Cook Museum and the railway, it ran south, along the stream, to end at Gunnergate/Gipsy Lane. A farm mostly of pasture and meadow, approx. 28% arable, it included three extra fields on the Prissick Hall side.

Mr. William Walker's, long, narrow, 186 acre farm, shows up as all the fields edging the west of Marton Road toward Cargo Fleet. Run your eye north over two miles from Gunnergate Lane, and you are still on Walker's land (interrupted only by the village). With two more fields on the University Hospital site, it too was about 23% arable.

It seems that these were both livestock farms. Another indicator that James Cook senior was a cattle man.

Marton village, where the Walkers lived near the church, served a large parish of tenanted farms. There were farm hands, weavers, a blacksmith with an apprentice, the bricklayer James Easton, the cooper John Lindsey. Some, like Robert Corps, were sailors. Between 1727 and 1733, Marton parish register shows:

1728 Wm. Anderson, Mariner, married Barbara Foster both of the parish.

1729 Lan[celot] Boys of Whitby married Jane Davison.

1733 Lancelot, son of Jane Boys widow was baptised 'husband drowned in the sea'.

1733 Geo.Masterman of Monkwearmouth
(Sunderland), Master Mariner, married Ann
Snowdon of the parish of Marton.

The crews of North Sea ships came from villages spread far inland throughout Cleveland. We can see it in the ships' muster rolls. Imagine two small boys John and James Cook, with their stick boats on the village pond, laughing and splashing, and a passing sailor saying 'Hoy! She'll sink that way. Bring her up into the wind.' As farm boys they had to learn to load boats. Riding sleds pulled by oxen, their father and his workmates, slid across the soggy flood meadows to the wooden jetties along the river Tees, to load boats with butter, cheese and hams, taking sacks of seed corn or coal back to the farms. Carts were only used where the dirt lanes improved. There were very few roads in Cleveland,

Marton had a tenant farmer called Thomas Dale, whose son James, born in 1725, later became a shipmate of young James Cook in the Whitby coal trade, sailing together in John Walker's ships. In 1764, the Dales ran the second largest farm.

Marton Farm, was occupied by the affluent farmer William Walker, and it is claimed his wife Mary taught the future Captain James Cook to read. Most women could not read. Most labourers could not read. Unless the small boy James Cook learned to read, he could be a labourer, like his father, and make little progress.

We know very little about Mrs Walker. Do we accept the family story of Thomas Walker Ord as she was his great-great-great grandmother? He was rather irritated by the local tale that she was a poor schoolmistress. In his *History of Cleveland* in 1846, he points out that she was the daughter of the wealthiest farmer in the neighbourhood, Mr. Dunn of Seamor. If so, she was a distant relative of Mr. Ralph Ward of Guisborough, who wrote in his journal that his Cousin Martin Dunn of Seamor owned Hargill coal pit. Not poor herself, she married the prosperous William Walker in 1725.

The words 'a poor schoolmistress' can be explained. There was another Mrs. Mary Walker at Marton. In 1722, Thomas Walker a taylor of Marton, married Mary Bent, spinster and schoolmistress. Has there been a muddle? Has someone grabbed the fame? There were still people alive in 1846 who knew the Cook family, but truth can slide. There was no school at Marton. Even as late as 1743 the Archbishop's visitation says there was only one old widow woman who taught reading to the poor children, and this cannot refer to Mrs. William Walker, who in 1743 was not a widow.

If we believe Ord's family tradition then, when she taught James Cook to read, William Walker's wife Mary was about 34, and may have included him in her lessons to her own children. Mrs. Walker's son William who was one year younger than James was probably a childhood playmate.*

It was the rule for a farmer's wife to teach her children to read, before they went to school at around age 8. Mrs. Walker may have included James as an act of kindness. Maybe his mother Grace was working at their farm? As a day labourer, his father may have worked both for the Mewburns and the Walkers, especially at harvest time

During the time the Cook family lived at Marton, things were uncertain about a large part of the parish, as owned by the estate of

*Real people in history do not disappear; they go on living their own lives. So, years later on 6th March 1755, four months before James Cook entered the Royal Navy, Mr. Ralph Ward 'Called at Marton to see William Walker's stoned horse'; he means a stallion, fully equipped. He writes that the following May 2nd William White, his steward from Loftus Grainge farm, brought the Chaloner mare to go to Mr. Walker's horse at Marton. The stallion was called 'Baboon'. Alex Pulman, the blacksmith, took the mare there 'to be leaped by him'. And on 17th Jack Arrowsmith came from Boulby taking one of the mares bought of Mr. Ward to Marton 'to get her horst with Mr. Walker's Babboon & returned same day with effect.' A good horse was vital to the rural economy, like a good vehicle now.

a Sir James Lowther. There were changes in its ownership, which might not affect the Walkers, but could make a day labourer worry about the future, and where they could live. With growing children to feed, where could the Cook family go? It turned out to be Airyholme, a farm high on the shoulder of Roseberry Topping, overlooking Morton-in-Ormesby. Again, not far, and a place where the Cook family were known.

This time, it was a promotion. James Cook's father moved his family to Airyholme farm, to become Hind in the service of Thomas Skottowe, the squire of Great Ayton. Local records make clear: at that time in Cleveland, the word 'farmer' was used for a tenant with a lease, and the word 'hind' for a steward of a farm not tenanted, but managed directly for the owner. So the Cook family moved hopefully to Airyholme as John and James reached the age for a proper school. Entry into a farm was usually in the spring. If there was any delay, the neighbours turned up to help to plough. Delays were dangerous. In a bad year for corn for bread flour, high prices meant the poorest people starved, and rioted.

Grace Cook had lived at Thomaby by the river, then near the marshy land at Morton, then at Marton on a slope of fine pasture, now she was to take her family to an even healthier place. Everyone knew that the higher into the moors, the less 'ague' they suffered.

A local doctor wrote, in 1762: 'The inhabitants of the dales or high valleys in Cleveland are little subject to intermittents [fevers] the exhalations from black peat mosses are not productive of intermittents, at least in the high moors, under a clear sharp air.' He means the fresh water mosquito could not breed.[1]

Unfortunately James' little sister Mary would die aged 5, new baby Mary died too, little Jane also died age 5, William died age 3. Gibbon the historian noted, that only one in nine babies survived. In moving to Airyholme, the Cook family could have hoped for better things. Yet the move showed Mr. Cook's determination to prosper.

3

SCHOOLBOY

Captain Cook's next boyhood home Airyholme Farm, is a place of far horizons. It sits high on the shoulder of Roseberry Topping, nowadays it is a conical hill rising sharply on the Cleveland escarpment, in James Cook's day it was more rounded; it fell in later due to mining. But Airyholme farm is much the same today, stone barns and the bleating of sheep. Arable fields edge the heather moors, skylarks twitter in the quiet sky. It has an air of being set apart. Holme is an Anglo-Saxon word, meaning almost an island.

The two small boys, John and James, had entered a landscape to start their imagination. On winter days, as they walked home from school, watching the clouds over Roseberry Topping, build into frothy white cloud oceans, coral cloud sands, purple forests, pearly gold cloud mountains hovering above, like paradise islands there, but not there, to disappear and re-appear as another imaginary cloud landscape* as they walked home again, tomorrow.

*This is best seen now on winter afternoons when the sun is low.

Each morning, in the 1730s as they walked back down the steep hillside to go to school, the Leven valley spread out flat below them, the view forty miles wide to the west, with the prevailing wind south-westerly, two practical young farmers would see the approaching weather. Is this the origin of Captain Cook's sixth sense of the fickle weather; was it something he had absorbed as a child?

It is said, he would come out on deck when the sky was clear and say 'Fog' and sure enough, there would be fog.

Roseberry Topping was used in folklore to warn of thunder:

> 'When Rosburye Toppinge wears a cappe
> Let Cleveland then beware a clappe'
> *(Ref. Cotton MSS)*

Over the centuries, Roseberry Topping has reflected the history of Cleveland. Known in Anglo-Saxon times as Osburgh (God's watchtower), later by the Viking invaders as Odinsberg, hill of the gods: Odin. The Norman conquerors kept the 'y' prefix, the name blurring into Osburgh y-Topping, tops being the local word for hills. Today's name Roseberry Topping smacks of Victorian nicety, but the R was already used in James Cook's day. Roseberry Topping was always a hill of legend. Listen to its story as told by Ralph Jackson in 1757 when, aged 21, he took his cousin Thomas Ward and their servant Jack, for an afternoon ride 'to the Bottom of Osbury Toppin' and walked to the top. He wrote - and if you emphasise the capital letters you can almost hear the cadence of his voice:

'The story or Naration of how this hill came by its present Name is this. There was a Prince whose name was Osburn, who had his Fortune told and that he was to be drowned, upon which his Mother enquired and found out this hill as a very remarkable one, and where no water was, and hither she came with her Son and lived in a little cave that is in the Rock to the west side till the Boy (the Prince) was so old as he could be left by his Mother, and one Day walking from his cave to the N.E. side he laid down and falling asleep a Spring of Water arose out of the side not quite at the Top, and he was drowned. This well I drank of,' says Ralph, pleased with his day out.

James Cook, just nine years older than Ralph, would have been brought up on Cleveland folklore. He and John surely played in the cave, drank from that same spring.

The boys would also play cats-cradles with string, on the way to school, a good lesson in knots for a future sailor. They would probably learn to knit by the age of 10, most local boys and girls did. And all the time they would be learning about plants and trees, birds and animals, winds and clouds and weather.

LIFE OF A FARM BOY

Nothing is known of the Cooks' working life at Airyholme farm, nor of James Cook's childhood there. To avoid fictionalising it, we can gain a good idea of their true life, by describing the lifestyle at Grainge farm at Loftus, of William White, farm Hind, or steward - both words are applied to him – of Mr. Ralph Ward. It is highly likely the Cooks knew William White through meeting him at the cattle markets. So let us go down the coast road, to Grainge.

Three miles north-west of Staithes, the cliffs drop hundreds of feet, sheer into the sea. Their landward side slopes gently, warmly facing south, good for growing com, and here stands Loftus Grainge farm. In those days it had 24 large fields, a small farmhouse with one extra room kept for Mr. Ward's visits, six tiny cottages for the farm hands and a blacksmith's forge. The good arable fields were planted with wheat, oats and barley, the pastures held sheep and prize oxen. Young horses, for the Ward family in London, were grazed at Grainge, where the hind William White, his wife Jane, and daughter Alice lived in the farmhouse. Every Monday, William White came to Guisborough cattle mart, called for his instructions at Mr. Ward's and had his dinner. Together they went to every Yarm Fair to buy or sell beasts and, at least once, William White went up into Northumberland to drive back sheep. Mr. Ward says:[1]

11th April, 1755. 'Wm. White who brought here 3 fatt oxen to go to Sunderland on munday next. Henry Mewburn of that place having Bought them of me at £51.'

15th Oct. 1755 'ordered Wm. White to go the next day to Dabhom for 20 bushells seed wheat to come from Mr. Pierse in a Boat Sent there to take in otes.'

19th April, 1755. 'Wm. White came here with 10 Steers he bought at Durham, and 4 at Darlington .... his steers cost in all ... £70. 10s. 0d.'

Feb. 9th 1755 'Wm. White being gon[e] to Kirby Moorside that morning to buy Seed otes.'

1st Sept. 1755 'Wm. White .... brought 5 packs of wool from Grang 5 packs of Wooll in a Waggon with 4 oxen & 2 horses .... to be sent to Darlington ... 90 Stone of it... at 10/6 p[er] stone. They returned about one. Fine day.'

William White was carrying large sums of money, twice or three times his wages for a year. With no banking system, honesty in those days was imperative. The punishment of the Courts for theft of the smallest thing was often deportation.

The life of a farm Hand meant travel, responsibilty and arithmetic. William White had to be able to count, to reckon up figures.It follows that so did Mr. Cook. Indeed his son James may have been able to reckon as well as read, before he went to school.

It did not matter if a farm Hind could not read. William White could at least sign his name; he was a churchwarden at Easington. Grainge farm paid ancient cesses to that church, of one and a half geese a year. Every June and December, Mr. Ward paid the half year wages for the men at Grainge, about £10 in all, and every year after Christmas, William White and his farmhand Thomas Jackson, brought from Grange 30 bushels of barley 'to make out at Steeping 60, for malt delivered at Oliver Preswick's Kiln' This was for Mr. Ward's household ale.

Year upon year William White appears in the records, we see him loading and unloading boats, and the sad fact is that he died working one Saturday, when he was drowned in Whitby harbour.

In 1736 James Cook's father would be expected to follow the same local pattern of life as William White; driving animals to Guisborough cattle mart, buying at Yarm fair, travelling to inspect beasts, going down to the river to collect corn from boats. Did he take little James with him? As the big ships passed, did the child ask:

'Where are they going to, father?'

'To London, son, to Norway - to see the World?'

Airyholme farm was not so big, nor so arable as Grainge, the soil was poorer, but its owner, the Squire Thomas Skottowe, may not have been so exacting as Mr. Ralph Ward. It was a farm which could be made to pay, given hard unremitting work. It was a step up, an opportunity for Captain Cook's father and his growing sons.

By moving to Airyholme, the boy James came under the direct control of the Squire, and would be expected to do as he was told, even as to his future. Thomas Skottowe was a kindly man, in that, the small boy James Cook was lucky.

What did James' 8 year old eyes see? With only one carriage road through Cleveland, and the steep lane up to the farm, the Squire would arrive on horseback. His high leather boots turned over, wide skirted riding coat of wool thick as a board, plain buttons, huge 'poachers' pockets, old lace at the neck, wavy brimmed hat above a square face (if later portraits of his son are anything to go by). Thomas Skottowe, then in his early 40s, had young sons of his own. He seems to have been a generous man, even at times too generous. Due to his help, a farm boy with little opportunity, was able to begin to develop, into the wide-horizoned, clever, truthful and famous Captain James Cook, R.N.

~~~

SKOTTOWE. *Azure a star or.*

THOMAS SKOTTOWE Esquire
1695-1771

We are able to approach quite close to the Squire. He states in a Deed, dated 3rd July, 1759[2] that he is the eldest son and heir of Thomas Skottowe of Norwich and wife Elizabeth, daughter of Christopher Coulson of Norwich. So it was through his mother he inherited the Coulson manor of Great Ayton. As Lord of the Manor he owned the freehold of the land and several ancient rights, including the Squire's social right to direct the local people.

Unlike his parents, Thomas Skottowe settled at Great Ayton. By 1735 he had taken his place among the Cleveland squirearchy, becoming a Justice of the Peace for the area for the rest of his life. For example, on Monday 16th September 1754, Ralph Ward, acting as a JP, says he joined him at the Cock Inn in Guisborough Market Place:

'I dined with the Justices at their Brewster Sessions, Mr. Robinson, Mr. Scottowe and Mr. Beckwith.' They were issuing Alehouse licences and permissions to brew beer.

Roger Beckwith JP lived at Handale Abbey, near Loftus; Ralph Robinson* a much respected popular old man lived at Ormesby. They were administering the East Langbaurgh Division of Cleveland, which ran from Guisborough down the coast, past Staithes to Lyth. The West Langbaurgh division centred on Stokesley. Thomas Skottowe and Mr. Ward attended both courts, and their influence was wide in Cleveland.

* *Thomas Scarfe had been a tenant farmer on his Ormesby estate.*

25

Thomas Skottowe had been married twice. His eldest son Coulson was the child of his first marriage, the others the children of his wife Ann.

Thomas Skottowe of Great Ayton
m. 1st Rebecca Ware   m. 2nd Ann Casrip

COULSON JOHN NICOLAS ANN THOMAS & SUSANNAH AUGUSTINE
b. 1718   1725   1730 1732   bapt. 1735 (twins?)   1736

Thomas Skottowe appears to have been by nature easygoing, and two incidents, across the years, show this:

• In December 1745, when he was 50, and James Cook's father was Hind at Airyholme, feeling was running high against Roman Catholics. They were suspected of fuelling that autumn's failed attempt by Prince Charles Stuart to reclaim the English throne. A letter written to the Gentleman's Magazine says:

27th Dec. 1745. 'Last Tuesday a number of Stokesly boys pulled some tiles off Mr. Pearson's Mass house, the damage of which might amount to 11 shillings. The papists could not see their place of worship insulted, without resenting it; therefore got a warrant from Mr. Scottowe against one of the boys (a sailor) who had been the most active in the affair. The constables apprehended the boy the next day; upon which his associates were called together to the number of about 200, and being joined by some young fellows, marched in order (with drum beating and colours flying) to Mr. Scottowe's, and declared to him that they all acknowledged themselves equally guilty with the boy charged with the fact. Mr. Scottowe could not forbear laughing at them; however, after giving them a gentle reprimand, he dismissed them recommending it to the papists to put up with the damage. Upon which the boys went to Ayton, beating up for volunteers for his Majesty's service, and enlisted about 30 or 40 boys; then marched to Stokesley Cross'.

There they made bonfires, destroyed the whole Mass-house,

tore the chapel to pieces and burnt it!

Thomas Skottowe seems to have had a calm temperament, tolerant with children, and humorous. They had let him down.

• Ten years later, one Friday in July, 1755, early in the morning, Richard Steavenson a well-heeled farmer from Brotton arrived at Mr. Ward's house in Guisborough in a tizzy. A woman of Marske had said that Mr. Steavenson was the father of her child, which meant he either admitted it was his and paid up, or a Bastardy certificate needed to be issued. The cost of such a child could fall on the whole parish. That afternoon, after a busy morning, Mr. Ward says he 'went to Mr. Scottowe's of Ayton to consult with him about Richard Steavenson's affair; but to little purpose. Stayed there an hour or two and came home.'

Perhaps the then 60 year old Thomas Skottowe, twice married and father of seven, had a more worldly opinion than the 75 year old batchelor Ralph Ward. Or perhaps the relaxed Justice of the Peace felt it was best not to make it their business too soon, that the problem would resolve itself.

The Squire may have been comfortable in his views; he was also kind and easy-going with money. Did he pay for young James Cook to go to school, even though he had sons of his own to educate? When James Cook was 8 and newly arrived at Airyholme, Thomas Skottowe's son John was 11, Nicholas 6, Thomas 1, and Augustine new-born. It would be strange if the boys did not meet, although they were divided by social class. Mr. Cook would have to visit Ayton Hall to get his orders. And there, familiar to the boys, there would be The Star.

The first stars Cleveland children learn are the Plough leading to the faint Pole Star, friend of navigators and all sailors; Orion, lifting its brightness over the horizon in winter, and the most brilliant lone first and last star to shine, the planet Venus. A single eight-pointed 'Star in the Heavens' was part of the Skottowe coat of arms, painted perhaps on the Squire's carriage, and in the church.

James was 8 and ready to go to school, and it has always been said, Thomas Skottowe paid for him. It is possible and sounds in character. After all, Mr. Cook would have had to pay for John.

The schoolboy James Cook, had moved into the shelter of a circle of influential men, which would affect his whole future. Thomas Skottowe, his first patron, may have been so for life.

AYTON SCHOOL.

Going to school was for those who could afford to pay. The choice of school reflected a father's level in society. Poor children had little chance but, the general feeling was that, as poor children could fall to the residents of the parish to pay them poor relief, it was best to school them in ways to earn their own living.

Mr. Ward's mother had endowed a charity school at Guisborough, in 1721, leaving in her will £13 for the school[3] 'for poor peoples children, and a proper discreet woman of the persuasion of the Church of England, to teach and instruct such children in Reading, Spinning, Sewing and Knitting' and a house 'to be provided for her £10-8 shillings a year'. The school taught about 35 children, who left at the age of nine. It vexed Mr. Ward that the children were often tired, and sometimes came late, having worked for their families since dawn.

For more classical education, there was the old Latin Grammar School at Guisborough, founded in 1561, with its schoolmaster who had to be a priest, and 'no Scot or stranger born.'

But the better-off tradesmen, were looking less for Latin grammar, more for business skills.

In 1759, when John Husband a Guisborough sadler was found dead on Freeborough Hill, along the moor road from Whitby, where he had been to buy bull hides, his 14 year old son Christopher came home from 'the writeing and arithmetic school' at Pickering, a boarding school. Mr. Pease, the Whitby grocer, sent two sons to Scorton school; James Pease entered his father's business, and Bristowe spent one year at Darlington school, before progressing to

Kirk Merrington school, for the education which would allow him to make his own way in life. Ralph Jackson gives the impression he too went to Scorton School. During his apprenticeship he attended the old Trinity School at Newcastle, under Mr. Turnbull, learning the accountancy he needed to be a Hoastman merchanting coal. Mr. Ward intended his nephew to be able to manage the money he would inherit.

At this higher social level, William Masterman, from Little Ayton, just down the lane from the Cooks at Airyholme, went away to board at Beverley School, before entering the legal profession, eventually to become a Member of Parliament.

The landed gentry taught their children to read and write at home, until about the age of six, when they were placed as boarders with vicars and curates, in order to learn their Latin and Greek, before going away to school. It was a respectable way for a poor but educated curate to supplement his pittance of an income. The young heir of Sir William Chaloner, of Guisborough went to Eton, aged ten.

This then was the social hierarchy of schooling. James Cook needed a school at his father's social level which, while quite lowly, was not poverty. So what was available?

There were very few schools in Cleveland. At Kirkleatham, there was a Bluecoat School for 20 poor orphans, but the nearby lovely building of the Kirkleatham school, founded by the Turner family was being turned into a library and museum of curiosities, after the Rev. Mr. Murgatroyd left with the Turner heir to attend Cambridge University, as his tutor.

Sir James Lowther had founded a school for poor children at Marske, and this had grown into a 'public' school for 30 children, but it would mean the expense of boarding, it was simply too far to travel. It was to be the Postgate School, at Great Ayton for the Cook boys.

The Postgate School had been established in 1704 by Michael Postgate a local yeoman farmer, for the instruction of eight poor boys. It soon became a 'public' school, with 30 children. Some paid a small fee. The school being intended to keep down parish rates for poor relief, some paid nothing. A charity existed to set up apprenticeships for very poor boys. All the children were instructed in their Church Catechism, reading, writing and arithmetic.

Great Ayton was a large village, of about 140 families, much grander than its neighbours. The little river Leven, trickled past its High Green, where the Postgate School stood, and dawdled through its Low Green fronting the Queen Anne mansion house of Thomas Skottowe. Between the two greens stood a ford and a mill. When the mill was working, the sluices went down to raise the shallow river to a level to work the machinery, and the river bed was used as a road, crossed by a dry ford. When the sluices were raised, to let out the water, the flooded ford turned into a quagmire. There was no bridge across the mud when James Cook was a schoolboy. But he must have been cleaner than most boys in school, as he did not have to cross the ford to get there.

As an 8 year old boy newly arrived from Marton, living slightly apart from the village, with a Northumbrian speaking father, James Cook would be partly an outsider. There are tales of him being unco-operative, unwilling to join the mainstream, as in the bird-nesting story where he would only go his way. Not that he would be above bird nesting, it was the duty as well as the hobby of country children, to help keep down the birds which over-ate the crops. A bad harvest meant poor people went hungry and animals starved. As boys, Ralph Jackson and his friend Billy Hudspeth spent hours and hours netting larks. There were many more birds, hares and butterflies then, and hares in particular could demolish the corn, and eat as much grass as a sheep.

James must have fitted in well enough at Great Ayton school; there is the account of what happened 30 years later, in 1767 when, as master of the *Grenville,* he was setting sail down the Thames on her voyage to survey Newfoundland. Before the pilot could stop it happening, a collier brig, the *Three Sisters* of Sunderland, caught by the Thames fluky winds, bore down on *Grenville,* fell athwart the hause and carried their bowsprit cap and jibboom away. Swearing loudly, according to one observer, James Cook then discovered the collier's Master was Thomas Bloyd, once his schoolmate at Great Ayton, and a convivial evening followed, while the two crews carried out repairs. *Grenville* was able to sail in two days.

No matter who paid, in sending James to Great Ayton school, Mr. Cook was probably doing the best he could.

Yet as a schooling for a career at sea, the Postgate School alone, was not good enough. Most of these small village schools were modest in their teaching, the charity schools were minimal.

Mrs. Sarah Osborn, the sister of Admiral Byng, writing on 29th May 1744 says: 'Poor Dudley still shows he only went to a farden* school. For Godsake let all boys have a propper school till 12 year old at least. Tis terrible to think when they are Captains yet will be a shame for them to write to the Admiralty.'

a Farthing was the smallest coin.

~~~

POOR PROSPECTS FOR A FARM BOY

It is said that the schoolboy James Cook had a talent for mathematics. His father, earning about £15 a year, had younger children, and James was the second son. To go on with his education James needed a patron, and it becomes clear that Thomas Skottowe was unable to help. The type of education required for James' future career, was not available to him. It **was** available to another clever poor local boy called William Stevens, and by looking at William we can see the education James Cook needed but did not get. As education changed little over those twenty years, it is valid to compare the fortunes of one boy with the other.

WILLIAM STEVENS

William Stevens was a clever boy from nearby Stokesley, whose father was a gardener who could not afford to educate him. On 18th April 1757, he visited the elderly Ralph Ward at Guisborough with a view to having his school fees paid. Ralph Jackson, who was then 26 and living with his uncle, writes:

'Wm. Stevens also dined at our house. He is a Boy little above 13 years old and lives with his father a little from Stoxley, and is surprixingly quick at the Mathematick having learnt Algebra by the help of a Printed book only, and several amazing Circumstances are to be found in him.'

Monday 6th June 1757.

'After dinner Wm. Stevens, son of Old Stevens near Stoxley (who has a remarkable genius) tho' only thirteen years the beginning of this year, and myself wrought some Problems on the Terrestial Globe. My Uncle has this day given him a Letter to Mr. Richardson, Schoolmaster at Darnton,* by whom he is going to be taught astronomy.'   * *Darlington*

By May 1758 Ralph Jackson was in contact with his own old Master on the Tyne to find an even better school for young William Stevens:

'Sunday the Fourth [of June.]

I had a letter in the morning from Mr. Wm. Jefferson….wherein he recommends Mr. Robt. Harrison, now Schoolmaster of the Trinity House, Newcastle, and Mr. Harrison wrote to me his terms, which are Two guineas and a half for Navigation and the same for Astronomy, but as the Lad is so promising a Genious he will abait a Guinea in the whole, or instruct him in circle Sailing and the use of the Globes for the 5 guineas.'

On Tuesday 13th, William Stevens and his brother set off on one horse for Newcastle; Ralph Jackson overtook them on the way. Next evening young William dined with Ralph at Mr. William Jefferson's where Mr. Harrison the Trinity Schoolmaster examined William Stevens' book, 'which he much approved on so far as related to the

Lad's performance, but said that Mr. Richardson had kept him too long upon one Thing.'

By Thursday, William was entered in Mr. Harrison's school, 'but,' says Ralph, 'as he only wants to know the Principles of Navigation and Astronomy being already able to work any question therein, he is to proceed to Geometry, the Conic Sections and Fluctions, which Mr. Harrison said he would himself refer to my uncle to pay for.'

Ralph Jackson caught the enthusiasm and began working out problems of Navigation himself, 'having got some lessons in the use of the Globes as also on Saturday…. I begun to use the Globes which my old Master Turnbull instructed me in a little at Newcastle'…. and…. worked some problems on the Terrestial globe.'

For three months Ralph read Keill's Astronomical Lectures, borrowed from the Trinity schoolmaster, Robert Harrison, and developed a lifelong interest in the stars. By November, he and William Stevens were working out problems on the Celestial globe. William had come to Mr. Ward's to show his patron his progress, to justify the charge of £10-8 shillings for four months school and board. For James Cook's father, that was most of one year's wages.

With Mr. Ward's patronage, William Stevens qualified as a surveyor and got the education which would take him into the East India Company, as a deputy Engineer. By the age of 14, he already knew more than James Cook, who was then 30 years old, and trying to learn surveying on the coast of north America. Younger and running ahead of James Cook, and a favourite of Ralph Jackson, William Stevens will re-enter James Cook's lifestory in 1768.

Maybe James Cook, as a boy, was equally clever at mathematics. In an unequal system, and without a willing patron, his education ended and he left Great Ayton school to take his chance at a much lower level of future prospects. It cannot have helped that he was thesecond son.

Why did Thomas Skottowe not help?

Could it have been because he was increasingly in debt? For those able to face debt, look at this:

THE SQUIRE'S DEBTS

It may in fact have been the Squire's limited help, caused by his debts, which started James Cook's career in the direction it took.

Thomas Skottowe, Esquire, was always in need of money. He sold off his Norfolk estates and mortgaged his estate at Great Ayton. In 1740 he granted the manor of Great Ayton to Mr. Ralph Ward for 3000 years, providing he could reclaim it with £2000. Instead he borrowed more and more, until the sum to reclaim it rose to £4000 by 1743, and to £8000 by 1754. This was, fairly, a fortune. He may have needed the money to buy positions for his five sons, for in an age of patronage little came free, and to find a marriage portion for his daughters. But it may have been in Thomas Skottowe's nature to spend. Ralph Ward notes in his diary:

'24th March, 1755. Fine day. Wind South, dined with Mr. Coulst. Scottowe to whome paid £200 for his Father: he beieng ill in an Eye & could not come himself.'

Throughout 1754-6, in Mr. Ward's journal, a pattern emerges of smaller debts building up and getting out of hand.

'1st December, 1755. Received from mr. Skottowe £40 being the remainder of half years Interest due 26th April last part. As Mr. Preston brought the money I returned a Receit by Him.'

'19th January, 1756. I dined at the Cock with Mr. Robinson, Mr. Skottowe & Mr. Becwith, having the Highway Sessions that day in all 13 of us dined. Spoke Mr. Skottowe about his Interest money.'

'3rd April, 1756. At home. Mr. Skottow & Servant came here about 4 in the Afternoon and paid me in part of Interest due 26th October last £140, went away about 6. Fair but close & cloudy all day.'

As the year progressed, things got worse.

'28th July, 1756. A fine hay day. Mr. Skottowe came here about 11 desireing me to lend him £500 upon a new mortgage. 1 promised him £100 in a month's time and the Rest about 2 months after, he did but stay to drink a glass of wine.'

'25th August, 1756.1 called at Mr. Skottows about the affair of his new Mortgage, who I spoke with and settled his coming here for £100 to be lent him on Monday 6th September.'

'6th September, 1756. Mr. Skottow came here with Mr. Preston & Dined here, to the former I lent £ 100 on his note which with £52.10s. lent him also on his note the 23rd August last being in all £152.10s.0d. it is agreed that I am to make up the said Sum £500, for which is to give me a new Mortgage to be dated 26th October next & that £160 is to be allowed me out of the said Sum £500 for 6 months Interest for £800 due the 26th April last past. Thick fogg in the morning with frequent drizzling rain, but fine afternoon.'

As Thomas Skottowe rode away in clearing skies, did he not care that by borrowing at interest to pay previous interest he was compounding his debts? That is a classic debtor's fault.

Mr. Ralph Ward appears to have been troubled. He was calculating, but thoughtful. We have to remember that, while much richer, he was a shade inferior socially to the Squire, that was finely understood. The day before the new mortgage was to take effect, he went up the street in Guisborough to speak to Mr. Preston, but the lawyer was out. It was three days later when:

'Mr. Preston calld at Door in his way to Marsk & Spok to me about Mr. Skottow's affair, in the Afternoon Mr. Skottowe himself came here to speak to me about reneuing his Mortgage and to borrow £1000 more, but I could not determine with him anything about it till some time after this.'

'12th November, 1756. I went about 8 in the morning with T.p. [Thomas Presswick] to Mr. Skottows at Ayton where met me Mr. Preston & his son with a new Mortgage on my Advance of £800, of which I paid him on two notes before, £152.10s & today £287.10s.

& he allowed me 6 months Interest due April 26th last & I gave him my note payable on demand with Interest also from said 26th October last, which made in all £800, he signed the Mortgage and a Bond, Mr. Preston & his son witnesses to both as also to my note. I got home betwixt 4 & 5.'

The new mortgage was fixed and would prove difficult to repay.

'29th November, 1756. Mr. Preston .... brought me Mr. Skottow's last Mortgage Deed from the Register Office.'

Mr. Ward may not have approved of the debt but he may have understood the reason; he sounds resigned, but Thomas Skottowe's cavalier attitude seems to have concerned him.

'20th December, 1756. A meeting of the Justices was today about Enlisting Soldiers, thay got only one Mr. Skottow desired £20 in part of £200 for my note I gave him the 26th October last.'

Thomas Skottowe was obviously short of ready cash, perhaps to pay the bill at the Cock? There is a carefree recklessness about that small sum which seems to show he had given up the idea of paying off the mortgages with real income. In fact during these years he was selling off his land.*

In 1755, both Major Waugh and Mr. George Duck bought land from Thomas Skottowe with money borrowed from Ralph Ward on mortgages. But Mr. Skottowe already owed Ralph Ward mortgages on the same land. Mr. Ward had just exchanged debtors.

As early as 1743 with the debt doubled, Thomas Skottowe already may have thought he could always sell Airyholme farm. There was no tenancy to complicate a sale, only his steward Cook's family to remove. It may have been the growing insecurity of his father's position, which caused the young James Cook to look elsewhere. While the Squire may not have funded James to schooling above his place in society, perhaps a mixture of guilt, expediency and generosity caused Thomas Skottowe to help find the boy a job. And the job may have come up in discussions of the debt, between Mr. Ward and Thomas Skottowe. James Cook, nearly 15, was about to become a draper and grocer's shop boy, at Staithes.

Looking back from his Will[4], we can picture Thomas Skottowe's life at Great Ayton. To the north of the house were eight large fields, farmed by a tenant. Apart from beds, furniture etc. the house contained pictures and books, the cellars were filled with wine, rum and brndy, the stables held a Chaise (carriage), horses, harnesses, hay and coals. The Squire owned a valuable ring, which he left to is son John, his wife Ann's eldest son. It may have been hers; there is sense of propriety about the Will. John lived on the island of St. Helena, so he received the easily moveable, the pictures, the books, the ring. What the Will does not show are the two large farms in the separate ownership of his son Coulson Skottowe.

James Cook's father, it is said, was helped by the Squire in 1755 to build a cottage in Great Ayton, on land leased to him by Thomas Skottowe. Both men were by then 60 years old. Airyholme farm was sold in 1758 to Mr. Bartholomew Rudd.
Down the lane at Ayton Grange farm lived the Squire's youngest son Augustine Skottowe with his family. Three other small fields, one medium sized farm, and a tiny plot were tenanted out. What the Will of Thomas Skottowe does not show are the farms the Squire had already sold off.
Thomas Skottowe, Esquire, had sold the Queen Anne mansion house, at Great Ayton, and moved next door into the old manor house. He continued with his life in polite society, drinking tea with his new neighbours at Ayton Hall, attending court as a JP, hearing land tax appeals. As we will see, he was ideally placed socially to influence James Cook's career in the Royal Navy. He lived long enough to see James Cook appointed to the Endeavour *and may have had something to do with it, but he died before the ship's triumphant return.*

4

GROCER'S BOY

James Cook, not yet 15, arrived in Staithes to work for William Sanderson the grocer, whose shop stood at the very edge of the sea, within a few yards of the breaking waves. James a farm boy from inland, was plunged into a seagoing community.

The old village of Staithes, hangs in a ravine cut by a tidal stream through 200 feet high cliffs. To stand at the top today, looking out over its huddle of pink-tiled and grey-slate roofs, set against a vast purple sea, brings a touch of wonder that such a place still exists. As you walk down the hill, sound quality changes in the cobbled street, there is a tang of salt in the air, the smell of seaweed, the screech of gulls. People disappear through alleyways into yards lined with cottages. James Cook would easily remember his way here.

In the harbour fishing boats, called cobles, still ride the tide. Striped red-and-white, blue-and-red, black-and-white, and built the same way as a Viking ship to make them sea-kindly, they are often named with hope*, Ambition, Pilot Me, Star of Hope.* Staithes boats bear a thin yellow line, so that wreckage can be identified.

The sea has always taken its toll. The parish churchyard is full of tombstones of the drowned, some have no bodies to accompany the verse, some the date, not of death, but the date the dreadful news reached home. The captains and crews are remembered here, even those lost in the East Indies. A popular tombstone verse reads:

Weep not for me my parents dear
I am not lost but sleeping here,
The Lord has took me in my prime,
though you are left to weep behind,
the pain of death did compass me
and bound me everywhere,
the flowing waves and raging sea
did put me in great fear
[*I cried*] for help but none was nigh
My precious life to save,
O Gracious God receive my soul
Since this must be my grave.

Here in the churchyard are men James Cook knew as a boy. Captain Miles Mewburn who sailed his ship out of Whitby, drowned aged 49 in 1750 with his crew; sand on the sea wind has worn away his epitaph:

'…………soon away/…………….doomed to swift decay
……once enjoyed but these/ with them lost in stormy seas,'

And Captain James Marshall, of the Staithes ship *Blessing*, in 1743 he was 32, a mild man, who survived to die at home:

'As with friends and foes, His gentle soul was meet for joys ….'
says his tombstone. *meet= meant*

In 1743, Staithes was one of the larger towns of Cleveland, stinking and rich on fish. Fish covered every available space, hung to dry on racks, in yards, in smoke houses. Women with lethal knives sliced open live mussels to bait the lines, they turned out with ropes to haul-in the cobles. The harbour was full of small boats. Large two masted 5-man boats lay on the flat reef, small skips splashed out to them when the tide came in; they followed the herring each season as far south as Yarmouth. Top-sail sloops sat beached, while bigger ships, brigs and Whitby Cats, stood-off waiting for a coble to bring out bread and nails from the shop.

Staithes was noisy with the cry of seabirds, and women fish hawkers, a smell of newly baked bread, and dung in gutters, barrels of urine, narrow alleyways full of crab pots, floats, pigs. The gates were shut at night to keep in the horses. Staithes men were men of the sea, their crinkled eyes smiled in the taverns as they told tales of sailing to Virginia, details of when the Baltic ice lifted at Riga, how to enter the harbour at Lisbon. There were Captains and cooks, men who sailed on colliers and large transports out of Whitby. The fishergirls sailed with the boats to Yarmouth, the captains' wives sailed too, some were drowned.

Into this seething small town in 1743, came the boy James Cook.

Fourteen was late for James to start work. Most boys left school by twelve. One possible reason for the delay may have been physical weakness. It is a medical fact that boys reaching puberty can outgrow their muscular development, tall, gangling and listless, until their muscles catch up. Drawings by Webber, and the portraits of Captain Cook, show this tall gangling frame, with a relatively small head. Another reason may have been that John had to be placed first, and a second placement fee saved up for James.

Someone knew of the job vacancy at Staithes, and someone knew of young James Cook at Ayton. The two met, and the most likely people seem to be the Magistrates of the Court, at Guisborough.

In Court, the Justices of the Peace (the Magistrates) could not act alone. There had to be a quorum. So Thomas Skottowe JP sat on the Bench with Roger Beckwith JP of Handale Abbey at Liverton, and both sat with Ralph Ward JP. And it is clear that Mr. Ward was involved with the grocer's shop, from the beginning.

In 1738, just after the schoolboy James Cook had moved to Airyholme farm, John Gill, a grocer of Staithes died, leaving his wife with the shop. His death appears to have been sudden, as he left no Will, and a grocer would have on-going bills to pay, orders arriving, approaching ships to supply. It was too much for a bereaved wife. On 1st February, Alice Gill 'for diverse good causes and Considerations' legally Renounced her rights to Letters of Administration of all her husband's property and business, to her husband's brother Samuel Gill, Gentleman of Staithes, and her own two half-brothers, John and William Clarkson. Alice signed, sealed and delivered this Deed in the presence of Ra.Ward, J.Gerec, Jn.Kirton and Fra.Wardale, the last named being a lawyer who was later Steward of the Manor Court of Seaton, which covered Staithes. The signature of Ra.Ward matches the signature of Mr. Ralph Ward of Guisborough on Boulby alum Works accounts documents.

Next day, 2nd February, a Bond of Administration in £800 surety, was drawn up[1], which obliged five named men to make an Inventory (sadly lost) of John Gill's goods chattels and credits, and to administer his affairs. They were:

Samuel Gill, Gentleman of Staithes.
John Clarkson, Yeoman of Woodhouse, Liverton.
William Clarkson, Yeoman of Handale Banks.
Thomas Gill, Sailmaker of Whitby, and
Robert Calvert, Inn Keeper of Whitby.

Samuel Gill, was the customs officer at Staithes. In 1727, Mr. Gill's wife and small son had died, and he was left with three little girls, Elisabeth, Sarah and Ann.

Samuel Gill's signature matches exactly the signature of her father's consent on Elisabeth Gill's marriage licence when she married William Sanderson who took over the grocer's shop.

WILLIAM SANDERSON

It is not often a man's name is handed down to posterity simply because a boy he employed in his shop grew to be a world-famous man. This fate happened to William Sanderson.

He married Elizabeth Gill on 6th September, 1741, she was 17 he was 30. Their first son Samuel, named after her father, was born in March 1743, and that may be why they took on a shop boy, James Cook, that year.

Sanderson's, was a shop on a plot of land, called a 'yard'. The Mulgrave rentals of Staithes 'yards' were for one rood of land, about a quarter of an acre. These yards later had cottages built around their inside edges that still exist today: Boathouse Yard, Barbers Yard, Mann's Yard, Chapel Yard, Elliots Yard, giving Staithes its uniquely dense layout, and shelter from a storm. Mr. Sanderson's shop and yard were under the cliff, where today's sandy beach lies, and rather exposed. It was finally demolished by a storm in 1812.

The shop was a 'double' shop, with one central door, and two counters facing each other, one sold groceries, the other linen and sailcloth. A later apprentice proves William Sanderson was also a draper. The business was always involved in sailcloth, and this may have been another link to Mr. Ralph Ward, who part-owned a sailcloth factory, next door to his house in Guisborough. The Administration bond of £800, is a rough value for the business. William Sanderson probably had to take a mortgage to buy it, and who better to ask than Mr. Ward?

The shop at the harbour edge, overlooked the fishing boats, huge five-man boats, brightly painted inshore cobles, tiny 'mules' and 'sploshers', which went with the large boats to the fishing grounds. There was Robert Campion's 'flat bottomed scoot' the *Mary & Jane*, bringing in coal from the Tyne, shovelling it into carts on the beach, when the tide went out. There were sloops like the *Darling* bringing in kelp to the north side warehouse, when the tide allowed, and the coble 'foy' or ferryboat, rowing out to the larger ships with sailcloth and replacement ropes.[*]

When the replica Whitby Cat 'Endeavour' came to Staithes on 9th May 1997, we were all startled at how close in she came to the harbour.

In 1817, Dr. Young quoted Staithes people who knew James Cook and the Sandersons: 'his companions were young fishermen and sailors, his leisure hours were often spent in making short excursions in cobles', and we know many of their names, such as John and Thomas Harrison, James Hutton, Richard Harland as, later, they joined Whitby ships as apprentices.

Staithes inner harbour was crossed by a footbridge, as it still is, and would have echoed with activity, with shipwrights sawing, caulkers hammering, rigging and sails clattering in the wind, fish hung out to dry on frames: the Manor Court Bye-laws for 1704-56 state firmly:[2]

'No sails, fish, or any other thing, to be hung on Staythes bridge or 5 shillings fine.

No stones to be taken away within 12 yards either side of Staythes landing place.'

No carrying uncovered fire out of the houses.

Clean your watersewers.

Any fighting or 'bloudshed' in the pubs, the landlord to report it within 10 days.

No hare coursing unless an authorised person.

It was the parish Constable's job to police the Bye-laws. He had this duty to the Manor Court of Lord Mulgrave, and different duties to the Justices' Courts of the weapontake[3] of Langbaurgh, at Guisborough.

To be elected Constable, a man had to have standing in the community, and a firm personality. As a Vestry officer, elected to administer the parish, subject to the Lord of the Manor's Court, the Constable was in charge of strangers. That court's 1704-56 Bye-laws for Staithes say: No 'strangers or wandering beggars' were to inhabit the parish. No 'lodging of wandering beggars without the appointment of the constable'. Strangers had to be vouched for. James Cook clearly had been. By 1754 the Constable of the parish was William Sanderson. He was a Vestry officer in 1749,* taking over from his father-in-law, Samuel Gill, who was acting in 1743, when young James arrived. The two men were in the house and shop with James. Mr. Gill was convivial and working with ships unloading coal in the harbour, outside the shop door. He would know James well.

* *His signature on his marriage licence[4] matches the signature on the church 'Terrier' of 1749. Years later the family boat was called the Terrier, but William Sanderson also liked dogs. The grocery shop probably had a terrier - for the ships brought rats.*

We only meet Mr. Sanderson much later in the diaries, in May 1753, when he arrived in Newcastle to stay at the Crown and Thistle Inn, at the low end of the Groat Market, and sent a message to young Ralph Jackson, who notes:

'I got a letter from my Sist[er] Dolly at Steaths off Mr. Sanderson I returned into the office and answer'd it by him, I carried it to one Place's Groat Market where I found him, he asked me to sit a while, but I stayed little.'

At age 17, Ralph was being virtuous about not drinking beer.

We know William Sanderson was a sportsman, walking up in the afternoon to Boulby to smoke a pipe, and joining his friends for hare coursing with greyhounds. Did he have a droll sense of humour or was he being pompous, when Mr. Ward showed some asperity about him on 20th December 1754, writing:

'A pay[day] at Boulby with John Jefferson and Mr. Sanderson dined with us. I received the case about his following the Idle Trade of keeping a pack of dogs and hunting'.

The Idle Trade is a local saying for retirement from work.
Mr. Sanderson was 49, a sceptical Mr. Ward 74 and still working.

Between 1743 and 1746, James Cook worked as a shop boy for

William Sanderson. As a 'Servaunt' was the word generally used.

In 1817 Reverend Young talked to Mrs. Dodds, William Sanderson's daughter, and to John Sanderson his son. They told him James Cook, was 'only placed on trial or on the footing of a verbal agreement, without any indentures'. At first, James may have seen his job as becoming permanent, and his future limited. Yet Mr. Sanderson would expect to prosper, to the point he could take on a proper apprentice, at a boy's wage. Would there still be a job for James then?

Or, it may have been agreed from the beginning, that James Cook's placement was a step up, toward another job.

That this was William Sanderson's practice is shown in 1764, when Ralph Jackson writes:

'2nd November. Visit of Mr. George Deighton of London and his nephew Thomas Pearson late an apprentice to Mr. Wm. Sanderson of Staithes but now going to London with his Uncle for business'.

A DRAPER'S SHOP ASSISTANT?

It is the Deighton family who show that William Sanderson was, among other things, a Draper. So it is quite correct to say that James Cook was an assistant in a draper's shop. It is just not the complete story.

The Deightons were cousins of the Wards and Jacksons at Richmond. Old Mr. George Deighton, aged 81, stayed for a few days with Ralph Ward at Guisborough in March 1758, and amused himself by cleaning some of the guns 'being originally a white and gunsmith', says Ralph Jackson.

In 1749, when the young Ralph Jackson began his diary in Newcastle, Robert Deighton was trading in drapery in London, and Robert's brother George Deighton junior was acting as his commercial agent. George would turn up in Newcastle on business, and take Ralph out and give him supper.

On 8th July, 1750, he treated the 14 year old Ralph 'to the play'.

A George Deighton was also captain of the Scarborough ship

Satisfaction. He was dumping ballast in 1748 at Newcastle ready to load coal. Was he the same George Deighton?

Ralph Jackson records:

'22nd Oct. 1756. I wrote to Mr. Deighton, and directed to him, Linen-Draper, Bucklers Berry, near the Mansion House, London'. Perhaps Nat Campion who dined that day had brought Ralph a letter?

18th Oct. 1757, Ralph Jackson, near Waterfall (Guisborough) 'met Mr. Robert Deighton of London.' Both George and Robert Deighton travelled on drapery business, which was probably their link to William Sanderson. The linen travelled by ship.

In 1759, George Deighton went to London into Partnership with his brother. He called Ralph Jackson up to the Cock Inn at Guisborough, to tell him so.

In London, the Deightons lived just around the corner from Ralph's brother George Jackson, and all the family called regularly, to drink tea.

So, even in 1764, through Thomas Pearson and the Deightons, George Jackson and the Ward family in London, remained linked to Mr. William Sanderson, and the friendship continued for years, among their children, who were still visiting the Sandersons in Staithes in 1780. They were a friendship group with influence.

~~~

JAMES COOK'S NAME

Let us return to 1743, to 14 year old James Cook, working in a grocer and draper's shop, and finding the first thing he needed was a name.

In Staithes, and Cleveland, there was a man's real name, for weddings and his headstone. There was his short name; Mr. Ward's tenant Duke Fogg was Marmaduke Foggthwaite. With so much intermarriage, and repeating of names, it helped if a few swops took place: William (alias James)[5] etc. Local men took their mother's maiden name as a Christian name; so Newark Beckwith and Newark Waller were probably linked on the maternal side; and Addison Brown was descended from Captain Addison; Burton Verrill and Verrill Burton were most likely cousins. A man's third name was his nickname - and many a risky story told! As for James Cook's nickname? At an informed guess, Staithes would dub him 'Yatton Jimmy', as one reason for a nickname, was to shout clearly over water, to find the right man quickly if boat broke loose.

When reading Ralph Jackson's journals we have to be careful, Mr. Bottom is Captain Longbotham. And there are four or five Ralph Jacksons, none related to our diarist, four William Wilsons, three Ralph Reeds.

When working in Staithes for Mr. Sanderson, there is a story that James Cook found a South Sea shilling in the shop till, and wanted it. Exchange it, insisted many a later teller of the tale, rejecting any suggestion of dishonesty.

'Put it back', says Mr. Sanderson angrily, in the story.

In fact it was a boy's job to change the rogue coins. With such a shortage of coin, there were all sorts washing around the system, especially in seaports. Most depended on their silver content. Mr. Ward rejected a Portuguese mondial in his interest money, it was legal tender but a bad coin.

In 1753, young Ralph Jackson 'weighed 2 x 36/- pieces = not weight so giver changed them.' 'Changed gold at Mr. Fosters', he says two months later. And, on board Mr. Drinkall's sloop at the quay, Ralph 'told off some Brass .... and took out the bad halfpennies', next day he changed the brass at Mr. Vickers. Brass was the nickname for small coins. 'He hasn't a brass farthing', is today's saying, for poverty.

During the three years, 1743 - 1746, when James Cook worked in the grocer's shop, Staithes was growing fast, due to the Alum Works at Boulby, in which Mr. Ralph Ward was the managing partner. The Works were perched on the cliff edge and took in supplies by sea.

To the northwest of Staithes the cliffs rise to 700 feet, the highest in England. They are made of alum shales, which were quarried, The process needed vast quantities of coal, brushwood, kelp (burnt seaweed) and urine. Boulby alum works ran the 'alum liquor' in a stone culvert, down to the works where the cliffs were only 200 feet high. There a shaft was sunk through the cliff, to a tunnel opening on a tiny beach called Hole Wyke, where a channel was blasted through the rocky shore. Into this narrow channel, ships sailed on the tide, to unload coal, which was winched up the 200 feet shaft, to the boiling houses. The ship then floated off out to sea, washed out the hold, and returned to load finished alum for delivery to London.

It sounds so simple, until you look at the cliffs, the channel, the sheer danger. The standard of seamanship needed day in day out, was breathtaking. And we know James Cook noticed, learned, and maybe even tried it, for he advised the same technique, 16 years later at the battle of Quebec.

When Mr. Ward was growing too old to run the Alum Works, he agreed to appoint a manager, Thomas Wardell. And it was this sociable man who wove together the Staithes group in friendship, for the rest of their lives. The main thread came from the marriages of Samuel Gill's three daughters. Elisabeth married William Sanderson, Sarah married Captain John Jefferson's brother Anthony, and Ann married Augustine, youngest son of Thomas Skottowe, Esquire.

Hence William Sanderson ended up related by marriage to both Thomas Skottowe and Mr. Ralph Ward.

This friendship, business and family group spread as a Safety Net, beneath the young James Cook. In the confined streets of Staithes, he would be always meeting them, they would not be able to forget about him.

In 1743, when 14 year old James Cook arrived, Mr. Ralph Ward was aged 63, Samuel Gill was 55, Captain John Jefferson 47. There was deference toward them from the younger men, Thomas Wardell aged 35 and William Sanderson 32.

These were the people surrounding the young James Cook in Staithes. Mr. Ward appears to have placed him there. He was under their influence and all of them were involved with ships.

It is time to learn more about them.

~~~

THE STAITHES' SAFETY NET

THOMAS WARDELL

Thomas Wardell, the Manager of Boulby Alum Works, was both an emotional man, and a good businessman. He pledged his warm loyalty to his employer, George Baker of Elemore Hall, near Durham. The Bakers had acquired their half-share in the Works through marriage into the family who owned the Boulby estate. George Baker was hasty and could be dismissive. The alum trade went up rapidly for a few years, swung down just as badly. It needed steady nerve. With warmth, patience and careful humouring of his employer, Thomas Wardell did much to keep the airy Mr. Baker and his partner, the measured Mr. Ralph Ward, in tune. Thomas Wardell cared about people.

One morning, looking out of his window at the Alum Works he saw: 'a poor brig breazing up, as if she would come against the rocks every moment, Thank God she got into Steathes and have sent Jack down to enquire after her.'[6]

At first Thomas Wardell, a widower, lived in a house on Skinningrove bank with his two daughters Nancy and Thomasine but, as they grew up, he sent them to his mother at Sedgefield to be taught. In 1755, when Mr. Ward finally decided he did not need Boulby Manor farm any longer, he let it to Thomas Wardell for a rent of £145 a year, plus £137 for the stock. Ralph Jackson and Thomas Presswick, Mr. Ward's secretary, went to remove the wine, some bottles had been there maturing, for 39 years.

In this old manor house at Boulby, beside its flat field which had been an Elizabethan bowling green, the friends would gather in the evening to smoke a pipe, talk over the day, drink ale: Mr. Ward, Mr. Sanderson, the two excise officers Mr. Samuel Gill of Staithes and Mr. MacDonald of Loftus, .and Captain John Jefferson. Eventually, a new house was built at the Alum Works to house Mr. Wardell. But wherever the warm hearted Mr. Wardell lived, everyone stopped at his door. It was Mr. Sanderson's habit to walk uphill to Boulby in the afternoon, smoke a pipe, drink tea. The two men were fond of greyhound coursing, and walked the fields with their dogs. Mr. Harrison the lawyer of Guisborough was another of their greyhound coursing cronies, often there.

Twice a year the alum workers were paid, and Thomas Wardell gave a dinner for his friends, it was a Works tradition, there was beer and laughter. Mr. Wardell found it helpful to keep in with the curate and rector of Easington. They were his next door neighbours, yet it was sometimes difficult to get Easington urine for the alum works. He shared the disappointment when Mr. Oldfield, the young curate, was passed over for the church living, but felt the new rector would succumb after a pipe and a glass or two.

Thomas Wardell threads through the days of Mr. Ward and Ralph Jackson, who never treated him with less than affection and respect. Though wily Mr. Ward did not fool Thomas Wardell, who warned Mr. Baker the Alum Works was 'in hopes of taking his farm, wee must have it, and soon too, but he does not know it.'.[4th Jan. 1755] Mr. Ward would have put up the price.

Mr. Ward's niece Elinor was married to Captain John Jefferson and lived at Staithes. They were Mr. Wardell's best friends.

MR. & MRS. JOHN JEFFERSON

We come to like Captain John Jefferson, he enjoyed life. He sailed his ship and his wife north to Newcastle to go to the races, visited the theatre and loved a game of cards. He kept open house at Staithes, and an open heart for his many nieces and nephews.

There is a beguiling moment when, after arriving at Guisborough in a chaise, (after leaving the stagecoach bringing them from a fashionable visit to London) the Jeffersons ride home on the farm waggon down to Staithes. We can almost hear them singing as the swaying oxen plod on.

When we meet Mr. Jefferson we have to give up any idea that the village of Staithes was an isolated hamlet of primitive fisherfolk. John Jefferson was both a wealthy, intelligent man, and an experienced, straightforward ship's captain. The best word to describe him is 'cheerful'.

His wife Elinnor Jefferson was shrewd, shrill of tongue, but liked to laugh. 'Nell will give me what for!' said their friend Thomas Wardell in a letter to his employer Mr. Baker, when he had forgotten to ask for a medicine for her husband.[7] Hospitable, quick witted, caustic, Elinnor Jefferson was a favourite neice of Mr. Ralph Ward; being most like him, astute and clever, she was more like a daughter. Twenty years younger than him, she was thirty years older than Ralph Jackson her first cousin, who found himself upbraided and smarting when he made a mistake with her butcher meat.

It is no good thinking of John and Elinnor Jefferson separately. They were a devoted couple.

Mr. Ward's eldest sister Dorothy Spencer, was an old lady in 1743. She owned the sailcloth factory, draper's shop and house, next door to Mr. Ward's house in Guisborough. Gentleman or not, she made him a convenient go-between, to her daughter Elinnor's home in Staithes. It became his favourite place. Elinnor Jefferson, was outspoken. He had better not get the messages wrong, except deliberately to tease her.

When Elinnor's mother Dorothy had married William Spencer of Guisborough, Dorothy's father, William Ward, had set them up in a sailcloth factory, partly to employ the poor. The Spencers had piled wealth upon wealth. Their children had prospered.

DOROTHY SPENCER (nee Ward)

THOMAS   RICHARD   ELINNOR   MARGARET   ESTHER
Merchants in London   Staithes   m. Adam Boulby unmarried

Elinnor Jefferson's sister Margaret had died. Her husband Adam Boulby owned shares in Whitby ships, and was left to bring up his daughters Dolly and Esther*, who were great favourites of the whole family, and spent a great deal of time with their Aunt Elinnor at Staithes. * *Esther died of a 'fitt' in London as a young woman.*

John Jefferson of Staithes was rich because he worked in a partnership with his wife's wealthy brother, Thomas Spencer, sailing ships in the Baltic trade. Thomas Spencer, who traded from London, had been apprenticed at Hull, and spent 18 years at Riga. John Jefferson based himself at Staithes, overseeing their Whitby ships trading with Riga, and in coal to London, and across the Atlantic. He was a ship's captain with a wide world-view of trade and culture.

John and Elinnor Jefferson had no living children. In 1728, the year of James Cook's birth, such a hopeful year, three children had been born in the large Jefferson family. Only one survived: Nathaniel Campion. Helped by his Uncle John, he would become a man of wide experience, a sea captain who sailed as far as Virginia, went frequently to Riga.

So, no, Staithes was not an isolated village of primitive fisherfolk. They were sea-going people with a wider vision, could speak foreign languages, and brought home souvenirs, sometimes a wife.

The extended Jefferson family of Staithes, was a sea-going dynasty. The daughters married sea-going men, Campions, Harrisons and Gallilees.

John Jefferson's father Mr. Anthony Jefferson was still alive in 1743, aged 81, but his mother Mary had died in 1740. Her name lived on, in true sea-faring tradition, in the names of the family ships.

ANTHONY & MARY JEFFERSON

JOHN	JANE	MARY	ANTHONY	SARAH
m	m	m	m	m
Elinnor	Robert	Paul	Sarah	John
Spencer	Campion	Harrison	Gill	Gallilee

These were the people James Cook lived among for three years, an extended Staithes family deeply involved with shipping.

Mr. Jefferson's sister **Jane** married Robert Campion, who owned the vessel *Robert & Jane;* and the open boat *Mary & Jane,* which sailed to Newcastle for coals, bought from the Hoastman William Jefferson and loaded most often at Jarrow quay. She plied along the coast and would sail as far as Cornwall. She was a touch Dutch in build, known as a scoot, and would beach on the flat reef at Staithes to unload coal. John Jefferson owned l/32nd share in her, Ralph Ward l/32nd, and Thomas Presswick, his secretary owned 1/16th. Mr. Robert Campion and his sons, Samuel and Nathaniel, captained the family ships, but the elderly Robert, crippled with kidney stones, preferred the short voyages of the *Mary & Jane.*

John Campion junior, of Staithes, was enrolled in 1743 as apprentice to Mr. William Jefferson at Newcastle. He was the older apprentice with young Ralph Jackson, leaving in 1750 to join the family ship *Thomas & Richard,* by then a Hoastman and able to trade in Tyne coal, though at first the independent way he did it, put Ralph Jackson in a huff, he thought him disloyal..

Mr. Jefferson's sister **Sarah** married John Gallilee. Their son John was master of the *Hannah* of Whitby, and later would be left his Uncle John's share of *Mary & Jane.*

The names Gallilee, Allely, and Mr. Yalloley (father of Ralph Jackson's apprentice friend, who had a market garden at Redheugh on the Tyne), all stem from the same root, and may be one of the old Norman French families in Cleveland. Gallilee men were respected as seamen, and we can see them in the Whitby records, captaining the larger ships.

Mr. Jefferson's sister **Mary** married Paul Harrison in 1724, their ship was the *Mary;* their son Paul was captain of the *Britainnia.*

John Jefferson's younger brother **Anthony**, in 1744 married Sarah Gill. She was 19, he was 40. Their first babies died, but their sons George and Samuel survived. At leisure, Anthony liked rod fishing: he fished with George Jackson. At work, he owned and ran ships.

It was the family ships which held the extended family together.

The ***Thomas and Richard*** named after Elinnor Jefferson's two brothers, was an older ship, half was owned by John Jefferson in partnership, plus tiny shares of l/32nd and l/16th held by Adam Boulby and his brother Thomas Boulby. This way, an owner spread the risk. She was listed at Whitby but sailed out of the Tyne in the Baltic trade; she was laid up at Shields in winter but would come down to Whitby for repairs. Nathaniel Campion was her master, then John Campion took over.

The ***Tryton*** was the other important Jefferson family ship, largely owned by Anthony Jefferson who had married Sarah. John Jefferson had a 1/16th share, Ralph Ward l/32nd. She was a Whitby Cat, with a crew of 13 including 7 apprentices. Captain Sam Gallilee took her to Carolina in 1747-9, she was used as a troop transport, and eventually owned by Samuel Campion.

Anthony Jefferson's other ships were the ***Sally*** and the ***Sarah***, and an old sloop the ***Midsummer***, shared with his brother Captain John which, with a crew of 5 under Captain John Salsbee, plied up and down the coast.

It was the sloop ***Darling*** which was Captain John Jefferson's darling; we can almost hear Elinnor Jefferson accusing him and laughing. He was happiest on her deck, down at Skinningrove loading paving stones for London; working her way into Hole Wyke at Boulby Alum Works with a load of coal; taking hams, eggs sunk in bran, and salted beef to London for the family there; unloading her coal at Mucking on the Thames, calling in at Rowhedge, on the Suffolk coast, to collect grapes, pears, and quickthorn hedging plants from their Aunt Margaret Gansell, for her brother Ralph Ward's fields at Guisborough. On calmer days Captain Jefferson would take his wife and her nieces Dolly and Esther on a daytrip to sea for fun.

Darling, rigged like a sloop, built like a tub, blunt bow, creaking, her crew sometimes under Captain John Addison, when could get a turn. At times he came home from London by coach. Women with social standing did not travel by sea to London, only maids, furniture and shopping were sent home that way.

Even with other sea-going families in Staithes, like the Marshalls

Captain John Jefferson was perhaps the most important man in the village. He was an official of the parish church and, all his life, he practised his religion without fuss and with friendly application.

Staithes is in the parish of Hinderwell. When James Cook arrived, in 1743, Archbishop Herring's visitation-returns that year show Hinderwell parish had 166 families, a few were Quakers. Probably about 300 people lived in the harbour village of Staithes. In summer half might be away at sea, the population made up with visiting fish merchants, and alum workers. The shop would be busy supplying passing ships.

A shop boy would be expected to go to Church and, having learned his catechism at Great Ayton school, would be ready, around the age of 16, to be confirmed in the Church of England, and it is just possible James Cook was confirmed by the Dean of York.*

*The Archdeacon of Cleveland whose responsibility it was, notoriously avoided such things as confirmations. He was Jaques Sterne, uncle of the future writer Laurence Sterne. The Dean often took over his duties, for instance, he married the Laurence Sternes.

Thomas Langstaffe, the Curate acting at Hinderwell, was a youngish man with a Cambridge degree. His allowance of £40 a year including surplice fees, was only just comfortable. The Rector of Hinderwell, being also Dean of York, was largely absent. There was a 'pettit' school, for the children to be taught religion, but all children and servants had to attend instruction during Lent, and church at Easter for communion.

With Mr. Samuel Gill and William Sanderson acting for its Vestry, James Cook would certainly attend Hinderwell parish church, and there he would be in contact with the influential and important Dean of York: Richard Osbaldeston.

~~~

REV. RICHARD OSBALDESTON.

This man, who knew the King, provides the link to James Cook's first recorded patron.

During the 32 years Richard Osbaldeston was Rector of Hinderwell, meeting with Samuel Gill and John Jefferson, one visitor must have been his elder brother William Osbaldeston MP, the one man we know tried to promote James Cook.

Richard Osbaldeston, who was noted for his unpleasant temper, his lack of courtesy, was appointed Rector of Hinderwell in 1715. He would not have lived much at Hinderwell, for by 1727 he was chaplain to the new King George II, and was one of George III's early tutors. He was appointed Dean of York in 1728. Yet he must have spent a certain amount of time at Hinderwell, for he signed the glebe Terriers, which list the property of that church, along with witnesses of local importance. In 1743, Richard Osbaldeston signed the glebe Terrier, alongside Samuel Gill (inhabitant). In 1749, John Jefferson and William Sanderson signed.[8]

James Cook must have seen the middle aged Dean in church and, as a family servant, may even have been sent to the Rectory with messages, indeed spoken to this man who knew the King.

The Dean's brother Willam Osbaldeston may also have met the shop boy James Cook.

~~~

WILLIAM OSBALDESTON MP 1688 – 1766

William Osbaldeston[9] was MP for the parliamentary seat of Scarborough between 1736-1747 and 1754-1766. He is not known to have spoken in the House, his function was more to grab naval contracts for his voters, and control the Customs and Excise jobs. In fact, at his first election his opponents objected that he had threatened to turn out the local customs officers, if they did not vote for him - a common enough act. Samuel Gill a customs officer, would certainly try to keep good relations with William Osbaldeston, who was related to John Hill, the Controller of Customs. Yet William Osbaldeston was not really a party political man, he was a Whig country gentleman, independent of mind. The Osbaldestons seem to have been related by marriage to Lord Milton.

It seems that, years later, John Walker of Whitby wrote to William Osbaldeston MP, who wrote to Captain Palliser of the *Eagle,* to get James Cook a lieutenant's commision in the Navy. Palliser replied with the sensible suggestion that the seaman Cook should apply for a Master's ticket, to which he was well suited. Palliser would later become MP for Scarborough himself though, being Yorkshire born, he may have known William Osbaldeston earlier. The Osbaldeston connections, were an acceptable way of patronage.

Why promote a young man he did not know? We do not know if William Osbaldeston had met the young James Cook. Yet other links which would later advance the young sailor in the Royal Navy, were already falling into place while James was still a young shop boy, at Staithes.

By the 1740s, the Ward family were already at the centre of the patronage system. They were able to promote the next generation, James Cook's generation. Mr. Ward's nephew, Ralph's elder brother George Jackson, entered the Royal Navy office in 1743. He too needed patronage. And his Uncle Joshua, Mr. Ralph Ward's younger brother, was in a position to help. Let us take a look at Joshua Ward.

5

PATRONS PENDING

JOSHUA WARD
25th June, 1686 - 21st December, 1761

No-one ought to avoid Joshua Ward, he was one of the world's great characters. He made his fortune from poisonous pills and gave it, and them, to the poor. He is included here to show just how close the Ward family stood to the very centre of patronage. Joshua Ward was the King's 'quack' doctor, meaning practitioner of alternative medicine, as we say now.[1]

When King George II dislocated his thumb, Joshua Ward cured it by a violent wrench, making the King yowl. The grateful King gave Dr. Ward an apartment in the Almonry Office in Whitehall, from which the poor could be treated at Royal expense. Joshua probably made clear to the King, and to everyone else, that was the reward he wanted.

Joshua Ward was a Yorkshireman, with that certain blunt independence of mind, added to a brusque manner which he shared with his brother Ralph Ward of Guisborough. But where Mr. Ralph Ward was sociable, though strict, and puritanical about not getting into debt, Dr. Joshua was tough, plain-speaking but believed in largesse. He was neatly over-generous to his family. Ralph Jackson notes on 5th October, 1757 that his uncle Ralph had written a copy letter for his mother to 'write over and send to Uncle Josa. about the Bounty he bestowed on her and ffather.' Dr. Joshua Ward was a rich, popular and famous old man, yet, for the middle 18 years of his life he had been forced to flee into exile, in France, charged with Treason.

Old William Ward, the wealthy Guisborough dyer, had had six sons; John the bankrupt MP who lived in Hackney, William, Edward, George, Ralph and Joshua. With the backing of their father's Yorkshire alum works, as young men William and Joshua had set up as Drysalters, selling alum and dyes, in Thames Street, London. This street, along the north side of the river beside London Bridge, backed on to the coal quays, where the Whitby ships then unloaded; the brothers were well placed for bringing in cargoes of alum. The alum trade, with such a long production time, of about two years, was risky, too slow to react to price rises and falls. Their mother Mary Ward's will in 1721 makes clear that Joshua and George were bankrupt. William too was not to be handed his capital legacy, just the interest. But by then Joshua had fled to France for embracing the Jacobite cause, of the Roman Catholic 'King over the water.'

Why did he do such a thing! The Wards were not Roman Catholic, they were English Protestants. They were industrialists, investing in land, country gentlemen with their sights set on Parliament. By 1715 Joshua had even become MP for Marlborough, when one of two rival mayors fixed his return, though no-one had voted for him. He took his seat at Westminster and voted as a Whig for the Septennial Bill before a petition unseated him.

As a drysalter, Joshua may have been involved with gunpowder. Did he sell it to the losing side? Or was his support for the Jacobite cause, of the exiled Stuart King, just part of his stubborn independence of mind? The 1715 Jacobite rebellion failed. Joshua fled to St. Germain, near Paris, where the exiled Jacobite court lived. They were just leaving. He stayed there.

The 29 year old Joshua had arrived in France at the worst possible moment to start making medicine and pills for a living.

His medicines were poisonous, there is no doubt of that now. Though they must be seen in the context of knowledge at that time. The medical profession used antimony and arsenic in small amounts quite freely, but it was well known that arsenic and antimony were poisons. Joshua Ward must have been convinced that the dosage in his pills was not dangerous. It was making them, which put him in danger.

The French were deeply suspicious of him - with good reason.

That year of 1715, the great French King Louis XIV died, and there were discovered still alive in French prisons, some of those poisoners the King had incarcerated 33 years earlier. In 1682, King Louis and his shocked ministers had been forced to act, when it became horribly clear that murder-for-sale, on a routine commercial basis, had taken over in France. Guilt ran to the highest levels of society even to the King's mistress. No-one was safe. The favourite method was poison; the favourite poison was antimony or arsenic. After shocking trials, multiple torture, executions and imprisonment, King Louis had prevailed, order was restored. From 1682 the sale of poisons was strictly controlled in France, private laboratories were forbidden. Which is probably why Joshua Ward nearly ended up in the Bastille as a prisoner himself, likely never to be seen again. He was rescued by John Page an English MP, a well-connected old friend, possibly by the medicine of money mixed with Jacobite favour. Joshua survived, recovered his position and was able to support himself for 18 years in France by the sale of his pills and drops. He thrived, and became known as 'The Quack', after he cured the French King's brother of an 'ague' when the French doctors could not. They scorned and ridiculed him, while he flourished and grew rich. They tried to undermine him. He became worldly wise, a trenchant, French speaking Yorkshireman.

Joshua Ward returned to England with a Royal Pardon in 1733. He was 48. The climate of opinion had changed. His old friend John

Page MP was an altruist, who refused favours for himself from his own close friend the Duke of Newcastle, that small fussy man who had every government appointment sewn up. It is possible the Duke arranged Joshua Ward's pardon, through Sir Robert Walpole's influence with the Queen. King George was a bluff man, who could see through people, but he admired his wife and followed her lead. We can imagine King George responding to Joshua Ward's straight manner, even as he yowled with the pain in his thumb.

> The Pardon reads:
> 'Writ of the Privy Seal. 6.Dec. 7Geo.II.
> Pardoned of all treasons by him committed
> in levying War against
> our late Royal Father King George.'

Back in England there was still no control over poisons.

Joshua could make any pill he liked. He set about becoming the most famous 'quack' doctor of his day, a mixture of osteopath, herbalist and chemist. He advertised his cures, trumpeted their worth, set himself up in style. He was attacked for being a 'Self Puffer', the newspapers were full of vitriolic protests. The Grub Street Journal ran a cutting campaign against him:

> 'But greater WARD, not only lame and blind
> Relieves; but all diseases of mankind
> By one sole Remedy removes, as sure
> As Death by Arsenic all disease can cure.'

The newspapers rampaged. 'Physicians use not this terrible Preparation', warned a doctor.

In the end, Joshua Ward issued an affidavit and made a dignified reply in the Daily Advertiser on 27 and 28 December 1734. He pointed out that 20,000 had taken his medicines since March, but the Bills of Mortality for 1734 showed a decrease of 3171; that the cancer patient he was supposed to have killed, happily still lived at The Dolphin in Bishopsgate, and another so called 'dead' man could be met alive at his own house in Pall Mall. He added firmly, there would be no more free medicine unless the person brought a certificate from his parish. Deaf, blind or those with disorders of the head must come Monday or Thursday mornings only.

Some startling cures - one wonders how - brought Joshua Ward untold wealth, fame, and patronage of the great. General Churchill promoted his pills throughout the aristocracy, Lord Justice Reynolds testified to the 'miraculous effects' of the remedies upon his maidservant. The shrewd Horace Walpole gave only qualified approval. Ward's Drop, and sweating powders, and his white, blue, red and purple pills, became a famous patent medicine of the day. The unstoppable Joshua was envied, sued, proved to have no medical learning, cartooned by Hogarth[2] in 'The Company of Undertakers', ridiculed by the poet Pope in 'The Instructions of Horace', but the public had enormous faith in him and when, in 1748, the Apothecaries Act restrained unlicensed people from making medicines, in order to ban the worst charlatans, Parliament inserted a special clause exempting Dr. Ward. If that is not influence and patronage, what is?

Dr. Joshua was known as 'Spot' Ward, from a claret coloured mark on the side of his face. Bulky and firm-spoken, he was notedly forthright when dealing with superiors in rank. Once, when corrected for turning his back when leaving the royal presence, he replied, 'His Majesty suffers no harm in seeing my back, but were I to break my neck from a regard for ceremony, it would be a sad loss to the poor.'

He was a deeply kind man. He bought three houses in Pimlico, and converted them into a hospital for his poor patients. He opened another in Threadneedle Street in the City, where large crowds attended each day, and fine ladies of fashion, like Lady Gage, sat by the door distributing medicines. The dying novelist Henry Fielding paid him a great tribute in 'Voyage to Lisbon', by saying

Joshua was both kind and very wise.

His wider public had ignored all the warnings, gobbled the pills, and made Joshua Ward rich. From the beginning, he gave much of it away. An epigram signed 'Conundrum' in a December 1734 newspaper points this out:

'Tis plain Ward's nostrums aren't dispensed for money all;
  His foes themselves declare them Anti-monial!'

Basically, Joshua Ward was a chemist. As a child at the Alum Works, he must have seen the fascination of making beneficial pure crystals from dirty shale rock. He attempted to manufacture porcelain and saltpetre and was the first in England to make sulphuric acid by burning saltpetre and sulphur. This process, which he patented, caused an intense stink like rotten eggs, all over Twickenham and Richmond on Thames, arousing angry complaints. The process, so like alum making, and the brightly coloured pills reflecting his childhood at the dyeworks, show both his home background in Cleveland and the development of early industrial and pharmaceutical chemistry.

Was it his knowledge of saltpetre, an ingredient of gunpowder, which caused him problems in both Britain and France? In 1734 he was attacked in a poem based on the Gunpowder Plot; entitled 'The Pill Plot', two lines of it read:

'As we long since escaped thy powder,
  Dost think we'll take thy pills?'

Public belief, blind faith, infallibility versus Poison? A closer look at his wonderous pills shows us medical chemistry at the time.

It puts the attempt to defeat Scurvy into its proper context.

DROPS, PILLS AND SWEATING POWDERS

In my childhood, a favourite advertisement at the cinema was for Carters Little Liver Pills, a man leapt joyfully over a field gate, another was for Bile Beans, one remedy turned the urine green. Patent medicines have always had glamour.

All the Ward family took Uncle Joshua's pills. The whole point of them was to purge an illness from the body. The public thought vomiting a good thing and to be encouraged; with luck it would also have brought up the harmful pills. On 5th December, 1752, Ralph Jackson in Newcastle found his master William Jefferson 'very ill for he had taken my Uncle Jos. Ward's Pills.' Ralph's mother Hannah suffered from gallstones; she took the Drop and Pill, suffered severe heartburn and turned a violent yellow. Cousin Matty Reed took Uncle Joshua's Sack Drop, dropped in white wine. Ralph took the Pills himself, once for a toothache 'which operated by puke extremely well, I also sweat much', he says. The toothache remained, 'a violent pain' which took him after three days to Dr. Bisset at Skelton, a renowned dentist, who killed the nerve. Yet something in the way Ralph recorded the Pill's use, gives the impression that one day his intelligence could have woken up to their danger, had not their popularity faded first.

There was definitely something sinister, about Dr. Ward's Drops and Pills. The French poisoners had first begun using antimony and arsenic for abortions. In 1762 in Greenwich, Ralph's sister Rachel was expecting her fourth child. She had at least nine babies, some dead at birth. In August 1762, Ralph's mother gave Rachel her Uncle Joshua's drops. And may have continued to do so. On 24th March, Rachel miscarried a girl child. Unsafe in their lack of knowledge, the Ward family loved and trusted Uncle Joshua and took his pills.

In London, Joshua Ward entertained his family and friends at his grand apartment in Whitehall. His niece, Elinnor Jefferson of Staithes would visit him, when she visited her brother Richard Spencer in Great George Street. Her husband John Jefferson arriving in his ship *Darling* would deliver him a ham. Ralph's brother George Jackson would call when he came up to the Admiralty. Ralph, and his sisters Esther, Dolly and Rachel took tea, when they were in London. The oldest nephew Thomas Spencer, the millionaire Baltic merchant, living nearby in Craven Street, was a regular support. Joshua felt close to his older sisters Ann, who lived with her second husband the Reverend Edwards in Greenwich, and Margaret who had married David Gansell of Doneyland, at Rowhedge, this was a small village with a quayside on the estuary running up to Colchester. The *Darling* frequently put in there, on her way north to Boulby. It was Margaret's son, the hot-tempered Colonel William Gansell, who looked after Joshua Ward in old age, on one occasion sacking the housekeeper, 'without a hearing' which his cousin Ralph Jackson thought not at all right!

Joshua Ward lived until 1761. He died on Monday 21st December, about midday. 'Colonel Gansell' says Ralph Jackson, 'convened his relations to Whitehall at Six in the evening,' and read the Will. A letter containing the sad news arrived at Guisborough on Christmas morning. Ralph read it carefully. There was one request by their uncle which had them bemused. 'My brother George says ... he has ordered himself to be buried within or near the outside of the alter rails in Westminster Abbey as can be'

A Self-Puffer to the last?

There is an intriguing post script to Joshua Ward's life. In February 1773, Horace Walpole, in writing to his friend Maquis du Deffand comments: 'There died five or six years ago at St. Germain, an old woman called Madame Ward, after her death they verified on the papers she has been a natural daughter of our King James II'. This would make her half sister to that other illegitimate daughter of King James, the Duchess of Buckingham of Mulgrave Castle, near Staithes.[3]

Could it be, Joshua had married in his young ardent days, and been exiled less for gunpowder, than for an explosion of love?

It is obvious that, with Joshua Ward's high connections, patronage would become available to his family. His friend Lady Gage was the travelling companion of Lady Sarah Osborne, sister to Admiral Byng, sister-in-law of Robert Osborne, Commissioner of the Navy. It was at the Navy Board and the Admiralty where, in future years, James Cook's patrons would be found. Which brings us to Ralph Jackson's brother, George, who probably had the most influence over James Cook's career.

Joshua Ward appears to have had this sculpture of himself made by Agostino Carlini, in order to place it in Westminster Abbey. It was an act of charity to rescue an impoverished sculptor, and was unfinished at Joshua's death. It ended up being given in 1793 to stand in the entrance hall of the Royal Society of Arts. In 1993 it was moved to the sculpture hall of the Victoria and Albert Museum, and there Joshua stands, with generously open hand.[2]

GEORGE JACKSON
1725 – 1822

George Jackson is the man most overlooked in Captain Cook's life. When James Cook was appointed to command the *Endeavour,* George Jackson was 2nd Secretary to the Admiralty. As all correspondence was addressed to the 1st Secretary, Philip Stevens, George Jackson's role has been forgotten.

George was the older brother of Ralph Jackson. He too came from Richmond, an inland town, so where did George get his passion for the sea? Perhaps at Staithes, just like James Cook? The Jackson family spent their holidays with their cousins, Mr. & Mrs. John Jefferson, at Staithes. By 1743, when James Cook arrived in the village, George, who was three years older, was about to start work in London as a clerk at the Navy Board but, it is likely, the two men first met, when they were young, in the small sea-going village of Staithes, where the boats beached outside the shop door.

George was sensible, sociable, his mind clear. In build less rugged than James Cook, in later portraits George's features are refined, the glance more sensitive than we expect from his confident pose. He was clever too, and a touch innovative, like the Wards. His grandson said, many years later, that what George meant by clever was 'a practical, scientific ability', which would fit his alleged appreciation of James Cook.

George Jackson made his long career in Royal Navy Administration, in which he rose steadily through the years, with the help of friends. None of his appointments would have been available without some patronage. His grandson said, he was appointed first under the auspices of Lord Milton. Was this via the Osbaldestons? Then there was Uncle Joshua's best friend John Page MP, himself the most loyal friend of the Duke of Newcastle, who controlled government appointments. And Uncle Joshua's friend's friend, Lady Sarah Osborne, sister of a Commissioner to the Navy.

Like James Cook, George was the second son. Both expected to have to make their own good fortune. George and Ralph's eldest brother, Edward Jackson, had served a sea apprenticeship with George Hill of Whitby, and in July 1744 left on the East India Company ship *Northampton*. as 3rd Mate. In the Indian Ocean, on the way back in 1746, the ship disappeared in a storm off the Isle d'Reunion. Her sister ship *Hardwick* brought the news home. When all hope had gone, George was the eldest living son, and the weight of family patronage moved to promote him instead.[4]

The bald facts[5] of George Jackson's career can be simply put:

At the Navy Board:

Clerk to the Clerk of Acts	24th June 1743 - 22nd Feb 1755
Chief Clerk to	
the Clerk of Acts	22nd Feb 1755 - 11th May 1758
Assistant Clerk of Acts	11th May 1758 - 11th Nov 1766

At the Admiralty:

2nd Secretary to the Admiralty	
	11th Nov 1766 - 12th June 1782
1st Clerk (Marine Dept).	ditto
Judge Advocate of the Fleet	19th Feb. 1768 -1st Dec 1822

Yet, what seems like a steady progress was, in fact, put at risk at the very beginning, when George did something reckless - for an ambitious man. At the age of 19 he got married.

His wife was his full cousin Mary Ward, only child of his mother's brother William Ward. Why did he risk it? Was Mary his childhood sweet-heart? Was she very beautiful, like one of her future daughters? Or was it a matter of having her money to establish them? William Ward had married into the wealthy family of Sir Francis Vincent of Stoke D'Abernon, who was Mary's grandfather. Mary was also the sole heir to 1/10th of her grandmother Ward's capital. At 19 George could not have married without his Uncle Ralph Ward's approval, he being trustee of Mary's money. George as the second son, was not then expecting to inherit his father's lead mines in Swaledale, and knew his parents lived too far over the horizon of their income. Mary was passing the age when she was expected to marry, and marry well. George, who was younger than Mary must have decided it had to be him. This ability to decide then act, was very much George's talent.

The young couple were married on 24th September, 1745 at St. Benet's, Paul's Wharf, in London, and soon moved to Fenchurch Buildings, a set of new houses, built over the old Sugar Loaf Alley, and near to George's work at the Navy Office.

The babies soon came. George and Mary were unlucky. Robert died aged 9 months, William died aged 4 weeks, Thomas Spencer Jackson was christened the day he was born and died within days. Mr. Thomas Spencer the Baltic merchant, brother of Mrs. Jefferson of Staithes, was godfather to them all. Commissioner Osborn of the Admiralty, godfather to the first baby, shows how well connected George was, but now the young couple with high hopes were broken hearted. Had Mary taken Uncle Joshua's pills?

By 1751, when the young Ralph Jackson was an apprentice in the coal trade in Newcastle, and James Cook was 23, an ordinary seaman on the collier *Three Brothers*, things at last began to improve for George and Mary Jackson, a healthy daughter was born. Thomas Spencer, Aunt Margaret Gansell, and Mrs. Turnpenny stood sponsors at the christening at nearby St. Olave's, Hart Street. The child lived. A second daughter arrived in July 1753, a third in April 1755. Confident now, they asked Mary's cousin Hester, daughter of Sir Henry Vincent, to be godparent, and Mr. Lane of the Admiralty, and Mrs. Spencer, the Russian wife of Richard Spencer their cousin. Following that birth, Mary's health fell apart.

George Jackson at 29, had to raise three baby girls, Mary, Catherine and Elizabeth. Known as Pally, Kitty and Bess, they grew up to decorate his life, loved by the whole family. Each summer he sent them to Guisborough, to stay with his mother, and came to collect them at the end of their holiday. George Jackson was to visit Staithes many times over the years, he and his daughters continued to meet Mr. Sanderson's family. George's horses were bred at Loftus Grainge farm, and he enjoyed shooting and dining at Boulby, fishing along Staithes beck with Anthony Jefferson. When he was 2nd Secretary to the Admiralty, even in 1774 long after *Endeavour*'s return, George would hitch a lift on a ship, and land by small boat at Staithes, to be met by Mr. Sanderson with a horse.[6]

George, rising steadily in the Navy office, with financial help and patronage, soon became a patron himself.

The year of 1755, had started so hopefully. On 22nd February, George had been appointed Chief Clerk to the Clerk of the Acts. There was the usual entry fee, or gift, to find. He applied to his Uncle Ralph Ward, who entered in his Journal:

'8th March, 1755. Much snow. Wind at NE with frost. Sent T. Presswick to Stokesley with a letter to leave with Mr. Scottowe and another for Mr. Matthews [Attorney at law] about remitting £300 which sum I intend to send Geo. Jackson who had got the place of Chief Clerk in the Navy Office conferred upon him and awaits that sum he has engaged to pay for his coming into it, now being in possession thereof as hee's been for a Week or 10 days past.'

Mr. Ralph Ward was calling in his loans to Thomas Skottowe to help advance his nephew's career, by paying George's premium or gift.

George now found himself in a position to help others along. That was how the patronage system worked. One of the first things to happen when Ralph Jackson left Newcastle in December 1756 to live with his Uncle Ralph Ward at Guisborough, was a request by letter from his recent Master William Jefferson for assistance from George. Ralph says:

'This letter recommended one Benja.Heslop, late apprentice to a Surgeon in Newcastle that I might write to my Brother to befriend him in a Place aboard a Ship of War, viz. a Surgeon or surgeon's Mate.'

'I wrote to my Bro. & to Mr. Wm. Jefferson my late Master at Newcastle the latter recommended a young Man to my Bros, favour, tho' I was [to] write to him.'

While they waited for a reply, the weather was snowy, but the

71

ships' captains were already preparing for the coming season. Ralph details how John Nichelson the butcher killed an ox at Grainge for John Gallilee of Staithes, who paid Ralph £13 -17s - l0d. During the business, William White happened the misfortune to cut the top of his foot with the bill or chopping knife. Grainge Farm may have been blood stained but it did not put off Ralph from the treat which always followed, a Tripe Feast at the Cock Inn. Though he was clearly raising his eyes to Heaven at the boring conversation there, between old Mr. Ward, Mr. Wardell and apothecary Proddy, as they discussed 'kelp, Snow Cawkers for horse shoes in the heel, and screws to fasten upon a Man's in frost'!

On 1st February, in heavy snow, the post arrived with a letter from London.

'This afternoon I received a letter from my Brother wherein he informed me of his having placed Benja. Heslop late of Newcastle Surgeon on board one of His Majesty's Ships of War (the Ferret). I wrote to Mr. Jefferson.'

So twelve years before the *Endeavour* appointments, George Jackson was placing men on Royal Navy ships, on request.

Second cousins were helped too. In May 1758, Mr. John Jefferson took William Pease of Whitby to London, to enter the Navy Office on 5th June, as a clerk to the Clerk of Acts, the job George had started with. 'On account of my brother's preferment,' says Ralph, he 'will by him be got into the Navy Office.'

From March 1755, through George Jackson, patronage in the Royal Navy was in place and waiting, for anyone connected to the Wards.

The Ward family had helped James Cook once, perhaps they would do so again? That July, 1755 he joined the Royal Navy.

~~~

6

WAITING FOR A PLACE

Let us go back to 1746, to Staithes, where 20 year old George Jackson visits in summer, and James Cook, a 17 year old grocer's boy, is thinking of going to sea.

Was James working at the shop, to save up to buy a place? It was usual for a lump sum to be paid as premium to become an indentured apprentice, even to an established grocer, such as Mr. Pease at Whitby. James Cook needed about £30 for a premium.

Ralph Jackson records only the side of the person he was representing but, for instance, widowed Mrs. Cornforth, who lived across the road from him in Guisborough, must have asked for his help:

'1763. February 2nd. Mrs. Ann Cornforth, agreed with Mr. Pease this afternoon, for her son Richard as an apprentice for 6 years from yesterday (he's going on 15 years old). She gives £42 as an apprentice fee and this day the Indentures were signed.'

So what kind of shorter apprenticeship was available? Apprenticeships came at all levels. A guild apprenticeship was usually for 7 years. Ralph Jackson served his time for 7 years as a coal fitter's apprentice, which brought him membership of the Hoastman Company of the Tyne, the Freedom of the City of Newcastle, the duty to carry a musket in its defence, and a vote for

Parliament. Ralph's schoolfriend Ralph Brockett, was apprenticed 3 years 'in the Chequ'd line[n] trade near Manchester

Sea apprenticeships were usually 7 years or 3. James was nearing 18, running out of time. The cost of a premium was usually related to the earnings. Two examples of local sea apprenticeships, show how:

1758   '11th   February.   Wm.   Reed's   son   Ralph[1]
to serve apprenticeship

    to Richard Knaggs.   6 years.

    RK to give him £28 viz.   £4 each year for 3 years

                                    £5   2 years

                                    £6   1 year

    Indentured'

Richard Knaggs, an up and coming Captain, had bought a new ship. This was the sort of opening that James Cook could look for as an apprentice.

    1758 '27th February. Apprenticeship-Indentures
    Robert Pulman
    (Brother of Alex Pulman) apprenticed
    to Richard Knaggs 3 years.
    '£31. 10s. at 3 several payments and 1/6d for every week
    the ship shall be laid by, or rather when he is at home.'

Both apprenticeships were agreed in February, the beginning of the coaling season.

In Richard Knaggs we see the future an indentured apprentice could aspire to, if he could acquire some money.

In 1756 Richard Knaggs had been master of the *Diamond* of Whitby, owned by Samuel Campion of Staithes. Ralph Jackson visited the ship at Shields because some of the loading keels had sunk in a storm, and insurance had to be talked out. To buy a ship, money had to be found, and people to buy shares in the vessel to share the risk. How did Richard Knaggs do it? He married it.

In June 1757, Richard Knaggs, judiciously and secretly married Tibby, the daughter of Oliver Presswick, and niece of old Mr. Ward's secretary Thomas Presswick, a Guisborough family who owned shares in ships. Captain Knaggs was soon buying shares in ships for himself, and even borrowed from Thomey Presswick to do so. Ralph Jackson was annoyed, especially when they could not easily get Thomey's money back from him.

Why did James Cook not find a place on a Staithes-owned ship?

Anthony Jefferson of Staithes' *Midsummer,* had six crew, and no apprentices at that time. She was handling general cargo to London.

John Jefferson's *Darling*, a sloop with six crew, bringing coal to Boulby, carried no apprentices in 1747, probably due to the difficulty in beaching at Hole Wyke. *Darling* took on a newly qualified seaman, Peter Webster, in August 1748.

The Marshall family of Staithes, owners of the Whitby Cat *Blessing* had their own group of family and friends to accommodate.

It is clear that James Cook belonged to the Gill/Jefferson/Ward group. Through them he must look further afield, to Whitby.

There appear to have been three classes of ships sailing from Staithes and Whitby: fishing vessels, **coasting** sloops and **Whitby collier Cats.**

There were only about 7 or 8 **coasting** vessels sailing out of Whitby with general cargoes as well as coal, including the *Elizabeth*, the *Edward,* and Robert Campion's *Mary & Jane* which needed only three men.

A typical cargo out of Whitby was taken by the *Darling* under Captain John Peters, in the winter of 1749: [2]

'46 tons of ash timber, 60 barrels spragg fish, 1 cask of hams, 1 barrel of pork, 7 casks tallow, 3 casks hams, 1 cask pork, 44 tanned hides, 1 box linendrapery goods returned.'

The following Spring she took '40 tons alum, 40 tanned hides, 3 casks tallow, 2 casks and 3 crates Hams of British Bacon.'

Ships coming in to Whitby brought crates of earthenware from Sunderland, 20 doz. glass bottles and coal. Robert Campion brought 16 tons of salt in the *Mary & Jane* from Blythnook.

These vessels were the general delivery 'lorries' of their day.

The larger ships sailing out of Whitby, the **Whitby Cats** were otherwise employed. There was a war on. A number of them had gone with the troops to America.

In 1743, the government agent in charge of these troop transports, showed them being paid a lucrative 14 shillings a ton, a calendar month. In his list were four smaller Whitby ships at least.[3]

Brig *SeaNymph* / Jos. Bailey	130 tons	6 guns
Snow *Greyhound* / Rob. Oliver	109 tons	6 guns
Brig *Tryton* / Jn. Boyd	123 tons	4 guns
Ship *Wm & Mary* / Arch. Montgomry	175 tons	6 guns.

Mr. Ralph Ward owned a share in the first three listed.

The *SeaNymph* and the *Greyhound,* had been delivering coal from Mr. Ralph Ward's colliery on the River Wear since 1729.

By 1746 the *Tryton,* (owned by John and Anthony Jefferson and with Mr. Ward having a share) was headed to Carolina, under Capt.

Sam Gallilee. Her 13 crew included among its 7 apprentices William Kirk, who went next to the *Midsummer* as a seaman, showing that Staithes found places for its own men first.

The transports carried guns and, as part of their pacifist religious beliefs, Quaker ships could not transport troops to war, only bring them home when hostilities ended. During the war, Quakers such as Henry and John Walker, were left at home to continue in the coal and timber trade. Naturally they took honest advantage, to expand.

With the demands of war, the press gangs were active, and vicious. To prevent being taken, a man needed an official 'Protection' from the Admiralty, and the terms were clear:[4]

Men over 55 had to provide a Certificate of their age from the Parish Register, signed by the minister of religion.

Men over 18, needed the same Certificate, plus the affidavit of a creditable person, usually a JP, that they serve in some British merchant ship. These were honoured by being ignored, though the ship's mate was often left alone.

A sea apprentice must produce his Indentures plus an affidavit of Protection signed by a JP.

As the 1746 coaling season opened, in February and March, the Whitby shipowners began to take out Protections for their new apprentices, most were employing just one. Newark Waller took on two. On 4th January, John Walker took out a Protection for John Dowson, on 6th February another for James Dobson. These may have been long-promised places. For three months no more apprentices were entered at Whitby, then two places were available and grabbed in July. The tide was running out for James Cook. It was no longer safe for him to stay near the sea; he had to find a place before he was 18 in October. William Sanderson would know he would lose James, the press gang would take him and, maybe, they had suffered some scares. The young man was 6 feet tall, not easy to hide. The smugglers' escape-runs through the roofs of the village houses had tiny trapdoors. Was it Mr. Samuel Gill, Mrs. Sanderson's father, the Customs officer, who found him a place? Or was the link Mr. John Jefferson's brother-in-law Adam Boulby, who had owned shares with Henry Walker in several ships, since 1740:

Greyhound	AB 1741	3 shares	HW 1743	2 shares
Sea Adventure	AB 1740	2 shares	HW 1744	2 shares.
Friendship	AB 1742	4 shares	HW 1744	6 shares.

A place came. On the 4th August 1746, James Cook's Indentures were signed with Captain John Walker, followed swiftly by a Protection on 15th August. He was safe! It had been a near run thing. He got one of the last apprenticeships vacant that season.

Somehow, the apprentice fee, of about £30, had been found. In three years working in the shop, with a boy's wages of less than £5 a year, he could not have saved it himself. So, who paid?

WALKERS OF WHITBY

Whitby has always honoured James Cook as her own. An apprentice, living as part of a seagoing community, the tall 18 year old would spend 10 months at sea, Christmas at home, and a few weeks at the beginning of the season, living in the warmth of the attic at the Walkers' house in Haggersgate, Whitby. Sleeping there, high above the narrow cobbled street, among the huddled roofs, and wild cry of seagulls, level with the top masts of his master's ships moored below the mud line of the tidal harbour. At work, rigging the ships in the short cold dark days, studying navigation and customs duties by candlelight; John Walker's sons said that, while the other apprentices larked, James Cook was solemn and studious, and the housekeeper provided him with a table and candles. A tendency to self-education? Years later when he returned as a famous man, the housekeeper Mary Proud could not contain her delight, rushing forward with: 'Oh Honey, James, how glad I is to see thee!' We can imagine him, standing there in the Whitby house, a tall man with brown eyes, smiling at her in memory.

The Walker family of Whitby were Quakers, with that mix of honesty and independence, thrift, humour and tolerance which caused Quakers to prosper. John Walker was 40, with a daughter Esther and three small sons, Robert, John aged 2 and baby Henry. He lived in Haggersgate, his elder brother Henry in Church Street. The house in Grape Lane was Mr. Walker's mother Esther's for her lifetime.

Downstairs in the 'blue room' the quiet old lady sat with her friends, taking tea from a silver tray. Quaker women had influence and tranquillity and, unusually for the times, equality with the men. They were brought up to be fearless. Addressing each other as 'Friend', or 'Esther Walker', they shared their lives and laughter. Their formal Women's Meetings put forward decisions to the highest level of the Society of Friends. God being part of the inner person, truth and practical work was their ideal. A Quaker household could blend business acumen, straight thinking and a beautiful holiness. A Quaker's word alone was binding. Oaths of any kind were forbidden. No Quaker swore. As seamen tend to swear - James Cook did in exasperation - no doubt there were a few muffled skirmishes in the apprentices' attic.

Mrs. Esther Walker came from a seagoing family and was rich in her own right. Her father Henry Stonehouse had been a Master Mariner. Her uncle William Stonehouse was a Hoastman of the Tyne, whose apprentice master was John Clavering. Her husband John Walker senior, sailed Whitby ships delivering coal from Mr. Clavering's mines around Chopwell in the wedge of hills south of the River Tyne, west of the Derwent valley. The coal was mixed to give different qualities and called Clavering Stella, and sometimes the mix was bad. The London agent wrote to his employer in March 1710:

'I have been twice down att the Gate* where I found poor John Walker att his witts end; he could not dispose of his Clav(ering) Stella tho' offer'd [to accept] 6d under the markett.'[5]

*Billigsgate quay.

The letter asks Mr. Clavering to compensate John Walker 'and lett him have a bulk of his best this next [voyage] if he can be perswaded to load.'

Inventories sometimes had to be made, perhaps following a death. At Christmas 1716 the agent wrote again:

'I wrote sometime ago to John Walker off Whitby to take an inventory and appraise our shipping as soon as they came to lye up but have not heard off him since.'

John Walker senior died in 1743 when his sons began to buy into more ships, maybe with their inheritance.

Henry the elder son was nearing 50 and, like most seagoing men had already made his will, committing his body to earth or sea 'as it may so happen' and ...'if at lande to be buried in the plainest manner possible ....',[6] there speaks the Quaker in him. Having three daughters, Rachel, Esther and Mary, he had put most of his money into land, farms, houses, a shop, an inn the Shoulder of Mutton in Sandygate. On Tyneside, to make supplying the crews with meat easier, he had a farm at Chirton, a small village just outside North Shields, and more land at Preston and Shields. His wife Ann was to have £80 a year from the profits of his shipping which his brother John was to manage. As trustees for part of his will, Henry Walker appointed Abel Chapman and Jarvis Coates, the shipbuilder. And it could even have been Jarvis Coates, who helped find James Cook an apprenticeship.

Jarvis Coates was a second or third cousin to Mr. Ralph Ward. The Coates family built ships at Whitby on the west side of the harbour above the bridge, where a channel cut in behind the Bell Sand to the firm shore. In 1717 the 237 ton ship *William & Jane* was built, in 1724 *Sea Adventure* a 248 ton, in 1728 *John & Dorothy* a Whitby Cat 99' x 25', in 1729 the *Lark,* all restricted to less than 28 feet on the beam, to pass through the drawbridge across Whitby harbour. Sometimes the ships hit the ricketty wooden houses built on the bridge. Jarvis let Thomas Fishburn take over management of half of his yard in 1748, selling it to him in 1759.[7]

Ralph Jackson met Mr. Coates at Staithes:

1757 Dec. 7th. Ralph says he dined at Mr. John Jefferson's with Nathaniel Campion and Jarvis Coates 'late a shipbuilder of Whitby.'

1759 Feb. 1st. 'Mr. Pease walked with me to Fishburn's new dock, and I went on board the Thomas & Richard, Nathaniel Campion Master, she is going to have new decks laid.'

Now, weave together a Customs officer, ship owners, a shipbuilder, their relatives and friends, the Staithes Safety Net operated to save James Cook from the Press. They got him to sea, with a Protection.

On the east side of Whitby harbour, upriver from the bridge, and across the water from Jarvis Coates' shipyard, the Whitby Dock company had set up in 1730, building a double dry dock in 1734, and then a single dry dock (recently rediscovered).

The new apprentice, James Cook, lived among shipbuilding and repairs, with lots to learn. Young sailors are interested in ship design and performance; later they opt for survival.

There appears to have been a shortage of materials, as ship building increased. Early in the 1745 season, Whitby ships like the *Dolphin, Endeavour*[8] and *Success* were taking coal to the Netherlands, and returning with sail duck, ells* of Holland cloth, chain. Henry Walker sent the ship *Henry & Mary,* under captain John Jefferson of Sandsend, who used 26 ells of Hessen Canvas on the way back, but the Walkers were not trading much out of Whitby. The Walker brothers were shipping coal outward bound, from the Tyne and the Wear, and timber inward to London.
ell = 45"…. 26 ells= 32.5 yards (30 metres).

At Newcastle, as the 1746 season opened, Mr. Ralph Carr's ship *Hull Merchant,* bound for America, loaded white crown glass, ironmongery, 18 dozen felt hats and other goods for Rhode Island, St. Eustace and New York. At Newcastle and Sunderland, the colliers were loading deck cargo like wheat flour or oil of vitriol, and sinking crates of glass in the coal, and were heading for Holland. A small fiction was being applied. They cleared customs cheaply for a British port, but went on to Europe, most came back to confess and pay their dues later. Sometimes they did not have a buyer in London, or a good enough price, and sometimes their agents met them at sea with new orders. In January, Whitby ships pleaded 'forced overseas by stress of weather'. Quakers were trusted to pay up. Some ignored the fiction.

John Boulby, took the *Loyalty* out of Newcastle in March, with 112 coals*, and deck cargo, cleared for Hamburg. John Watson cleared the *Friendship* for Portsmouth on 15th January, with coal but took it to Dort, in the Netherlands; he paid up on August 18th.
Coals are given throughout in Newcastle chauldrons of approx. 8 cwt. [8 hundredweight] (20 cwt = 1 ton)

John Walker was sailing out of Sunderland, where Whitby colliers were loading at 88 or 92 coals, clearing for Yarm, Lynn, Harwich, London, but unloading at Scheedam and Rotterdam, Amsterdam or Middleburg. John Walker, master of the *Nightingale* brought back Holland sailcloth from Rotterdam, '3 foreignmade sails of 92 ells', from Dort. [9]

James Cook was entering a world of competence, danger and shrewd buying and selling. His shop experience would not be wasted, especially with sailcloth. The Walker brothers were operating a shipping line, captaining, building and managing ships and cargo. They were training their own apprentices and, in 1746, were employing freelance experienced captains. Among these were the three brothers, Matthew, William and John Jefferson of Sandsend, a different Jefferson family to the Staithes Jeffersons. It was John Jefferson of Sandsend who would become James Cook's captain.*

* Ralph Jackson followed the local pattern of speech. He usually called his cousin at Staithes, Mr. John Jefferson. The Sandsend John Jefferson, he usually called Captain. Which, from now on, we will too.

7

SEA APPRENTICE
1746 -1749

The FREELOVE¹

It took from seven to ten years to become an elite Whitby seaman. It was arduous and exhilarating, dangerous, often boring. The bitter cold and sea sickness, the cutting wind, raw eyes, fear in the bones, were balanced by milky blue days, torpid green water, fresh fish, flashing sunlight. Or a night sea glinting with stars. It was repetitive, tedious, a slow accumulation of knowledge which could save a man's life - or tell him he was about to lose it. We are able to skip over the fear and the tedium. James Cook had to suffer it. He learned to work with the wind and the tide. He learned, in those long hard years, skill to take him around the world.

FREELOVE
August 1746
When 17 year old James Cook entered into John Walker's service in August 1746, he may have been sent to the *Freelove.* She was new, built as a collier at Great Yarmouth during 1746. At 341 tonnage, 106 feet long and only 27 feet on the beam, in order to pass through Whitby harbour bridge, she was very similar to the future

Endeavour (368 tons, 106' x 29'3"). *Freelove* proved a sound ship. She was finally lost off icy Greenland in 1792.

'Freelove' was a Quaker term for offering good faith. James Cook was sailing for a Quaker who believed in this principle of trust, and the attitude on board was meant to be based on Quaker manners, quiet, care, and lack of showy behaviour. It seems to have affected James Cook for life. Perhaps too, so did Quaker fearlessness.

His indentures were dated 4th August, but he was not safe to go to sea without a Protection certificate. When this was signed on 15th *Freelove* was on the Tyne loading coal and paid light and buoyage fees of 1 shilling 2 pence on 12th August at Newcastle. He probably joined her at sea as she passed south.

Freelove[2] paid 1 shilling 2 pence again on 27th Sept. and 31st Oct. and seems to have loaded at 182, 173 and 179 coals. *Freelove* then disappears from the coal ports of Newcastle and Sunderland until 9th July, 1747.

For a new Whitby ship, the usual place to go during these missing winter months, was across the Atlantic, taking about 6 months: there is no proof that happened. There are no muster rolls for *Freelove's* spring /summer voyages. Yet Jamaica or Maryland remain possible, from the pattern of voyages by other Whitby ships.

FREELOVE
1747

Early in February, 1747, Henry Walker's ship the *Henry & Mary,* under Captain John Jeffels, coming in to Whitby from Scheedam, took 'out of his Majesty's wharehouse' from on board the ship,[3] '1 foreign-made sail of 128 ells value £10-13s-4d'. And his ship *Esther* from the Coast used 'a parcel of foreign-made sails of 217 ells value £8-18s-8d.' All that year Whitby ships were bringing in staves, spars, handspikes, deal planking. One ship, the *Ingeber Maria* came into Whitby from 'Berg and Christiana' with deals. Whitby yards were building ships called Cats designed to use the awkward River Tyne.

The Tyne was not the best of rivers to move coal. It was shallow, with sandbanks; it twisted, so that sails kept losing the wind. The early coal mines were upriver above the old arched bridge at Newcastle, through which colliers could not pass. Keelboats rowed the coal downriver to load the ships. From Newcastle bridge down to the river mouth, on fuller tides, ships loaded from dirty coal staithes, served by waggonways from the collieries.

Even to enter the Tyne was treacherous and took feats of seamanship. Across the river mouth there was a sandbar, which shifted all the time and, at high tide left only 21 feet depth of water, which could be reduced by the trough of a big wave. A Whitby Cat drew about 15 feet laden. The colliers settled for mooring at Shields, where there was a depth of 30 feet, they moved upriver only on the higher tides every two weeks. To guide ships in from the sea, North Shields had a Low Light and a High Light. Lining them up from out at sea, indicated the hidden channel beneath the churning waves to cross the bar; the gap was only 600 feet wide. Once across, the sudden turns then needed, to reach deep water, still caused many a wreck.

A Tyne Commission engineer Mr. Messent[4] describes inside the bar:

'The channel was abruptly reduced in width to four hundred feet opposite the Low Lighthouse, the contracted channel being called the Narrows. Shields Harbour, about a mile and a half in length, consisted of a comparatively narrow, tortuous, deepwater channel, with large shoals dry at low water, some of which, the In-Sand and Middle Ground on the south, and the Dortwick Sands on the north side of the harbour, extended from the shores to and beyond the middle of the river. It required very careful navigation to take a laden vessel out of Shields harbour at high water (the only time possible), and keep clear of the shoals.'

The Tyne was not a place to make mistakes. Whitby Cats were designed flat-bottomed to float off the sands. Even an experienced captain like Sam Campion found himself aground and stuck on the Dortwick Sands.

James Cook would be learning the tricks of his trade and keeping his Apprentice Book. The apprentices were set navigation problems which they had to solve mathematically and illustrate, e.g how to calculate sailing angles for a big ship to protect a little ship from pirates.[5] And no doubt, how to cross the Tyne Bar, allowing an hour each way at high water for the wind direction.

By July 1747, *Freelove* was back in the routine coal trade, at Newcastle. In the muster roll for her next voyage, her Master, 32 year old John Jefferson of Sandsend, refers to 'the last voyage from London to Whitby. It sounds like one home visit, but there had been three trips to the Tyne for coal; *Freelove* paid light and buoyage fees on 9th July, 4th Aug., 10th Sept., loading at 184, 180, 176, coals. They had just come back north to load at Newcastle.

And now, at last, we can meet her crew. In 1747, an Act of Parliament made ships' Muster Rolls compulsory. The Musters for Whitby ships begin on 29th September.[6]

1st *FREELOVE* (Muster Roll)
29th Sept. 1747 - 27th Dec. 1747
Captain John Jefferson, mate Robert Watson, carpenter Thomas Harwood, the 56 year old cook Matthew Hill, and all nine apprentices, including 18 year old James Cook, mustered on *Freelove* in London on 29th Sept. 1747. They were nearly all from the Whitby area. Thomas Gibson was the senior apprentice, and 15 year old Donald MacDonald, was son of the Customs officer at Skinningrove, a close colleague of Samuel Gill, and friend of William Sanderson.

Freelove did two round trips to the Tyne for coal, then returned to Whitby for the winter, where her crew signed off on 17th December. For the last six weeks they had had no cook, Matt Hill had signed off on 9th November at Shields. James would have taken his turn to cook the meat.

Apprentices usually went home for Christmas. James would return to the farm at Airyholme, to the clear sharp air of the hills. We can imagine him, 6 feet tall, wind-tanned and toughened after a year at sea, helping his father haul straw and hay to the cattle overwintering in the warm dark byres. Seeing the breath of horses in the frosty air, their harness jingling down the steep lane to Ayton, hearing his sisters laughing, the soft Northumbrian of his father's voice in the barn, maybe his older brother John advising on local girls, his mother making the Christmas goose pie, saving the goose grease to rub on her family's chests for winter colds. James could tell his father of his adventures, his frights and achievements. It was a sea apprentice's ambition to haul the weather-earring at the far tip of a yard, hanging out dizzily over the sea, proudly braced on the footlines, high on the surging dipping yard, clinging on with one hand, or none.

Whitby town now slid into winter, dark afternoons, a quiet sucking harbour, some noise of ship-building in the icy mornings. It was smokily cosy. Seagoing men were home, the taverns full, with tall tales and laughter, the houses full of souvenirs, Portuguese silver, Brussels lace, Dutch crockery, rum. The *John & Jane,* had come home from Jamaica, though *Mary* was still away on transport service and *Tryton,* with her Staithes crew, was in Carolina.

2nd *FREELOVE* (Muster Roll)
26th Feb. 1747/8 - 22nd April 1748

Whitby apprentices would be back in January, to study navigation and to help rig their ship. *Freelove,* moored in the harbour below Walker's house, with her top yards lowered and lashed down for the winter, top masts removed, now had to be re-rigged, with a cats cradle of good hemp ropes, sails repaired, cabin painted, her stores and meat ordered. Beasts would be slaughtered on Henry Walker's farms, an owner had to provide his ship's bread and meat. An apprentice had to be fully kitted out with wool stockings, tarred coats, his sea chest mended, his school books complete.

We can almost hear Mary Proud, the Walkers' housekeeper

complaining of mud in the house, though we know she was fond of James.

The crew joined *Freelove* on the 26th February. By 1st April, they were unloading 30 ballast at Mr. Burdon's ballast quay at North Shields. Her apprentices were in two watches. John Walker liked to combine older with younger ones. Thomas Gibson's group of four stayed with the ship until 7th June. James Cook's group of five left *Freelove* along with her mate Robert Watson, on 22nd April, because Captain John Walker had other plans.

~~~

The *THREE BROTHERS*

1st *THREE BROTHERS*[7] (Muster Roll)
14th June 1748 - 14th Oct. 1748
He had bought a new ship. Was she named for John Walker's three small boys? She was another club ship. John Walker as her main owner had farmed out his risks, with 17/64ths sold: 6 parts to Henry Walker, 8 to Anthony Pearson, 2 to Jacob Linskill and 1 to Jona Lacey, a ropemaker who, by taking a share in up to 7 Whitby ships, made sure they bought his ropes.

For *Three Brothers'* first voyage Captain John Walker took her out himself. She left Whitby on 14th June, with two mates, Robert Watson, and 35 year old John Newton of Sandsend, whose career had faltered. As master of the coaster *Elizabeth,* on a voyage to London in October 1747, he had been removed after 11 days. 'Ship taken', says the muster roll. Was the ship captured by pirates and ransomed? Or did John Newton go bankrupt? His same crew continued their voyage, his ship's new owner changed its name to *Joseph & Ann.*

Walkers' boys, had taken about 7 weeks to rigg *Three Brothers,* and now Thomas Gibson, and 16 year old Richard Sanderson, had transferred across from *Freelove.* Thomas Dodds, aged 20 - seemingly from old Thomas Dodds the Newcastle Hoastman's large and well-educated family - was leading James Cook's group. *Three Brothers* sailed out of Whitby to Newcastle, with 10 apprentices, 5 of them older, split into two watches. John Walker was taking no chances. Would his new ship leak too much, would she be sea-kindly or a brute? Would she carry too much weather helm, be skittish, awkward, a trial of their strength and skill, would the crew hate her?

It was a nervous crew. That February the Press boats had been active. Between the great dangerous sandbanks from the Humber to the Thames, as ships were forced into confined deepwater channels, the Royal Navy was waiting. One seaman each, had been taken from the Whitby ships: from *John* coming from Haverdegrace, from *Ann* returning from Jamaica, from John Stonehousc's *Free Mason* coming from Wivenhoe. Sam Campion had even lost an apprentice out of the *Hopewell* on 10th February

Three Brothers was larger than *Freelove,* she settled her first harbour dues at Newcastle on 25th June, 1748, unloaded 78 ballast at St. Anthony's quay, and took on 232 coals. They did not get the weight correct. *Three Brothers* would consistently load at 220 coals in 1748 and 1749.[8]

John Walker must have been content, for he discharged himself at London on 14th July.

On the dirty Thames wharf, they unloaded their coal, and took on ballast. *Three Brothers* left London river under the command of her chief mate Robert Watson; three days out they met the *Freelove* at sea and Captain John Jefferson came aboard, changing places with mate Watson. The two mates had clearly ironed out her problems and, by 20th August, Captain Jefferson was dumping 80 ballast at the 'Ewesburn', on the north bank of the Tyne.

Ouseburn, a deep stream entering the river close to Newcastle, was one of the few moorings upriver for larger ships. Their ballast of flint, chalk and sand dumped there for generations, formed the base material for the pottery and glasshouses by the Ouseburn. So the colliers often took away extra cargo of new glass. That summer Whitby colliers were carrying blue glass, pig iron, cork, wainscot boards, shumack, brandy, flax and spinning wheels.

After a quick voyage, two seamen left at Shields on 12th September. Two days later, Captain Jefferson dumped 64 ballast at Joyce quay, and would take on more Tyne coal. Though built as a collier *Three Brothers,* being new but tested, was attractive to the Admiralty. Her seakeeping qualities were now known, and her leakage, her planks were eased.

On 14th October 1748 in London, the whole crew signed off. After serving four months their dues to Whitby Seaman's Hospital were calculated, so that John Walker could pay up to that date. Captain John Jefferson signed off that day too, and entered the Transport service; so did the crew. *Three Brothers* was to be 'taken into Transport' by the Admiralty, and Captain Jefferson had to ready his ship to transport troops home from Flanders. The war had ended.

2nd *THREE BROTHERS* (Muster Roll)
14th Oct. 1748 - 20th April 1749
This was a lucrative venture, for their new ship. Thomas Gibson and Robert King had completed their apprenticeships, they quickly signed on as full seamen, pleased the war was ending, not so vulnerable now to the press gangs.

There were eight apprentices. James Cook was just two weeks off 20, Wm. Beilby 20, Walker Chandler and Ralph Newby 18, Edward Smith and Richard Sanderson both 16, the experienced Donald MacDonald 15 and the new boy, 15 year old Luke Collingwood, a Scot born in Leith. They expected adventure. First the ship had to be altered, stalls-built for horses, quarters for men. Any small space the apprentices had would now disappear. They would be skyscraping in the freezing rigging. Winter sailing was hard.

Other Whitby ships were signing up for transport too: ships like

Thomas Holt's brig *Olive Branch*, Wm. Webster's *Ridley,* Jn.Linskill's *Streatlam Castle,* and Chris. Richardson's *Unity,* a ship which had spent the previous winter in Maryland. On London's river in great activity, among the swirling apprentices, could be seen the tall fit gangling James Cook.

John Newton signed on *Three Brothers* as 2nd mate, most long distance voyages carried two mates, the troops from Flanders were to be taken to peacetime quarters. Within a week a Scot who lived in London, John Wood, signed on as 1st Mate, bringing with him a cook and three London seamen; on 2nd November a carpenter from Gravesend arrived; the re-fit speeded up. *Three Brothers* was to be crowded. For the first time the ship carried a steward, to make sure the food was not stolen. Whitby ships going to America usually carried a boatswain,[9] *Three Brothers* did not. There are mixed views as to where she sailed that winter. *Kippis* writing in 1784 says they carried troops to Liverpool and Dublin. All we know is, the Mate John Wood signed on Alex Furrow a Peterhead man like himself on January 17th without saying where.

At the end of that season of winter gales, grey heaving seas crashing on bitter cold decks, the boys clinging on to lifelines with calloused hands, hearing eye-opening tales of war from gambling soldiers, dealing with terrified horses below, in the stench of overcrowding, *Three Brothers* came back to London on 20th April 1749. James Cook was ending his apprenticeship, the war was over, he was lucky to be safe. He was tall, strong, hardened to awful conditions. It was just as well. That day when he and the crew signed off, they signed on again for a summer coaling season, there was to be no home leave, no respite.

Back they went to the coal trade.

3rd *THREE BROTHERS* (Muster Roll)
20th April 1749 - 26th Sept. 1749
At this point we would expect John Newton to become 1st Mate again. Instead, John Wood sailed as Mate to Captain Jefferson. John

Newton signed on as able seaman. Was he stepping down to widen his experience of distant ports?

By 17th May, Captain Jefferson was dumping 90 ballast at Burd. quay on the Tyne, and loading coal. *Three Brothers* shipping dues at Newcastle show in 1749: 17th May coals, 20th June coals and on the 7th Aug. they dropped 90 ballast but loaded no coals.

So James Cook's first freelance voyage was under the experienced Scot, John Wood. He was no longer tied to any ship or master, in fact expected to move from one to another to build up expertise. His friends, apprentices from Staithes, had sailed further, well on their way to becoming Whitby's elite seamen. After a late start James still had a long way to go. By the end of this voyage on 26th September, he was almost 21 and had been at sea for one and a half years continuously. On 27th September, 1749, with *Three Brothers* riding at Shields, waiting a few days for the highest tide, James and her crew signed on again for the late season coaling voyage. He would not be able to do without his pay until February; there was little choice for him but to work.

He still had a lot to learn. Much sea-lore was passed on through word of mouth by sailors who could not read. They told stories, rhymed about landing places, sang about dangerous currents and tidal flows.

4th *THREE BROTHERS* (Muster Roll)
27th Sept. 1749 - 8th Dec. 1749

The Baltic seas were icing up. Whitby ships were heading home. Cleveland was sinking into autumn, leaves falling, fields empty of crops, game being shot to fill the winter larder. The stars stood out hard and bright in the evening sky. But if the North Sea stayed calm enough John Walker could fit in some coal deliveries to London, to top-up his profits. William Woodcock a young Scarborough carpenter joined the ship to make essential repairs, and John Grainger an older London seaman. John Newton of Sandsend now took over as 1st Mate. The watches of 8 men were complete and, with the old cook John Atkinson, a County Durham man born at Hamsterley, banging his spoons wanting to be on his way to London where he now lived, *Three Brothers* took on coal and left the Tyne before Saturday 7th October.

Eleven days later, Ralph Jackson arrived with his father at the house of the Hoastman William Jefferson on Newcastle Quay, to start his own 7 year apprenticeship in the coal trade. The following week, on board *Three Brothers* James Cook celebrated his coming of age, his 21st birthday.

It is through Ralph Jackson's diaries, we can see into James Cook's life on the Tyne, shipping coal from Newcastle.

RALPH JACKSON Apprentice

Ralph, aged 13, appears to have been on a four week trial, to see if Mr. William Jefferson liked him and thought him suitable, after all a 7 year apprenticeship bound a master as well as a boy. So during those October days, young Ralph was carefully counting the pocket money given to him by relations, and trying to find his feet in an energetic, busy, hilly city of Newcastle. John Campion took Ralph for a walk to the Forth, a popular garden outside the west city wall, down by the river, where men played bowls. Ralph says he signed on at the 'erithmetick' school and began learning 'substraction', at which he was quite adept looking at his pocket money accounts; he had spent little, apart from giving a half penny to a poor man. William Jefferson would later do something about Ralph's bad writing, meanwhile he took him shopping to the Saturday meat market near St. Nicholas church, to learn to buy meat for ships' captains. And on Monday 30th Ralph went to the Sandhill at the bridge end, where he saw the 'soldiers fire.......it being the King's birthday.' King George II was 66 years old, a short blue-eyed man, well enough educated and a good soldier. German or not, England had accepted him.

Three Brothers was now due back on the Tyne. If not in time to hear the royal salute, those on board would toast the King as all loyal Englishmen did. As for the Scots, it was only three years after the failed Jacobite rebellion, of Bonnie Prince Charlie, and many were careful to show their loyalty to King George. But a lot of Tyne keelmen were Scots, there were agitators on the river. Quakers avoided violence. The top of the tide being 2nd November, a quick turnaround was possible for the ship, and she sailed again for London.

The coal trade began to tail off for the 1749 season. The tide rose lower each day, in its constant two-weekly rythm, with less water, more exposed sandbanks, fewer ships floating in the river channel. Ralph's month's trial was up. William Jefferson gave him the ultimate test - could he play cards? For two weeks they played cards, first at Mrs. Hudspeth's house, then in Henry Hudspeth's room and, on Wednesday 14th November, Mr. Jefferson of Staithes arrived. Now *he* liked a jolly game of cards! Ralph remembered what his cousin Mr. John Jefferson had taught him. William Jefferson the Hoastman was satisfied. On 16th November, 1749, a Friday, Ralph Jackson was bound his apprentice.

Pride had been saved all round.

Newcastle was a fine city, with a castle and gardens inside its medieval walls, fountains in the streets, rich merchants' houses, a new theatre, coffee houses, sports fields, space for a boy to grow-up.

Ralph's new home was a tall narrow house, with the kitchen downstairs, office and parlour upstairs, Chinese wallpaper in the best rooms. His own room was near the top among the chimney pots, beneath an attic full of shovels for the keelmen. His street, of medieval houses with jettied floors, the Cheshire Cheese inn, busy shops, a smelly distillery, faced the inside of the city wall which ran along the Quay. Between the houses, narrow alleys ran back flat to the base of the high mound on which rose All Saints' church. Crowded unsavoury alleys full of sail lofts, smoky lodging houses, breeding fever, but with one wider lane, the Broad Chare where the Trinity School stood. Outside the city wall, the windy open Quay bristled with fishwives, sailors, cargo stacked high, and the Can House, where respectable Mrs. Margaret Bone, the Can Wife, issued food and drink to the keelmen, and where they got paid. Ralph soon learned to give her his sassifras, which she brewed for his dawn 'coffee', for everyone worked with the tide, and kept irregular hours. And always the dangerous dirty river water, rising and dropping beside the quay.

The tide in the river, began to rise higher each day. *Three Brothers* was due to come in at Shields. On Thursday, Ralph, boyishly solemn, went to see a ship launched on the high water 'which was the first I ever saw'. Another ship was launched at Dent's Hole *(pronounced Holla)* a scoop in the north river bank. Down at the river mouth at Shields on the full tide, James Cook on *Three Brothers* arrived. His ship was to be moored and laid up there for the winter. Up in the rigging her yards were coming down, her sails coming off for repairs, her iron rusty, her greased ropes stretched and frayed, it was dirty work for hardened hands, the crew filthy. Yet the weather was good enough, for on Friday 8th December a master of a ship came up to see William Jefferson presumably to load coal. That same day *Three Brothers'* crew signed off and went home. A lucky crew, not one of them had been lost at sea. James was going home after two years.

The easy way to go to Great Ayton, was to catch a local sloop delivering coal down the coast and up the Tees, a morning's sail. Perhaps it was one of our beautiful sharp winter days with blue satin sea, ships sit like pearls and, with visibility clear for nearly 80 (sea) miles, Staithes can see Tynemouth.

A week later, William Jefferson sent Ralph home to Richmond for Christmas. The boy had survived his first weeks at work; in January Ralph would be 14 years old.

James Cook was now 21, with choices to make.

As a freelance seaman now, he had to find a ship for himself.

8

SEAMAN
1750 - 1752

The MARY

The *MARY* (Muster Roll)
8th Feb. 1749/50 - 5th Oct. 1750.

If John Newton had shown James Cook how to step down to progress, then William Gaskin of the *Mary* showed him the limits of his future. Captain Gaskin was only 27 years old when appointed master of the *Mary,* one of the ships owned by John Wilkinson, a Hull merchant who sailed his ships out of Whitby. The Gaskin family had owned ships for two generations; William Gaskin was gaining experience to command his inheritance. James Cook had no family money behind him, if he thrived in the merchant service, his children could achieve, maybe, William Gaskin's state of prosperity. At 21, James Cook was already working, not for himself but for his future son. Unless anything out of the ordinary happened, he was already limited.

Years earlier, in 1702, a previous William Gaskin had shared command of a ship *William & Mary*, a square stemed 'pinque', one of ten coal ships sailing out of Whitby in the days of John Walker's father, who was then master of a collier *Owners Adventure.*

By 1750, Mr. Jos. Gaskin owned one old ship *Fortune* of Whitby, and the *John & Mary.* William Gaskin had captained *John & Mary* when he was only 24, dumping ballast from her in March 1748, with Joseph Gaskin aged 21 his mate. During 1749, they had loaded once a month with Tyne coal.

The *Mary* was another club ship, 11 shares were held by others: Anthony Pearson 5, Jonah Lacey 1, Jacob Linskill 1, and Henry Walker had held 4 since 1744. James Cook was part of Walker's club of ex-apprentices, reliable seamen they had taught.

With the war over, Whitby ships began trading further abroad. In March, *Three Brothers* took coal to Dunkirk; in May, Thomas Linskill captained her to Gibraltar; in July, John Jefferson took her with 224 coals to Lisbon. Most Whitby colliers were delivering to Holland.

William Gaskin was seeking a crew to sail to St. Petersburg. To a young seaman, wanting to build up his experience in the Baltic trade, it would be irresistible. James Cook decided to join the *Mary.*

One week before, on Friday 26th January, his 14th birthday, Ralph Jackson had returned from Richmond to his Master's house on Newcastle Quay. As the new week began, he says workmen were 'mending our Keel' at Mr. Charlton's landing place. Old George Weddle *[Shop Owner?]* came down to the house to play whist, there was not much happening, but the river men were putting their minds to the coming coal season. On Wednesday Jacky Campion appeared at the house. The *Thomas & Richard* was fitting out, down at Shields. The Whitby men, and James Cook, were arriving on the river.

Ralph walked out on to the open Quay 'to see Jacky go away' knowing they were all invited to dinner on the ship. So early next morning he went to seek a hacking horse to ride down to Shields about 9 o'clock. They all dined on board the *Thomas & Richard* and

'Jacky and they drunk a pint of Punch', he adds, a little shocked. They rode back to Newcastle by 6 o'clock, in time for Mr. William Jefferson to go to the cockfights at Jack Dowson's.

The Newcastle merchants began to act, there were cargoes to arrange. Mr. Deighton arrived in town and could be found at the Bridge End Coffee House, arranging for goods to go on the *Ann & Mary* to New York. School started for Ralph. Still a child to William Jefferson, while his master entertained visitors in the parlour, Ralph stayed in the kitchen downstairs. On Tuesday, 6th February, as his master was busy with Mr. Webster in the office, - perhaps the Whitby ship *Blessing* was fixing to load coal? - *Mary* dumped her 76 ballast at 'Bland' quay. On Thursday the carriageman arrived from Richmond with a letter from Ralph's father, and that same day downriver at Shields, James Cook signed on as seaman on *Mary*.

Trade accelerated. Mr. James arrived at the Bird & Bush in Pilgrim Street and on Saturday Jacky and 'Mr. Gallant' *[Gallon?]* came upriver to the house. The Campions' boat *Mary & Jane* was probably loading too. The keelmen were being paid, coal was coming to the staithes. Ralph joined the crowd to see 'Mr. Blegdon's large ship being launched', the tide was ripe for *Mary* to leave.

By Friday 16th *Mary* would be away, crossing the Tyne bar at high tide, heading out into the choppy North Sea.

Apart from 22 year old James Cook, sailing as a plain seaman, William Gaskin's Mate was William Mellanby aged 23, with Daniel Cambell and four apprentices, led by John Watson of Whitby. (Robert Watson was now captain of *Three Brothers,* these ships were very much family affairs.)

James' fellow seaman was Francis Allely. They were headed for St. Petersburg for a whole summer's trading, there was plenty of time to talk.

Francis, a member of the Allely family of Whitby, who owned the big collier *Greyhound* in which Mr. Ralph Ward held a share, had acted as mate of *Friends Glory* to Dantzig, early in 1748. So he too had stepped down to sail further. Though *Mary* was headed for the Baltic, by February the pack ice would not have broken up in the sea approaching Riga and St. Petersburg. They must have traded elsewhere first. But their main destination was Russia.

From 1741 to 1761 Russia was ruled by her Queen Elizabeth, a lady built large, untidy, easy-going, owning as many as 15,000 dresses. She was helped in her rule by the enlightened and cultured Count Shuvalov to develop Russian culture and education, to encourage science.[1] While ruling with foresight, Elizabeth bought hats. She had the magnificent Winter Palace completed at St. Petersburg, a wonderful new city begun in 1703 by her father, at the mouth of the river Neva. It was a city of stone, built on piles for it stood on a marsh, and it was beautiful. St. Petersburg was Elizabeth's new capital, it was growing rapidly, sucking in trade and goods, from the commonplace like coal, to the luxuries of silk, tea, finest English woollens. A young captain like William Gaskin could make his fortune if he traded well. St. Petersburg was a radiant, beckoning city. For British seamen, this would stop when, in 1757, Russia entered the Seven Years war on the enemy side, but in the summer of 1750, *Mary* with James Cook on board was heading into a peacetime adventure. William Gaskin was to gain enough experience to allow him in future to move easily between ship owners, who were confident in letting him command their vessels. James Cook had his eyes opened to a wider, sophisticated world: St Petersburg had public toilets.

That summer in Newcastle it was hot, Ralph went bathing in the river. The theatre was open. His Master treated him to the Play 'of the Mourning Bride, and the Endkermain was the Contriguinge Camber Maid', a bedroom farce. Ralph helped Billy Hudspeth, his master's young nephew, to learn his multiplication table, and bought Dilworth's arithmetic book. He saw a monkey alongside Captain Clifton's ship and, taking up a shovel, Ralph helped to clean out the ship's 'degs' [*Dregs?*]

Autumn approached, the winds turned biting, Riga and the sea approaches to St. Petersburg began to ice up. British ships now had to escape home or be trapped. *Mary* was back in London from St. Petersburg by 5th October 1750. That day the main crew, including James Cook, were discharged. They were young men with money in their pockets who wanted a good time after 8 months at sea. The apprentices, captain and mate stayed with the ship. She would not have returned empty and was probably carrying Baltic timber. *Mary* needed repairs. On 20th November John Hutchinson, the carpenter from Skelton in Cleveland, 'Happened misfortune to crush two of his fingers' and was discharged to St. Thomas Hospital. They urgently needed a carpenter and managed to find another Stockton man, Thomas Johnson. He and other seamen wanting to go home to the north signed-on on 30th November. By 5th December they were discharged at Whitby and *Mary* laid up there for the winter.

So where was James Cook? Was he in Wapping, lodging at the Bell Tavern at the top of Execution Dock stairs? And was that when he first saw the little seven year old girl who would one day be his wife?

Wapping lay on the curve of river downstream from London Bridge. Stairs led up from the dirty river wharves, through timber yards and coal depots, spilling wind and stench into the narrow Wapping High Street, with its overhanging many-storied timber houses, more foetid alleys, full of ale houses where the coal heavers waited for jobs emptying ships. They were employed and paid by 'Undertakers' at the ale houses, which meant they often drank their pay. Near the river, amid poverty and filth, Quakers worked out of Wapping Meeting House offering rescue, comfort and help to wretched children, mothers and the sick. Dr. Fothergill, a famous Quaker botanist, physician and Yorkshireman, was their official guide at Wapping.

Yet beyond this greasy fringe to the industrial river, north of Wapping High Street, lay open market gardens. Good houses stood along Broad Street, Old Gravel Lane, Princes Street. Here lived the better off, the richer ships' captains from Cleveland, like Henry Gofton, of Adam Boulby's ship *Lyon,* and Charles Peacock a blockmaker, who would write a seaman's will for another Loftus man. Daniel Weston, the Quakers' cashier, owned three houses, stables and cooperage in Old Gravel Lane.

Zachariah Cockfield, a ships-chandler, had moved from Whitby in 1737, to marry Sarah Sheppard, daughter of a wealthy Quaker who owned wharves and wharehouses in Wapping, a timber yard in Cinnamon Street, and chandlers on Wapping Wall. In 1750, he and Joseph Sheppard were in court, accused of stacking so much timber against a neighbour's chimneys in 1748, and 1749, that the chimneys collapsed. The timber trade was clearly thriving.

The HOPEWELL

HOPEWELL
Between 5th Oct. 1750 - Feb 19th 1751

In February 1751 the Muster Rolls show James Cook's previous ship is listed as the *Hopewell* and he and his shipmates, Robert Clarke, Robert Storp and the cook Henry Pearson, all gave their abode as Sunderland. The Muster Rolls can be misleading if they are read too strictly. The way the question was phrased was clearly the northern expression, 'Where are you from?' or 'Wheer d'ye hail fra?' This can apply to birthplace, where you live, or where you have just come from. They said they came from Sunderland.

Sunderland was growing too fast. On the tip of the south headland at the mouth of the River Wear a rival coal river. Sunderland with its parish church of Holy Trinity built in 1719, its large green churchyard, and its almshouses, had the air of a country market town under stress. Much of its coal went to Holland, many of the houses were Dutch in style, the second church built in 1769 certainly was. Sunderland was considered a 'loading port' where sailors could find a ship.[2]

In the next Muster Roll (February 1751) James Cook's previous ship is stated as 'Hopewell Saml Ca'Campling' London. Ca' could indicate the writer spoke Lowland Scots dialect: it means 'going by' Or was Campling a mishearing of Campion? We can almost hear the writer asking him, 'Whoses' *Hopewell?'*

There were other ships called *Hopewell,* but in Henry Cockerill's *Hopewell,* from February 1744, Henry Walker owned 1/64th share. In 1747, the 27 year old Sam Campion of Staithes, had been Mate on Henry Cockerill's *Hopewell* of Whitby. Now at 30 he was her Master.[3]

Sam Campion arrived at Shields on 30th October 1750, *Hopewell* dumped 32 ballast at Jarrow quay, and set off for London. They were back in Whitby on 29th November, where the ship was laid up. Her crew list of 12, does not include James Cook. Did he hitch an unpaid lift north from London on her, around 17th October, spending only 10 days in London after leaving the *Mary*? Did he arrive at Whitby on *Hopewell*?

James Cook did not join the *Hopewell's* next voyage. He may have been looking for a ship at Sunderland, but he was looking for a longer voyage. On 14th February Captain Sam Campion sailed *Hopewell* out of the Tyne for Rotterdam. Five days later James Cook joined the *Three Brothers* at Shields.

RALPH JACKSON.

It is through Ralph Jackson that we learn what was happening in the Tyne coal trade. Young Ralph Jackson was not doing so well in his own work. During that Christmas of 1750, he had been enjoying himself at Richmond with his parents and sisters, he was reading *Robinson Crusoe*. But on 1st January, his father received a letter from William Jefferson 'calling Me to Newcastle'. A bound apprentice had to obey his master, so Ralph set off next morning on the long ride to Newcastle, calling on the way at Mr. Hutchinson's in Durham but Billy his friend was not in. Billy was William Hutchinson, the future Durham historian, who may have been at school with Ralph, and was to remain a friend into adult life. Ralph rode on to Newcastle where he left his galloway pony at Mrs.Pinkneys and walked downhill to find his master was at Court. Waiting, walking in the Exchange until William Jefferson came out. Ralph was then told off. He had not completed the last year's fitter's accounts, before the new coal season.

A long inky day's work later, he was allowed to set off back home again to Richmond, intent on buying his first wig, to show he was grown up really.

That January, the weather was bitter, the freezing air cutting. When Ralph finally returned to Newcastle there was dangerous ice in the river. Yet William Jefferson took on a large ship on 28th January. Despite the pitch black mornings and piercing cold, traffic on the river was starting. Friday 1st February saw Jacky Campion going downriver in Lumsdale's wherry, and Ralph was sent down to Shields with a letter for Mr. Presswick, owner of the Whitby ship *Ann & Elisabeth*. William Jefferson had made his point about work. So he allowed Ralph to give the keelmen their orders on the Quay each evening. We can imagine him, a leggy 15 year old instructing the burly keelmen twice his size, these rowers had muscles like iron balloons. The coal trade depended on their brawn and skill. All along the river, carpenters were mending keel boats, the coal trade was starting work. *Hopewell* loaded and left for Rotterdam on 14th Feb.

Tuesday, 19th February, was busy. At midnight Ralph got up to let Jos. in to the tall narrow house, and again at 4am down the narrow stairs to let him out again. Each day the water surged higher in the river, high tide came in the very early hours. That day James Cook and the rest of her crew signed on aboard *Three Brothers* which was rigging at Shields.

> 'Giddy topmasts thick as rushes;
> Crowds of boats and dirty keels;
> Ballast hills like gooseberry bushes;
> Altogether - Canny Shields.'
>
> *Local song.*

Shields was throng with boats, white-sailed pilot cobles going out to escort ships across the bar, a rough and colourful fishing fleet, gutting fish under the cry of gulls, dirty colliers groaning in the tiers, and big ships safe and sighing in the famous mooring of Peggy's Hole. There were leather backed keelmen shovelling coal into colliers, there were open, broad-beamed wherries moving cargo and passengers, and Foyboats manned by six strong rowers, acting as tugs guiding ships upriver through the tortuous channel to the coal staithes, or even up to Newcastle quay. And smoothly among them shot the small scullers, with a veteran seaman who knew his navigation, tides, and mood of the river, keeping the merchants and ships in contact. Vital North Shields, where James Cook and Ralph Jackson were walking on the same crowded shore, crews walked in groups, among sail lofts and uproarious pubs, where shipowners had houses on the hillside, where just inland, the Walkers had farms. There was filth and the stink of coal gas dispersing along the quay. Merchants were making their fortunes. Shields Quay faced the Dortwick Sand; when the tide dried it out, poor people surged over it picking up lumps of lost coal. And, across the uneasy river, beyond another line of moored ships waiting at South Shields, steam rose from hundreds of shoreline salt pans.

Back to THREE BROTHERS

5th *THREE BROTHERS* (Muster Roll)
19th Feb. 1751 - 30th July 1751
Robert Watson was now 30, a fully qualified master mariner, John Walker appointed him *Three Brothers*' Captain, promoting him from the smaller *Freelove.* The Mate John Swainston, was a 32 year old Guisborough man, who had last sailed up from London in the *Jane,* and two more Guisborough men signed on next, both from the *Isabel & Mary*: John Jackson aged 22, and John Gofton the carpenter aged 24 - a younger member of the Gofton family, once of Waterfall and friends of the Wards. Donald MacDonald now out of his apprenticeship, joined as seaman, James was with old friends, among them Wm. Beilby. Sailing with 6 seamen and 6 apprentices, they were headed for Norway and the timber trade. All about them ships were jostling in the river hoping to load coal, but the season was off to an erratic volatile start.

Normally a collier Cat would load and sail within the days of the highest tides, but both trade and nature were at odds on the Tyne. The day after James Cook arrived downriver, young Ralph was on Newcastle quay by Mr. Foster's distillery watching the excitement: 'In the afternoon I saw the Great Cop[p]er for the distilhouse w'ch held 40 Hogsheads & it stook fast in the narrow part of the Key.' Anything which interrupted the flow of spirits was serious. Coal supplies were unpredictable too. Long Benton coal was too slow to come on line to the north bank staithes. On Thursday 21st William Jefferson sent Ralph to tell his keelman Anderson not to take a fit tide. Ralph was taking over the work of Jacky Campion who was leaving. With his Hoastman's apprenticeship complete, Jacky was sailing with the Baltic ships. Old Mr. Robert Campion was moored and waiting, in his usual place for the *Mary & Jane,* at Jarrow Quay, near his friend Mr. Daniel Railston's. The weekend came and went. On Tuesday Ralph went to see if the waggons were going up to Long Benton pit. In the short hours of daylight, all along the Tyne the ships waited, they needed a high tide to take them out over the dangerous shoals at the river mouth, and now they were in danger of losing their slot. It meant lost profit and less work for seamen.

A new factor entered the stalemate. Near the coal staithes, there was a new pit. 'Thursday 28th Feb. In the morning as we went down to Winkhamlee,' says Ralph, 'we saw the Alderman's Pit at work, viz. Alderman Ridley's Biker Pits.' It meant erratic movement in the price of coal, and ships' masters playing off the Hoastmen, one against the other on prices.

Nature did not help, the river flow was awkward. On 1st March keels went aground and Ralph was out at 1am seeking keels at the bottom of the quay, yet Mr. Jefferson's other keels were working as Ralph paid the keelmen, and that Saturday a ship was launched 'over the water'. Suddenly, the coal trade unblocked. On Monday Ralph could find no keel at all at Winkhamlee and had to go back to Dents Hole for Andersons. The Whitby masters came upriver to deal. Tuesday brought Mr. Robert Campion to dine and deal at William Jefferson's. Wednesday brought Mr. John Jackson, the master of the

Constant Jane: the Jacksons of Whitby began most of their ships with the name *Constant.*

Jacky Campion was ready now to leave William Jefferson. He had paid his farewell visits the previous week. Now on Thursday 7th March, it was time to go. It is in his leaving that we find the most likely date of departure of the ships for Norway, including *Three Brothers* with James Cook aboard. Other Whitby ships headed for the Sound did not leave until the end of March. They were still waiting to load coal, grindstones, lead, and white glass: the *Roberts,* the *Sea Nymph,* the *Olive Branch.*

Not all the ships got happily away. William Railston, a ship's master at Shields, was dangerously ill. One Monday night, William Jefferson tried to get a doctor. Ralph was sent to find Dr. Askew, but he was away at Durham. Early next morning they succeeded in getting Dr. Lambert to go down to Shields. He was too late. By Friday, William Jefferson was going down there in sadness to attend Captain Railston's funeral.

The seas around western Norway do not normally freeze up; timber was loading in fiords and harbours of the long indented coast. Some was for pit props, some for building ships, deal for floorboards for the new houses sprouting up everywhere, pine for furniture, spruce and fir for ships' masts, some wood was just to burn. James Cook would become an expert in timber, a good thing for a seaman of a wooden ship, which can be cut out and repaired as she sails along.

We hear no more of *Three Brothers* until she arrived back from Norway on Tuesday 30th July. High tide was early that morning, and late in the afternoon, but the days were long and light, and she probably came in on the afternoon tide after the loaded ships left.

The early summer coal season had been bad on the Tyne, Ralph had been out every day on the dirty coal staithes. Even one Sunday, which people dedicated to their religion, several 'underladen ships sent up to Mr. Jefferson to ask could he fill them, and Mr. Gallilee came up to give on his ship for Tanfield coal.'

That July was lost in a heatwave so severe that fish died gasping in the river. Rubbish turned putrid. Disease blossomed.

Ralph Jackson took ill. His throat was sore, his head ached, in the evening he had a 'stoury' of honey but he got worse, he missed Church, took a sweat and was very weak. Two days before *Three Brothers* came in to Shields, he was still wobbly: 'in the afternoon I took a walk with Billy to see if they had led any Friars Goose *[coal]* & they had led about five keels'. This colliery near Gateshead on the south bank of the Tyne was an object of great interest because it had a huge beam pumping engine. Next day 'on the morning I was pretty well', he says. A relieved William Jefferson rewarded him, by sending him to Wickhamlee at 5 am all that week. Coal was loading. *Three Brothers* arrived. On the unhealthy stinking river, there was coal for her captain to buy.

The day after they signed off, James Cook and the crew of *Three Brothers* signed on again immediately and, as they were making ready their ship at Shields, upriver William Jefferson's maid chose his busiest week to make her views felt. Jenny 'took the pet and ran away' says Ralph anxiously. She was petulant by nature, wild tempered, stupidly stubborn; she also ran the whole many-storied house and did all the cooking for the wifeless William Jefferson with the help of only one charwoman. Their washing went out weekly to Mrs. Dixon the Blewwife's, but the overworked Jenny threw regular fits of vile rage which hurled the whole household into war. Ralph was frightened of her and worried. Mr. Jefferson sent for her father.

6th *THREE BROTHERS* (Muster Roll)
31st July 1751 -26th Oct. 1751
21st Nov. 1751 - 7th Jan. 1751/2

The day William Jefferson's peace was being destroyed, *Three Brothers* was loading coal. The ship would make two sets of runs to London that autumn and winter, probably three round trips, a break, then two more.

On board, James Cook was with the same crew, except that the ship's cook left and 28 year old Richard Milner took his place. The Muster Roll says Richard was born and came from Shields, but then it also says James Cook was born at Yatton ('Where d'ye come from?'). Richard more than likely belonged to the sea-going Milner family who later built the famous *Endeavour* at Whitby. Their family ship, the *Friends Glory,* was about the same size as *Three Brothers.* John Walker now discharged one apprentice, and enrolled Robert Brown aged 15. As a new muster roll could not be taken out until the old one was signed, John Walker signed for the master on 30th July. He too was at Shields.

The weather was hot, Ralph went bathing. His Master sent him to the Newgate prison with sixpence to give to a man sentenced to be hanged. Ralph decided to buy a bird, a cage, and all the 'accoutrements'. His mother affectionately sent him some birdseed, which he seems to have forgotten. On a slack tide, Ralph and Billy Hudspeth went to see a puppet show. They were boys, their minds unformed not making connections.

By the 28th October after two short trips, *Three Brothers* was back at Shields. Her crew discharged that day. They had been at sea since February. For a whole month, *Three Brothers* rode in the slurping tidal river; her captain, mate and apprentices stayed with her; she may not have needed repairs as her carpenter had left, they were simply waiting.

During the first two weeks of October the coal staithes had been working but there was no new carriage of coal coming on; the keelmen were being paid, the coal stocks were being run down. John Jefferson arrived to dine at their house. Ralph took in £50 on behalf of John Gallilee, but there were no more captains arriving.

It was the second week in November before the coal staithes were busy again, the tide shifting. Loading coal in the cold afternoon just before dark, gave way to loading in the frosty early morning hours, and Ralph was out there on the reeking black staith in clouds of coal dust, in his leather breeches, woollen stockings, and tarred coat. The

Baltic ships were returning. Jacky Campion turned up to dine; then Mr. Nathaniel Campion, and Mr. Cockerill, and on Monday 11th John Jefferson arrived again. The Whitby ships were clustered at Shields. Captains were willing to sail, but the coal stocks were dwindling. On 15th Ralph hopefully went down to Wickhamlee staithes but 'the waggons were not on'.

It was an indescribably dirty trade. The coal dust inhaled by Ralph as a boy affected his health in later years. James Cook at least escaped industrial disease at sea. But in the thronged streets and packed buildings of Newcastle quay, contagious fever arrived from distant ports, sickness thrived in confined rooms up narrow alleys, and in crowded inns. On the 19th November a working Monday, Ralph again took seriously ill. There were no antibiotics in those days, if a throat infection got out of control the sufferer choked to death. Fifteen year old Ralph struggled through the week but was too ill. By Friday he was in bed, unable to write…. his diary is empty.

Along the diseased River Tyne, John Walker, like other shipowners, decided to get out and risk a last voyage. He and his Captain Robert Watson made up a reliable crew from their ex-apprentices, who were now qualified seamen discharging from other ships at Shields. Thomas English and John Rowntree came over from the *Trew Briton*; John was from Stokesley and was almost certainly from the Rowntree family who had been James Cook's mother's childhood friends at Thornaby. Two Durham men joined: Ralph Hutchinson who came from the *Liberty* and Richard Williamson from George Yeoman's *Swan*[4] a popular ship belonging to a Whitby family linked to the Walkers. Mark Kitchin[g] of Loftus was now a qualified seaman and he too joined from the *Noble Hope,* a ship well-known at Staithes, owned by Matt. Noble, captained by William Proud, or by Thomas Trattles, who lived on a farm near Hinderwell church. *Noble Hope* is pronounced *Noorble Hoorp* in a Tyneside accent. This ship was nicknamed *'Hooble Hoop'* (water pipe). A wet ship?

Among old friends on *Three Brothers,* James Cook signed on as if he had not been anywhere else. Clearly he had not been at sea and, after long months away he must have been anxious to see his parents at Airyholme. Now he could tell his own tales, of Norway timber, dark forests, legendary seafarers, fiords and fish. All seamen love a yarn. The culture of northern England was full of storytelling. Like the giant Wade and his Wife, to explain the standing stones on the Mulgrave estate. Like the Whitby Bargheist who, in unquiet rest - it was told - took Whitby sailors from their new graves back to the sea, a tale inherent in the later story of Dracula, written at Whitby.

As Christmas 1751 approached, *Three Brothers'* crew collected for this last voyage of the year, most came from the same area of Cleveland, they knew each other well, which would help if the weather turned foul. In fact the weather was quite open, the coal staithes were working but, by the time *Three Brothers* was approaching London through the dangerous shoals of the Thames estuary, the seas were breaking up badly. On 7th December, Ralph says it was a very stormy night as he came home from work. James Cook was lucky to reach safety.

Young Ralph had come through the putrid fever. He was now a useful worker. It was as late as 22nd December when William Jefferson sent him home for Christmas. This time the Fitters' accounts were complete.

It is almost certain, the crew of *Three Brothers* spent Christmas in London. Did James stay at the Bell Tavern in Wapping? The ship left soon after, for by 7th January she was back at Shields, her crew signed off. Next day her captain, mate and apprentices all signed off too, the ship was laid up at Shields for the winter. By the 20th January there was deep snow, and a muffled silence fell over the land.

In the white world of crusted trees and silent smothered moor around Airyholme farm, James Cook had something to tell his father. His drive to seek wider experience across the North Sea had paid off. From all his past apprentices, John Walker had chosen James Cook to be Mate of a collier the *Friendship.*

9

MASTER'S MATE
1752 - 1755

The FRIENDSHIP

The year of 1752 opened with deep and dangerous snow. Ralph went plunging through the pasture at Richmond trying to collect his invalid sister Hannah's pet sheep. Mr. Allen their neighbour and relation, had given him a German flute for Christmas, he was teaching Ralph how to play the notes. With 26 inches of snow, business was at a halt, the roads so impassable that Michael Vitty a miller, carrying corn, perished in the drifts. It was not until the 10th February that Ralph could struggle back to Newcastle. It was soon clear William Jefferson had grown used to a quiet house, without pesky apprentices:

'Friday 14th. In the morning when I went downstairs my Master was beating the dog for tearing the Magazene and he [h]it me two or three slaps for lying it there but asked me pardon after he had done it, and I went to Mr. Akenhead's shop to buy another.'

The coal season was running late. It was 22nd February before the Whitby captains began to arrive and John Gallilee and Samuel Campion came up to dine at William Jefferson's to buy coal.

Jenny the housekeeper was having bad moods, one night she 'took one of her huffish fits' and went off until 11 o'clock. Another day she would not lend Ralph the key to the stairfoot door, so he was locked out. If he tried to be kind she turned on him. She bullied him. He was frightened and fed-up.

Yet in his work he was learning and slowly, on the river, coal at last began to load. Captain John Jefferson of Whitby, James Cook's ex-captain, arrived at Ralph's house on 1st April. The Whitby ships were rigging at Shields, and 23 year old James Cook was about to enter a ship for the first time as Mate. Of course, it is a sailors' tradition to hate the Mate.

1st *FRIENDSHIP* (Muster Roll)
30th March 1752 - 8th Nov. 1752

Yet James Cook's *Friendship* years were in many ways just that. Old friends, ex-apprentices, met in distant harbours, always a familiar face looming as another ship came alongside, shouts and beckoning, passing the ale, and quiet conversations in the dark watches of the night, hove-to amid the myriad of riding lights of other ships. Or in sunshine, cutting through a choppy sea to the sound of a sea-shanty as another sail went up, laughing as they creamed past friends on another collier. There were accidents, and deaths too, painful tragedies. Walkers' ships would go down, and James Cook was lucky to leave *Three Brothers* for within a few years she too was lost.

Friendship was not a brand new ship. In 1740 Newark Waller had owned her; by 1744 Henry Walker owned 9 shares and John Walker was paying her dues, so the brothers were operating her.[1] She was sailing out of Newcastle in 1746, undertaking 6 or 7 voyages a year, regularly loading at 160 coals, so smaller than *Three Brothers.*

John Walker had captained *Friendship* himself on the earlier voyage, now he handed over to an experienced man. Captain Richard Ellerton was 45, his previous command had been over Nicholas Jackson's *Constant Jane.* He was to be James Cook's captain for three of the next four years, and to earn his deep respect.

Friendship was slow to leave. The weather was bad. On 12th March Ralph Jackson drank tea on board the nearby *Thomas & Richard* with Captain John Campion. Ralph says he came home in a remarkable hurricane of wind and rain. And there seems to have been a shortage of men.

Friendship's voyages were to be marked by changing crews, most stayed for only one round trip. The ship carried only two young apprentices. John Woodill came from Loftus, sailing with his seaman brother Thomas. Charles Rois of Tynemouth discovered that no-one could ever spell his name. The ship's carpenter was James Dale, who had been born at Marton the year before James Cook, and may have been his childhood friend. One, Thomas Carter, came from Pinchinthorpe below Roseberry Topping. The others were Whitby men. This first short-handed crew of acquaintances, sat in Shields until 16th April until John Walker managed to produce three more seamen. Thomas Dodds, James' fellow ex-apprentice, came over from *Freelove*, and we, learn from his entry that *Freelove's* captain was now William Gaskin. One man came over from the Whitby ship *Blessing,* and Charles Rois' brother John came from the *Harwood.* At last, with six crew to a watch, they sailed out of the Tyne and headed for London.

April had fine days, Ralph walked uphill to the Shield Field sports, the fishermen were bringing in salmon, and he bought fresh oysters for a penny on Newcastle quay. The shipping trade grew busy. John Jefferson, James Cook's previous captain, who had dined at the house on the 1st, rode out to Benton Pitts to see the coal, and Hoastman William Jefferson ordered Patterson's keel to load Captain Jefferson's ship *Richard & Ann* of Whitby. Ralph got into trouble for not properly arranging her loading.

By 11th, 'in the morning there was a great many ships sending up', says Ralph, scrambling for the tide.

The ships left. Trade fell quiet in Newcastle. Ralph spent some time with his new musical friend the apprentice William Kent. His master took the boys to play skittles at the Shield Field, and took his nephew Billy Hudspeth and friend Lionel Trotter fishing in a hired sculler. Ralph would walk by Newgate across the Barras Bridge the highest way to the Shield Field to watch the horseshoes game and the cockfights and, one day, he saw the soldiers reviewed on the Town Moor by General Campbell. On 23rd he notes 'this day I have served my Master as apprentice two Years and a Half.' He was now 16 and William Jefferson honoured him with a key and half the desk in the office. Nothing much seemed to be happening in Newcastle except the troops in bright uniforms were milling around the town.

Friendship was back in the Tyne on 12th May after her first round trip, when all the crew except the captain and mate Cook signed off.

By signing off, men may have been avoiding the Army's strong-arm recruitment. Trouble began. Ralph heard on the Quay of Robert Parker a cooper, 'being run in the Neck quite into his heart with a knife done by a Soldier, it was done at Mr. Pickney's sign of the Black Bull in the Bigg Market'. Down on the Quayside it was no less raucous; one morning he saw a fight 'between two or three women against one man.' Ralph was a boyish 16, and adults were still amazing to him. Amid recording his work with the keelmen, the ships loading, his visit to the Excise office to take out a Brandy Licence for Mr. Railston of Jarrow quay, he thinks it worth noting when 'Petro the Man that makes Nets and all sorts of sweetmeats was at our house.'

The lull in the coal trade vanished. Ships captains once more began to arrive at William Jefferson's to buy coal, John Gallilee and John Gallon of Staithes, John Clifton of Lynn.

On 21st May down at Shields, three crew rejoined *Friendship,* five new men entered to work under the mate James Cook. Captain Ellerton now had his complement of men and could sail. It was a quick trip this time. By 16th June they were back in Shields. The cook, the carpenter James Dale and seaman Thomas Woodill left, but they signed on again on 24th June. It is as if they were nervous to hang about while coal was loading. New men were entered. This chopping and changing went on all season. Yet not much time was lost. *Friendship* was coming in regularly about once a month to load Tyne coal.

In early June, Ralph was reading a history of the Trojan War and interested in his music. While his master smoked a pipe in the evenings, he studied sonatas and, one evening, the apprentice Billy Kent played Ralph's German flute, Mr. Williamson a Bass Viol and Lionel Trotter the small viol, 'which was very harmonious', says Ralph satisfied. When now we read their names coldly listed in the Hoastmen's records, it is nice to recall their summer evening of melody.

James Cook on *Friendship* had arrived back at Shields. But people all along the Tyne, were waiting for something. In the third week of June each year, Newcastle underwent a vast happy upheaval. James Cook would learn the difference between his work and pleasure.

NEWCASTLE RACES!

Newcastle saw horseracing at its best, with rich merchants taking tents beside the course to entertain their guests, and all the colourful ragbag of characters to be found at a major race meeting. Excitement began to build the week before as the boys went to school and, all around town, inns and lodgings were filling up. The gentry were arriving. The stables were full. The racehorses were being pampered. The excitement grew, and every ship's master who could manage it, wanted to moor in the river, who cared if they missed a tide? A small collier like *Friendship* could take coal and leave space.

On Thursday 18th his master sent Ralph up to Mr. Wilkinson's to see if he could get lodgings for Mr. & Mrs. Jefferson of Staithes who had arrived on their ship. He came back breathlessly to say it was 'a Guinea a Week for a Room to Lodge in, but they never took anybody that eated.' So it was planned they would eat at Mrs. Hudspeth's. Mr. John Jefferson could spread bonhomie wherever he was. Newcastle streets were filling up like a theatre. Ralph walked up into the High Town and listened to 'The Tall Man play upon the

French Horn,' one of the 'Sights'. And after work on the Saturday, and hauling hay at the stable for his master's mare, Ralph and young Billy hurried to see the Sussex Boy, he was, says Ralph in wonder, '7 foot and two Inches high, he marked the Length of his hand and finger upon my hand, the former was 10 inches and the Latter 3.' His middle-aged cousins, Elinnor and John Jefferson of Staithes, arrived at the house on Monday, he could not wait to tell them.

His master William Jefferson had laid down the law, there would be a great shortage of hire horses, so no-one but old George was to have his mare. While Ralph was at work on the Quay, the stately John Jefferson took young Billy up to the Moor to the racecourse. Mr. Allen of Richmond was there, Billy told Ralph. After breakfast next morning a horse had to be found for Mr. John Jefferson, so he took both boys out to find one. As Ralph went afterwards to the Quay he saw Mr. Allen coming towards him, adding one more to the lively dinner party at the Hudspeths. Ralph fetched his flute, Mr. Allen played and, even better, kindly loaned Ralph his horse. Billy and he were desperate to get to the race meeting, followed closely by Mr. John Jefferson and William Jefferson. After the first heat they all went into Mr. Charlton's tent, with its flags flying, and there 'got some Boyled Beef and Tounge', then Ralph and Billy raced off to see the other two heats, between 'one Seby the Winner' says Ralph, and 'one Scot, two four year olds nigh 16 hands high. It was thrilling for the boys, the glowing horses, the colour, the streamers, the pedlars and the cheers, they all returned home tired to supper in the parlour. A happy Ralph went off to return Mr. Allen's mare.

In the morning he paid Mr. Allen's price, by collecting a parcel from the Carrier but, after a fruitless search for the popular Mr. Allen in the crowded town, he left a note in his room window at 'Mr. Parkers the Turk's Head inn, (also the name of a sailor's knot). The Jeffersons had returned from dining at Mr. Cooper's and were drinking tea at Mrs. Hudspeth's when Ralph got there. Mr. John Jefferson sent him and Billy straight to the Playhouse to speak for four seats in the side box. Who were they for? An excited Ralph got dressed up. John and Elinnor Jefferson with the two young Hudspeth girls in their ribbons, and the shining eyed boys went up to the theatre. Billy and Ralph eagerly 'went upon the Stage' to sit, from where they spotted Mr. Allen, and watched the play 'the Conscious Lovers, and Damon & Philida the Enterment'. Ralph and Billy came home joyfully content behind the coach the others rode in.

Tactful Mr.& Mrs. Jefferson. Thursday 25th, being a serious race day, with important guests dining at both houses, the boys were to keep out of sight. Billy sneaked Ralph into their house for some strawberries, and afterwards they went up to the Moor to see the horses run, they decided to become racing experts. Ralph solemnly records: 'There was eight started but three distined [*disdained?*] the first heat, and Mr. Carr drew his horse so there was four started the next heat. Mr. Bowes got the first and second heat and Mr. Branderling the stakes.'At Robt. Hill's [*tent?*] they got some meat and Mr. Railston came alongside. They had been good. On Friday, William and John Jefferson took the boys to the course and into Wm. Bulman's tent, and they ended up at the Turks Head with Mr. Allen. Horseflesh was the talk of Tyneside. Horses were wonderful! Ralph got up very early next morning to see Mr. Allen leave, and was allowed to ride his horse as far as the bridge.

Quietly, downriver, *Friendship* - crowded out of her moorings - had sailed. There were no Races for James Cook, a humble Mate.

That summer of 1752 there may have been too much coal. Prices dropped. On 13th July the selling price of Tanfield coal was lowered by 2s-6d per chauldron, Captains rushed to buy. John Gallilee gave on his ship for Hutton coals. Mr. Gallon arrived to load the *Mary & Jane*. Ralph was loading the *Sukey & Nelly* of Lynn, whose Captain John Clifton was a regular customer. Yet between 20th and 30th July, James Cook was on board *Friendship* as she lay idle at Shields. There was a new ship there too. On 25th Ralph was sent to take out a sufferance for Mr. John Richinson, master of the *Success* of Whitby, for 88 chauldrons of coal 'the first she ever made.'

There were two men on *Friendship's* July trip who would be of great interest to her crew. Daniel Cambell, the 29 year old Scot who had been James Cook's shipmate, had just returned from Greenland, whaling in the *Revolution,* Captain Anthony Skinner's ship, and 28 year old John Hall had sailed to Greenland on Richard Lydell's *Neptune.* This adventure into whaling would continue until war came. Whaling was high risk for high rewards, extreme sailing, dangerous icebergs, deadly. To survive was an accolade. From them, James Cook would learn a lot about ice.

During that busy summer, Ralph had a 17 year old's confidence in his life at Newcastle, apart from being nervously fed-up with Jenny. He and Billy Henderson, Lewis Hick, and young Billy Hudspeth would go in the Trinity School yard to play shuttlecock. They were attracted to go up to the High Town to see 'the Duke of Hamilton's Lady one of the celebrated Beauties of England.' Ralph made a board to hang receipts on in the office, and learned to make boot blacking, with 'ivory black'. He began to make a 'Dictionary of Luck', writing in it all the Latin, Greek, Italian and French words 'as occur in music' and he practised his German flute, outside high on the lead roof, though William Jefferson seems to have encouraged the boys to go up the Chare to old George Weddell's roof instead.

Ralph even took Billy Hudspeth on holiday to Richmond where they bought ribbons for Billy's two sisters, Bella and Ann, and, as they walked down the street they bought a bell for *Dogo* the dog, and explored the castle ruins. It was holiday weather. A typical late summer storm was brewing.

James Cook on *Friendship* was at Shields on Thursday 20th August ready again to leave. He must have been caught in the raging storm as he sailed south. On Saturday 29th, Ralph was on board Mr. Till's sloop when he saw 'two or three Sloops, & Brigantines come up, some wanted Masts and some Boltsprits with several other misfortunes by the violence of the Storm on Tuesday night & all Wednesday the wind at ENE, all the storm.' A wind direction to force vessels on shore. A severe test for a ship's Mate.

Nature may not have won all that battle, but in the next fixture she was to be the outright winner.

THE CALENDAR CHANGES

In September 1752 an act of great importance came about, which had ordinary people studying the heavens and talking of the stars. For a long time Britain's calendar had been out of step with the universe. The British could no longer pretend they were right and, on 3rd September, a New Style calendar was adopted. To correct the error, 2nd September, a Wednesday, was followed by the 14th, a Thursday. A lot of people were confused. 'Give us back our missing days!' cried some. Others asked for their missing Sunday off. Some asked for missing wages. Many sensible people accepted that 1st January would now be the first day of the year but, all the same, continued to celebrate old Christmas Day in mid January for years afterwards. Ralph Jackson and James Cook were both 11 days younger than their birthdays imply.

Their mathematical understanding of the heavens, made Captain Ellerton and his mate James Cook sign on their next crew on 14th September, but the captain, mate and apprentices who had served continuously from 30th March to 10th November are entered correctly as having served 7 months; it was only the end of October by the Old Style calendar.

AUTUMN 1752

In Newcastle during that same short September, Ralph was going to Trinity School between the high tides. He and Billy went to school from 7am to 9am, then Ralph went to work and back to school in the evening. Jenny and he were fighting, she called his uncle names and hit Ralph with the iron coal rake. Young Billy cried out not to hit her back, whereupon William Jefferson walked into the kitchen and was very angry. But when he calmed down, he took Ralph aside and told him the truth about his family. He probably explained to him about his old uncle John Ward, and that Jenny may just have been right in calling him a 'lieing, thieving, scandalous fellow.' Ralph must have been shocked. In his young determination to be a good man, he had been undermined by a relative he felt obliged to be ashamed of. William Jefferson was kind, he must have talked to him sensibly. But his old uncle Ralph Ward now had questions to answer. From this time on, Ralph Jackson applied his mind to his religion, paying more attention at church, and reading such books as 'The whole Goodness of Man'.

On 28th September, the Quay was deserted, most people, sighs Ralph, had 'gone to see the unfortunate Owen MacDonald publicly executed for the murder of Robt. Parker Cooper and his body was given to the surgeons to be anatomised'. Jacky Campion was in town, competently loading his ship with coal. So Ralph asked his friend Ralph Morton to go with him as he had never cleared a ship before, and his master had told him to clear Mr. MacMillon's *Two Brothers* of Newcastle. For the first time, William Jefferson had gone away for a few days and left Ralph in charge. On his return, Jacky Campion was welcomed to the house in the evening and 'told of his voyages this summer and about the Customs at Riga', and we can imagine Ralph's rapt face in the candlelight as they listened to his tales, and William Jefferson smoking his pipe and sometimes asking a question. The ships were home from the Baltic, the days growing short.

The northern counties do not have languid autumns like the south of England. Two weeks, one howling wind and the trees are stripped bare. In Newcastle men were wearing their 'wide coats', the weather was rainy and miserable, but on 31st October (Hallowe'en), the night before All Saints Day, William Jefferson invited the young man Lionel Trotter and the boys to a merry evening 'we spent in played Cards, Catching at the apple upon a stick, and also in the water, and cracking nuts', says Ralph gratefully. He says at least once that William Jefferson was a kindly master, he appears to have been a tolerant, crisp man. Ralph Jackson had had to ponder family secrets he did not like. Ralph now began to constrain his own behaviour.

Downriver at Shields, on 27th October, *Friendship's* last crew had signed on in the rain, and left for London where they all signed off on 8th November. Two days later Captain Ellerton and the Mate James Cook signed off there too. It had not been an easy season but they had managed to sail regular voyages. Coal prices had not been good. The profits did not augur well for the Mate of a smaller collier on the fringe of John Walker's business.

During this year, 1752, Henry Walker of Whitby had died. His ships he left in the management of his brother John Walker. But Henry's daughter Rachel had married John Yeoman, who would have to have a more prominent place in the shipping firm now. John Walker would keep James Cook in work for the next three years, but always limited to the smaller ship *Friendship*. Why did Mr. Walker not transfer him to Mate on the larger Cats, going further abroad? The *Friendship* was the right size only for the North Sea. James Cook's career was not going far. It was discouraging.

WORKING ON THE TYNE
1753

'A boy from the Freelove came to the door
Nathl. Jatkin Master, Mr. Jo. Walker owner.'
Ralph Jackson   9th July 1753.

It was about this time, that John Walker of Whitby started to trade with William Jefferson. Ralph, now 17, at work with ships and coal, began to meet more of John Walker's men and visit Whitby.

The morning after Christmas Day, 1752, Ralph and his sister Dolly, rode down to Staithes to spend a holiday with the Jeffersons. Mr. Fox, from the Guisborough sailcloth factory arrived too and, at night, 'the blind man sang several songs and Play'd several Tunes upon the Fiddle.' Ralph went on the sands next to Mr. Sanderson's shop to gather shells for his sister Rachel. Ralph played cards and jaunted off to Whitby, where on 28th December he walked along the upper harbour. 'In the afternoon I went with young Mr. Pease and saw the dry docks'.

There was dangerous flooding that winter of 1752/3. With the rivers in spate, the horse boat at Stapleton could not take people over the river Tees to Darlington. At Newcastle, there was a 'fresh' in the Tyne which damaged 15 ships. Keels and wherries were torn from their moorings. The coal season was disrupted. Unable to work, Ralph and Billy, intent on being gentlemen who could shoot, were made to play cards for money, to buy shot and gunpowder from Mr. Kirton's shop on the Quay. William Jefferson was under pressure! And his cousins were reporting flooding on his inherited farms at Croft on Tees. As if that wasn't enough, John Campion of Staithes arrived.

'22nd February, this day my Master was very angry at me because Mr. John Campion told him that my Far[ther] was saying at Staiths that he fear'd I show'd little improvement at Newcastle.' Ralph tried a flurry of conscientious work.

Sam Campion's ship was lying at Simpson's quay at Shields neeped-on, the Campions came upriver to see the coals at Mr. Bowes staithes. Next day (27th) the ship lifted off on the tide, but went aground at the high end of Dortwick Sand. Ralph took a boat out to her, ate dinner with the Campions, then went with:
'John Campion and one Watson Master of one of Walker's ships of Whitby down to the Fort and went on board the Peggy Man of War where we saw the Prisoners that she had taken of a Cutter.'
The Royal Navy was in the Tyne. In peacetime, their job was to stop smuggling, and they had caught a French cutter with uncustomed goods, brandy, rum, tea. In port with Walker's ships, James Cook was nearby on *Friendship*. Did he too go to visit the Royal Navy?
Friendship had been laid up in London at the end of 1752, but by 2nd February 1753 her crew had collected there to sign on under

Captain John Swainston, *Friendship*'s new Captain. He had last captained the *Three Brothers.* James Cook had his friends aboard, Chas. Rois, Thomas & John Woodill and Francis Sutton, Daniel Campbell, and two men from the Yarmouth ship *Herring.* With *Friendship's* topmasts struck down, but mizzen rigged in case she broke loose from her Thames moorings, and had to be sailed free and brought back, she would need to be fully rigged to sail north to the Tyne, tarred and caulked on the way. Nearly all her first crew left at Shields on 20th February, two days before John Campion made trouble for Ralph. The Captain and Mate James Cook stayed aboard at Shields for six weeks. Were they waiting for repairs or insurance against bad weather?

On 2nd March, Ralph was sent to the Insurance office to know 'what they had a hundred for the run up to London they told me a Guinea and a half so I told my Master for Sam Campion wanted to insure'. William Jefferson dropped ink on a bill for £30-12s-4d and made Ralph go down to Shields to get Sam Campion to renew it. Ralph writes down his work in order to prove it. William Jefferson relented, he made the boys have a raffle with dice, for pocket pistols. On 16th March, he told them 'he had heard that Sam Campion's Ship was lost.'

The second *Friendship* crew signed on, 1st April

Ralph was determined to be diligent. 2nd April saw Captain John Jefferson, James Cook's ex-captain, who now lived in London, and had arrived at Shields on his ship *Richard & Ann*, come up to the house to dine and buy coals. Ralph filled out the accounts: 'Park coals Shipt per Wm. Jefferson in the Richard & Anne of London
 Mr. Jno.Jefferson Master
 192 Chalders April 13, 1753.'

Ralph went to buy Captain Jefferson a kitt of salmon for 8 shillings, maybe as an apology in advance.

Hoastman William Jefferson, seeing the effort, gave Ralph a book, 'The Whole Duty of Man,' to read. Ralph was growing up, and started to get shaved on Saturdays; testing his strength at the Shield Field with his friends playing spell and knor.[2] He was reading

'Salmon's geography', bought glass thread and frostings from the glasshouses for his sister Rachel to make her pictures, and enjoyed the spectacle when 'the Free Porters were going to weigh a Horse for a wager in the weighhouse upon the Sandhill.' He bought three papers of snuff and, that summer, he started smoking. But not drinking. Mr. Deighton, convivial at the Peacock Inn, had taken Ralph to Mr. Fairlum's glass wharehouse in the Close, then to Mr. Fleming the booksellers, to buy Gayles Tables, Ralph admits 'I did drink two glasses of Cyder against the check of my own conscience to the contrary.'

The Crown and Thissell pub stood at the foot of the Groat Market, its landlord was Christopher Place, whom Ralph's family knew from his brother in Swaledale. Mr. Sanderson was there, but could not tempt Ralph. On 5th May, 'I got a letter from my Sist. Dolly at Steaths off Mr. Sanderson I returned into the office and answer'd it by him .... when I found him, he asked me to sitt a while but I stayed little.'

For Ralph, life was intoxicating enough on the Tyne, with ships arriving from New York, Greenland, Virginia, Russia.

On 13th June a West India ship *Experiment* came in 'lying nigh the high Crain. I went on board and saw the curiosities as 2 or 3 Tortesses alive, a Parrott & Parrokeet, a Negro Boy, Munkey & pinapples with other curiositys I was a stranger to.'

The *Experiment* had been built by a group of Newcastle merchants in 1752 and had sailed on 5th October, under Captain John Scaife, for Jamaica. She had returned after nine months with sugar, rum, pimento, coffee, cotton, mahogany, lignum vitae, as well as Ralph's curiosities.[3]

For James Cook too, the ships on the Tyne gave a glimpse of far-away lands, of a wider experience he was missing. Unlike Ralph, he was a grown man of 25, but without young Ralph's social advantages and financial backing. James Cook was stuck.

That summer, 1753, Ralph prepared for his Confirmation in the Church of England. James Cook would have been Confirmed at 16.

29th April 1753, Sunday.

'I went to the Garthead* heard Mr. Jno. Westley preach.

I came down into my rooms and Prayed.'

* *an open place, outside the north east city wall of Newcastle.*

On 2nd July at the Trinity chapel Mr. Maddison preached from the 37th Psalm & 38th verse 'Keep innocency & take heed to the thing that is right for that shall bring a Man peace at the last.' There was always something innocent about Ralph.

On Sunday 8th July, at church, Mr. Swinbourne preached from 16th chapter of St. Luke, 12th verse. Ralph went out of their pew up to the choir and there received the Blessed Sacrament. He says, he was 'confounded as I took the bread in my left hand.'

Ralph continued a steady Christian for the rest of his life, as were most men at that time, which must include James Cook.

Next morning, 9th July, his master sent Ralph up the Broad Chare to find Mr. Wm. Jefferson's boy who had a message.

10th July. 'After I went upon the Key Mr. Nathaniel Jatkin, Master of the *Freelove,* Mr. John Walker of Whitby came up and fixed to load Tanfield [coal] with my Master.'

'16th July. Mr. William Jefferson Master of the *John & Esther* dined at our house.' This was another Walker ship.

By 15th August Ralph's Father, sister Rachel, and brother George who was on holiday from the Navy Office, were in Newcastle staying at Mr. Fish's inn, the King's Head. The men walked to see Fryer's Goose engine. In good company, Ralph played his flute and Rachel sang.

'I took leave of my Sister very Chearfully altho' I knew she was with God's will to go to London with my Brother.'

Rachel was to have a London season, the correct way for a girl to meet a husband. Within two years she would marry Captain William Wilson an East India Company captain, of increasing wealth and fame.

Ralph's diary stops at end of August 1753. There is only one entry he considers important enough to enter before March 1756.

Wednesday 29th May, 1754.

'My Master came from the Exchange and brough[t] News that Mr. John Campion of Staithes Master of the Thomas and Richard was lost in Bullrow at Riga in going from one ship to another and never more seen, this News came by a Letter from on board the Ship to Mr. Fish, called by some flying fish from his quickness in walking I imagine tho! I believe his name is Thomas Fish, the above Mr. Jno. Campion was hall'd up by an arm by the same sailors that were weighing their anchor in order to come from Riga about a week after Mr. Campion was so unfortunately drowned.'

LEAVING The FRIENDSHIP

4th & 5th FRIENDSHIP *(Muster Rolls)*

The last voyages on *Friendship* in 1754, with James Cook serving as Mate to Captain Ellerton, found ever-changing crews. They kept four apprentices, aged 14, 15, 17, but one, Francis Sutton, was 20. They mustered on board the collier at Shields for round trips on 9th August, 7th September, and 4th October, for the monthly voyages.

That autumn the weather was wet and wild - Mr. Ward tells us in his diary. As *Friendship* headed toward the Tyne, at the end of October, violent rain brought great floods on land. Wind from the North or North-West, thwarting ships beating northwards, pushing them away out to sea denying them a harbour, *Friendship* battled into Shields on 5th November.

Mr. Ward had been down to Boulby, to see the great flood, of Staithes beck, at Dale House mill bridge, but decided it was 'not so high by 3 or 4 feet as that in June 1725.' By 7th, the excessively high wind had veered south. Mr. Ward called in at Grainge and 'ordered a good.fire to dry me being very wet.' These were not conditions for sailing. It was 15th November before *Friendship* collected a different crew and left on a last voyage to deliver coal.

Returning north, *Friendship*'s crew met severe frost, much snow, and no thaw until 3rd December. But it was windy enough to allow them to make way towards Whitby, two more frosty days with the wind at the West, keeping them struggling, with ice on deck and iron-hard sails; heavy rain followed and, at last, they got into port by the 10th December. Once safe, the night grew fine. That's sailing!

As James Cook was laying up *Friendship,* in Whitby, the gales returned from the South East with more heavy rain. In atrocious weather they secured the.ship by 18th December. The crew signed off. Mr. Sanderson may have had quite enough of storms and floods threatening his shop. It was during those miserable days he made his threat to retire to the 'Idle Trade'.

James Cook stayed home until February. He found his father was building a house, to the side of Ayton Low Green. Did he help?

February 1755 opened with frequent snow showers and, some days, a hard bright frost. Cattle were being slaughtered on farms for ships' captains. Mr. Ward had two oxen of 110 and 74 stones slaughtered at Boulby for Mr. Jefferson, two for John Gallon and Richard Andrew. On 15th February, James Cook and *Friendship's* crew signed on at Whitby. That day the 'wind South and a brave thaw' says Mr. Ward. It was raining as *Friendship* ploughed through the waves to start the coal season on the Tyne.

During James Cook's *Friendship* years, seagoing men were growing more uncertain. A phoney war began, seamen were being taken by Royal Navy press gangs. The Muster Rolls, which had started with writing very clear, now began to fudge the facts. In 1754 Francis Sutton and two other names were scribbled out. Francis, born in Andover, arrived in Whitby to marry the Walker's servant Alice Gill, and was taken on as a very late sea apprentice. In 1753 he is neatly entered on the Muster Rolls as servant aged 21, by 1754 his age drops to 20, in February 1755, no age is entered for any man. Quaker honesty had given way to protective omission. Other captains like Sam Campion had been doing this for years.

It was a season riddled with fear. The Mate James Cook was on his third round trip delivering coal when *Friendship* was stopped by the Royal Navy; probably somewhere off Yarmouth, as it was 18th May, and a week later they were in Shields. War had not been declared but the 'writing was on the wall'. No seaman was safe who looked over 21. Francis Sutton, of indeterminate age, was pressed into the Royal Navy. Captain Ellerton was 47 and protected by custom. Had the Mate James Cook argued, he would have been pressed too.

Francis Sutton was taken. He later drowned on the King's ship *Ramillies*. Many years later, Mr. John Walker asked Captain Cook to help Alice Sutton *nee* Gill. Her son Francis had been drowned too, and a lawyer would not release his pay. John Walker signed the letter 'thy real friend'. James Cook was not a Quaker so would not usually be greeted as 'thy Friend', the greeting between Quakers. Their letters show affection between the two men.

Meanwhile, it was 1755, James Cook was 26, Mate of a collier, the weather was dry, clear and cold, wind northerly, as a jolted and thoughtful crew arrived back in Shields, without Francis Sutton. One thing James Cook must have decided: there was no way he was going to be pressed. Respecting Captain Ellerton* as he did, they must have talked it over. Mr. John Walker would have to be told. By 14th June *Friendship* was back in London. On 17th June, James Cook volunteered for the Royal Navy. He did not just launch himself on their mercy, knew the Royal Navy had none. His entry appears to have been controlled, even organised.

Letter to Mr. John Walker 'please to be remembered to Captain Ellerton if still living.' [4]

10

THE ROYAL NAVY
1755

In 1831, E.H. Locker, writing about Greenwich Hospital, quoted a note from the Quaker John Walker which said James Cook 'had always an ambition to go into the Navy.' The timing was right in 1755. At War, the Navy was no longer on the beach on half pay.

Yet the sea can get into a person's bloodstream, they want to sail and sail, further and further. James Cook did. He was skilled in the North Sea trade and was just as liable to be pressed into the Royal Navy from an East India ship. To volunteer for the Navy was to protect himself from the abject cruelty and almost certain death of a pressed man. To join the Royal Navy meant service on wider oceans. To James Cook it would be a practical step. But knowing of the terrible conditions on Royal Navy ships, it was also courageous.

James Cook volunteered at Wapping on 17th June 1755. The press gangs were on the river, he would be glad to get on board the *HMS Eagle* a 60 gun ship under Captain Joseph Hamar, moored at Spithead off Portsmouth. A prime seaman among so many pressed 'very indifferent landsmen', and an impressive six feet tall, it took only a month for him to be promoted to Master's Mate. He kept his Log from 24th July; full of rough spelling it records the coals, casks, and stores coming aboard, working on the ropework. He would be carrying his apprentice indentures and his 'good testimony' to prove he was an experienced Mate. These probably got him the Master's mate's job. His posting to *HMS Eagle* may not have been by chance.

Thomas Bisset, Master of *HMS Eagle* had settled his wife at Plymouth, but a Bisset family owned the timber yards lining one side of Execution Dock Stairs in Wapping, the stairs that led to the Bell Tavern. Did the two men already know each other? It seems in character that James Cook would navigate his entry into the Navy.

Also on 22nd February, George Jackson had been promoted Chief Clerk at the Navy Board, responsible for getting ships ready for sea. *HMS Eagle* had come out of the dock on 8th May with only her lower masts and bowsprit standing. She needed experienced men to fit her with masts, yards and rigging. With so few seamen on board, James Cook must have been a welcome gift to Thomas Bisset and his captain. Was he a gift from George Jackson?

On 27th July, the volunteers on board *HMS Eagle* received 2 months pay in advance. Now able to buy himself extra food, James Cook's calculated change of career began to payoff. He knew a lot about groceries, useful perhaps in his later approach to scurvy.

HMS Eagle sailed on 4th August to cruise between the Scillies and Ireland, to protect the notoriously rough waters of St. George's Channel. The ship was lurching, dangerously short-handed, and every vessel they intercepted was boarded to press men for her. There was little that was nice about the Navy. On 1st September 'a Monstrous great Sea' carried away the driver boom, Captain Hamer feared for their safety and returned to Plymouth for repairs. Once in harbour, he began to procrastinate. He wanted to put the ship into dock. Exasperated, the Admiralty replaced him with Captain Palliser. They had no time for complaints.

Hugh Palliser was five years older than James Cook, he had been at sea since the age of 12, had been in battle, had served in the West Indies and off India, and had just returned from convoying transport ships to Virginia.

A Yorkshireman, Hugh Palliser was one of those men who always know best and, as they are often right, infuriate people; when they are wrong they do not like to admit it. When they see wrong they cannot be quiet. James Cook would see this in Palliser right from the beginning; he had been on restrained Quaker ships. But Palliser was a sailor's sailor, a total professional, an enthusiast!

HMS Eagle headed out into gales and squalls on 8th October, chasing every ship they found in the western approaches, English, Swedish, Dutch, and fishing boats returning from Newfoundland. Vessels were harried. Two they caught were French. Sea conditions were appalling when they sighted *HMS Monmouth*, to help capture another in a hard gale. Their prizes were sent in to Plymouth, while *HMS Eagle* with 200 prisoners aboard continued to cruise down to Biscay to join Vice-Admiral Byng's fleet. They were present when the French man-of-war, *Esperance* burned in the ocean under pulverising British guns. They were filling up with more prisoners they could not feed. *HMS Eagle* had been storm damaged so much she was ordered back to Plymouth, where on 27th November Captain Palliser wrote bluntly to the Admiralty. He had too many men on board from other ships, given him to make up a crew, no-one knew who they belonged to, only three were worth keeping. He begged for 'a few good Men' as he had 'so very few Seamen on board'. *HMS Eagle's* crew was dangerously unskilled. James Cook succeeded to the Boatswain's job. In February, he spent a few days in hospital. They had all suffered.

HMS Eagle's men were due to prize money. Forceful Palliser would see they got it! Master's Mate Cook would get his share.

By early March they were at sea again, fighting, harrying the French, taking prizes. James Cook was in command of the ship's cutter, raiding the French coast. In May *HMS Eagle* joined Admiral Boscowen's fleet off Ushant to take part in the blockade. *HMS Eagle's* men were dying. She had so many sick and prisoners aboard, Palliser was sent back to Plymouth. He was highly indignant at his men's condition, he protested. His surgeon and four men died as they arrived in the harbour, 22 had been buried at sea, 130 were put into hospital, including the two surgeon's mates, he landed 143 prisoners, he was ill himself. The sickness and death was due to lack of clothes, he thundered, the men were nearly all landsmen 'Naked when they came on board being for the most part Vagabones not one in Twenty of them that had more than Shirt and one ragged Coat,' he demanded payment for the extra clothing he had had to supply to the sick. That deathly *HMS Eagle* cruise had turned both the loud angry Palliser and the quiet Cook into hardened crusaders for better conditions.

Palliser was a bruiser in any position he took. A prime example occured during their next cruise in the bitter winter seas of Biscay. About 180 miles South-West of Ushant, at one o'clock in the morning, with *HMS Eagle* awash in driving rain, they saw a sail. Palliser gave chase and cleared for action. His more senior captain in *HMS Medway* did not. When the sail turned out to be French, *HMS Medway* signalled Palliser to shorten sail to give them time to clear for action. Of course he did not; he attacked and took the 50 gun *Due D'Acquitaine. HMS Eagle* suffered badly. With Palliser effervescent with anger, she was taken in tow by the other ship, and all three headed back to Plymouth.

Palliser was brave. He was young and had no time for those he disagreed with. James Cook was circumspect. Maybe he learned to be with Palliser. He had Palliser's support for years, as Palliser rose in the Royal Navy, from Newfoundland surveyor, to Commodore, to Governor, to maybe choosing the vessel to be named *Endeavour.*

James Cook was serving under one of his country's most brilliant sailors, punishing the French in a war which, by the way, had not yet officially begun.

When War did begin, James Cook would cross the Atlantic Ocean and start a new chapter of his life, a new opportunity, if he survived.

~~~

THE SEVEN YEARS WAR
1756 - 1762

For the past two years, James Cook had been involved in aggressive blockading by the Royal Navy, in a war that had not been declared. Since 1754 Britain had been nervous about French intentions, heavy patrolling of the seas by the Royal Navy was to prevent French arms and garrison build-up and there was cruel press gang activity to bolster the fleet. So, what was the conflict about?

The Seven Years War was about the expansion of trade. Who would control the fur and timber from Canada, the gum from Dakar in Africa, the luxury goods and spices from India and China, sugar from the West Indies? As ocean trading grew, coin was short in Europe. In Britain it was seeping away. Russia only accepted bullion. China only accepted gold and silver. A lot of silver came from Spanish colonies. If Spain joined France against Britain, they could strangle Britain's trade.

This war would be global. In Europe, the usual place to fight, France, Russia and Austria fought to control Silesia. It had coal. In America, the French fought to stop British colonies spreading west. Spain held the lands around the Mexican gulf. France held Louisiana, the Great Lakes, the St. Lawrence, and the land north into Canada. Together they encircled the English colonists on the Eastern seaboard, hoping to push them back into the sea.

Across the open plains of north America the Indians followed their own way of life, hunting the buffalo, and crept through the silent forests tracking the deer, the moose, and the Europeans. These Native Americans had a huge confederacy around the Great Lakes, forged over 300 years by the Iroquois. Naturally, they followed their own plans to stop colonist expansion into their lands.

For the Royal Navy, we could say, the Seven Years War was about fish. After the last war ended, France had been allowed to keep her fishing grounds on the Grand Banks off Newfoundland. In these foggy waters of the Gulf Stream, the 'Bucaloo' trade in cod brought thousands of tons of dried fish home to Europe, vital to feed the French.

The 'Bucaloo' trade was a nursery for prime seamen. So many sailors were thrown on the beach when the last war ended in 1748, they had to find work somehow. French sailors were ready at two weeks sailing distance to man the French Navy, tough, expert anti-British. It meant France could start a war all over again.

The Seven Years War did not begin as a war for timber, but when Russia became an enemy, one source of first rate mast timber dried up. Britain was self-sufficient in timber for Royal Navy ships until 1764, but anxiety was showing long before that, and some Royal Navy vessels were being built in America. In 1759, as the British fleet eased down the St. Lawrence estuary to attack Quebec, there must have been a few greedy-eyed boatswains and ships' masters looking at the superb timber lining the shores, one of whom must have been Thomas Bisset, Master of *HMS Stirling Castle*. The banks of the St. Lawrence would soon become known as Britain's woodyard.

Numbers of ships:[1]	In 1755	In 1760
France	88	103
Spain	61	71
Britain	191	250

Even so, with international trade expanding, clearly there were not enough Royal Navy ships to police the world oceans. With barely enough to guard essential trade routes, the East India Company had started a navy of their own, the Bombay Marine.

The British people were clear about one thing. As an island nation, the first duty of the Royal Navy was to protect them, in home waters.

Britain a nation of 8 million people faced France, a nation of 22 million people. Any invasion which landed, would overwhelm Britain. Only the Royal Navy blocked the way. From 1754, without any war being declared, they had begun to deny French ships the freedom of the seas. James Cook was involved in a brutal stand-off.

1756 WAR DECLARED!

'I was minded to set about this work
again' *Ralph Jackson 2nd March 1756.*

Ralph Jackson at 20 was now a well-dressed young man. His sister Dolly had sent him a steel chain for his watch, he had a black satin waistcoat, a blue coat, white cotton stockings, and an amber-headed cane 'exceedingly pretty .... gift of my Bro. Wilson before he went out in Feb. last to Coast and China.' Ralph went to Messrs. Langland & Gudricks to collect his silver seal for his letters.

But the year 1756 began in dread, with the imminent threat of war, the gulping fear of French invasion and the Navy press gangs pitiless. On 6th March, returning from Long Benton staith between 8 and 9 o'clock, Ralph saw 'the Tender's boat board Mr. Shadforth's ships where five men were press'd.'

The *Thylow,* the Royal Navy tender, moved higher up the river to opposite Mr. Watsons, and Langdale Sutherland Esq., Collector of Customs for Newcastle, was ordered to clear no ship at the Customs House. Young men hid. '8th March….John Dent (my Master's servant) laid with me this night for fear of the press gang who we heard were to go about people's houses at three or four o'clock in the Morning and which I hear was accordingly done in Pandon Street.'

The coal trade could not operate without the keelmen so, next day:

'Mr. Baker fitter came to desire my master wou'd meet the Company at Mr. Winds in Pilgrom Street...in the evening the company met again to consider of means to preserve the Keelmen from the Press and yet the Regulating Captain partly demanded a Hundred or a Hundred & Fifty Men. I believe they came to no other determination than that the Captain might take that number as he would come at them.'

Two days later Ralph 'saw some sailers who were going to Liverpool to a Greenland Ship there carried on board the Tender all 24 in number.' Next morning the embargo was taken off all coasting ships, and confined only to those bound overseas. The collier captains left their crews hiding at Shields, and began to come up to the house to buy; Jos. Martin master of the *Warren* of London dined. Ralph was dismayed, affronted by injustice when 'I saw Davd. Greehound press'd from his protection….' The embargo was laid on again. A keel of coals was an untrustworthy '£4-6s-0d. @ 12 shillings per Chauldron for 8 chauldrons'. William Jefferson was having trouble. With his cash in the hands of one Charles Admondson the man came back to confess: two women had picked him up and he supposed they got the money from him. His captain took him back on board, but next day Admondson returned to their house; To Ralph's surprise 'the norseman complained of his ill usage from his Master who beat him sore after they got on board.'

Ralph managed to get Protections for his Master's keelmen, with one extra for a young Scotsman. There was fear on the river, men disappearing. A letter came from Ralph's father 'to enquire for one

George Mowat that was impressed on his road to Scotland, went to the Rendevous but upon the books being examined no such man as George Mowat Watchmaker appear'd. I was told that if he had been impress'd and told his occupation he would not have been detained as none but seamen and watermen are wanted at present expect *[Sic]* a landsman choose to enter.'

Britain waited bitterly for invasion. The embargo was taken off, as *Thylow* went from her moorings with a large number of pressed men. The Earl of Northumberland met the Army at the Moor Head. There was one guinea reward for entering HM 58th Regiment of Foot under Lord Charles Manners. Soldiers were quartered in the town.

At Newcastle it was still possible to shut the gates and man the city walls. Newcastle was a rich target. Gentlemen began cleaning their pistols. Merchants sent their children inland.

In north Yorkshire, there were long stretches of sandy beach and several harbours, hard to defend. This was the duty of the Deputy Lieutenants, Justices, and Constables of parishes.

On 6th February, 1756, there had been a national patriotic General Fast. Mr. Ward did not eat all day, and attended church at Guisborough, 'which was So Crowded with people I never see the like before,' he wrote in his diary.

Mr. Cholmondley Turner sent him a message, asking to have the road mended for his coach, as the Justices and Constables of the Weapontake were to meet at Guisborough court to set up the Watch on the coast. Mr. Sanderson would be there, standing at the market cross listening to Mr. Spark read out the King's orders. On 8th March, Mr. Turner at the Cock Inn, read to the Justices a letter from Lord Rockingham *Custos Rotulorum,* about procuring recruits for some newly raised regiments. Mr. Ward wrote uneasily 'the press is very Hott in Whitby & Geo. Mewburn and John Hawman [auctioneers] came here at night', to buy 40 sheep.

Tempers were hot too. At Stockton, at the Black Lyon Inn, the gentlemen at the town, 'being Cordially met Togeather', news arrived that two men taken up for the King's Service, had escaped.

The under-Bailiff taking the blame, entered himself instead and promised 20 more, but managed only one, a likely young fellow who entered for Sea. An argument about the blame flared up between the gentlemen, high words flew between Mr. Baker and Mr. Sutton of Stockton 'which lasted some hours, but at last Subsided,' laments Mr. Ward.

Mr. Wardell wrote to Mr. Baker, from Boulby on 11th March:
'Honrd. Sir,
….as all trade is now Stopd by Sea: no fish taken now, the fishermen dare not Goe to Sea, nor even stay in the town of Staiths for fear of the Press Gang Comeing there: all goes on very well here, I Beg my Duty to Mrs. Baker and the dear Little ones: from your most Obdt. Hble Servt. Thos. Wardell.'[2]

People waited, and waited, watching the sea for invading ships. The warning beacons stood ready on the cliffs.

But the watch was taken off the coast on 12th April, by the Justices, including Mr. Skottowe and Mr. Ward, who says:
'The Watch which have been kept for Some time in all the Townships of Cleaveland, all the Cunstables appearing for the East Division, Mr. Murgatroid, Mr. Smith, Mr. Sanderson & Mr. Scurfield of Stockton dined with us.'

It was just a temporary lull in their fear.

At Newcastle, during these unstable days, Ralph was loading Whitby ships for wary captains. Mr. Fargus Foster, master of the old ship *Fortune* of Whitby loaded with Long Benton coal, while Isaac Newton, once her master, loaded a ship of his own. Matthew Jefferson, now Master of the *Richard & Ann* of London, loaded with South Moor coal 'with which the Owners uphold double coal or 16 to the Keel.' The whaling ships were trying to sail. Ralph went upriver to the Crooked Billet inn to say goodbye to Captain William Hedley who was leaving in *Resolution* for Greenland. Captain Robert Hedley's *Neptune* bound for Holland, which had been waiting at Mr. Headlam the shipwright's anchorage in the river, now bought beef at £1-4s-0d a cwt. ready and anxious to sail. Master Edward Dillon's 'galley' *Good Intent* of Falmouth was loading Tanfield and Main Seam Top coal, on 18th May, the day War was finally declared in London.

Two days later Ralph went to the coffee house to read the Declaration. Come Saturday morning, he listened to the Proclamation of War being read out 'by Mr. Bruce Sargeant at Mace on the top of the Court stairs, the Aldermen standing below.' In towns and cities, across the country, the same ominous Proclamation was being read out to the public. In Guisborough Mr. Ward and the justices heard it at the market cross.

'I sincerely pray for God's assistance now in this time of need,' Ralph writes.

A disturbing bright star hung eerily over Newcastle for five nights. Superstition ran wild.

When the June raceweeks began, Ralph was too busy taking out Protections for their keelmen, he notes quickly:

The King's Plate of 100 guineas was won by Mr. George Scurfield's horse *Dunkirk,* 4 heats. Mr. Wm. Bell of Swalwell's grey horse *Trimmer* won the £50, 'he belonged to the late Sir Richard Hilton'. Robert Shafto Esquire's horse and his chestnut colt won, and Mr. Fenwick's horse *Matchem.*

Ralph was now skilled on the water. He bought a quarter share in a boat, paying £1-8s-6d., with John Dawson and Mr. Wm. Addison. They called it the *Mellnion.* They were to use it for fishing on the river. But were they safe? The war was odd, it was too quiet.

William Jefferson was loading colliers from distant ports: the *Jos. & Samuel* of Bridport and *Molly* of Ipswich loaded Hutton or Marley Hill coals. Ralph took Mr. Jos. Tipple, master of the *William & Mary* of London to the glasshouse to buy glass; the common bottles were Is-9d. a dozen, 2s-3d for 'champain': too dear he thought.

Then on 19th July Master Frampton of the *Brilliant Star* of Lymington said he had seen an engagement off the Kentish Knock, and news broke that the British Mediterranean fleet had failed. The British naval base, Port Mahon in Minorca, had been taken by the

French. Shock ran through the country. How could the Royal Navy fail? Within days, Ralph was at Mr. Hindmarsh's the Glover, in the Flesh Market, when he saw Admiral Byng's effigy burnt, after it had been carried around the town 'for his ill behaviour in the Mediterranean.' That week, Admiral Byng was arrested as he landed at Portsmouth. For his failure, he was Court Martialled, and shot on the deck.

Ever afterwards, it has been seen as a famous miscarriage of justice, a dreadful example of a badly drafted Act of Parliament operating in the way no-one intended. And George Jackson was present in the Court.

ADMIRAL BYNG EXECUTED!

It seems, George Jackson was there in his capacity of Clerk of the Acts at the Navy Office. Years later, his grandson wrote that George Jackson had been 'quite within measurable distance' of it, and had 'the proceedings taken down in his own handwriting.' But George afterwards wrote Ralph a letter:

'my Bro. tells me, that Adml. Byng is Sentenced to be Shot, but recommended to his Maj.'s Mercy, wch greatly affends & affects the good old King, the Court Martial find him Guilty by the 12th Art. of war made in the 22nd yr of his present Majesty, but don't find him guilty of Cowardice or Disaffection therein mentioned, so that it must be Negligence. Or An Error in Judgement in not going down to engage the Enemy.'

Expecting invasion of home waters, the Royal Navy had sent Admiral Byng with only a small, badly prepared fleet to protect Minorca. Sailing into battle, in thick rain, the line of ships misjudged a signal, entangled themselves, could not regroup, and split up. The battle and the island was lost.

London was jittery with fear. The French army gathered their battalions across the Channel. They could be seen from the south coast. The British government was weak and needed a scapegoat.

Admiral Byng was blamed for government failures. His letter of explanation was published - Ralph saw it before he left Newcastle, he saw the angry bonfires lit. The government had held back the justifying half of the Admiral's letter. The public, the King, the Navy itself, felt he could have done better. But no-one expected the death penalty to take place.

Byng was tried under new legislation, which was faulty. The law was only eight peacetime years old, and badly framed as it allowed no discretion in punishment. Byng was first to feel its effect.

Mrs. Sarah Osborne pleaded for her brother's life.

The Admirals of the Court Martial asked to be released from their oath of secrecy to explain their difficulty with the law. The House of Commons agreed, the House of Lords refused.

Admiral West, who had been in the forefront of the battle, protested the severity of the law to his cousin, Lord Temple, 1st Lord of the Admiralty: 'The court have convicted him, not for cowardice nor for treachery, but for misconduct, an offence never till now thought capital, and now it seems, only made so because no alternative of punishment was found in that article they bring him under.'

In spite of a great rumpus in Parliament, Admiral Byng was executed. Ever since, it has been seen as a wrong done to a brave but cautious man.

A few minutes before he died he gave a letter to the Marshall for Mrs. Osborne,[3] 'My dear sister.:....all has proved fruitless.... Persuaded, I am, Justice will be done to my reputation hereafter .... If my crime is an Error in Judgement. .. .1 forgive the Judges if the Error in Judgement is on their side.'

She was in no doubt. She buried him under a stone inscription:
'To the perpetual disgrace of Public Justice
The Honourable John Byng Esq.
Admiral of the Fleet
Fell a Martyr to Political Persecution.'

Every Royal Navy officer knew now, what the penalties were for any failure. It stiffened resolve, maybe past the point of reason. The war must be won. The cost of any failure was too high.

RALPH JACKSON MOVES TO GUISBOROUGH

Ralph Jackson was 21. With his apprenticeship complete, he moved to live with his uncle at Guisborough. The elderly Mr. Ward tried to give him a sporting start to learn the business. On 3rd January, 1757, Thomas Presswick took Ralph down to Grainge farm where 'we went into Wm. White's house and got some goosepye it being Xrmastime'. They rode on to Boulby Alum works 'where we found Mr. John Jefferson of Staithes with Mr. Wardell.' Nat Campion and John Gallilee were going greyhound coursing with Thomas Wardell, but Thomey and Ralph went down to Staithes with Cousin Jefferson, where Ralph stayed all night - with his uncle's permission. 'We played at cards', he says happily.

At Guisborough in the winter evenings, he read a good deal to his uncle: they were reading 'some small books wrote by Edwd. Synge a Bishop .. .in Ireland'. For himself Ralph was devouring a Treatise on the Spanish Inquisition by John Coustos, once a prisoner 'a most horrid Court indeed', he shudders. The snow fell, deep and heavy. There were practical things to master - with a cut-throat razor. 'I shaved Jack and he shaved me by way of learning ourselves this being the first time we either of us shaved anybody'. Jack Pearson was his uncle's servant. Both lived.

Mr. Ward enjoying the new company, made a point of teasing Ralph. He bought a 'strong brown mair for his own riding, rising 6 years old,' and let Ralph ride her. Eventually Ralph found he had his own horse. One happy evening when John Jefferson, Nat Campion and Mr. Wardell came to stay the night, 'My Uncle sat up till past ten and drank punch pretty freely'. It put Mr. Ward into bed with gout. Ralph sat with him in the little downstairs sick parlour that February. 'My Uncle is a most useful and entertaining companion' he says, after old Mr. Ward had recited this poem to him:

> 'Like apes we toy till twenty & one,
> As bold as lions, till forty is done,
> As cunning as foxes, till 3 score & 10,
> Afterwards asses, and no more Amen '

During one long candlelit winter night, Mr. Ward told Ralph of a journey he had made in 1715 to the very north of Scotland, to buy kelp for the Alum Works, during the dangerous upheaval of the Jacobite rebellion. While his friend had been called home, he had gone on.

And one evening 'My Uncle showed me a Copy of a letter that he had by the Post in 1726. It was dated October 2nd 1726 but no Town mentioned it was signed…..Pottowske, advising him that his Life was to be taken before Christmas…..but this he is persuaded was only a Scheme of the Duchess of Buckingham's and Mr. Moore's who at that time were his professed Enemies'. The Duchess, who owned Mulgrave lordship alum and Mr. Moore the Loftus alum works, obviously did not like having such a successful rival alum works at Boulby, wedged between them. They thought they had been robbed by John Ward, and won a court case against him. Ralph Ward had clearly prevented them from taking the Ward family money.

The Duchess of Buckingham had been known as the proudest woman in England, the last woman in fact to have an effigy of herself carried in procession at her funeral in Westminster Abbey. She was an illegitimate daughter of the exiled King James II, and had married the Duke as his third wife. She made him build her a town house; it is now known as Buckingham Palace. At Mulgrave their old castle was too draughty and mean. She evicted her steward from his own house on the hill and rebuilt it as the present Mulgrave Castle. No minor personages, such as the Ward family, could be allowed to stand in her way. We wonder how much sleight of hand Mr. Ward used to defeat her.

As Ralph began to learn his uncle's business, the old clerk, Thomas Presswick took a back seat. He taught Ralph as much as he could, though Thomey sometimes shocked Ralph by becoming too happy in drink. Thomas Presswick would work for Mr. Ward for nearly 58 years. 'My worthy friend', Ralph called him. But it was the younger Jack Pearson, his uncle's man servant, who stayed close to Ralph for life.

Dr. Bisset describes Jack as 'a robust peasant type'. Jack was an out of doors man. Many years later Ralph calls him his gamekeeper. It is likely Jack stayed at that because he could not read.

Meanwhile, if the French invaded and conquered Britain, and French law was imposed, the Justices, like Mr. Ward and Mr. Skottowe, would be executed. Old men like Mr. Ward could not, even would not, run away. With those winter tales, of bold journeys through a country at war and death threats at home, wily Mr. Ward seems to have had it in mind to save Ralph, his heir, by persuading him to flee into the wild moors, with a trusted servant who knew how to live off the land. And the man for that would be robust Jack Pearson, who lived in the house, ready for orders, ready to go.

11

MASTER MARINER
1757

Two years of harsh Royal Navy life had passed for James Cook. He was still Master's Mate of *HMS Eagle* under Captain Palliser.

Thomas Bisset, Master of *HMS Eagle* had left on 28th April 1757 to help complete the building of *HMS Pembroke*. It was about this time that Palliser received a letter from Mr. William Osbaldeston, MP for Scarborough, written at the behest of John Walker of Whitby, suggesting that James Cook might be commissioned. Palliser, who also became MP for Scarborough years later, and may have known William Osbaldeston suggested, fairly enough for the pay was better, that James Cook took the exam for Master 'by which he would be raised to a station that he was well qualified to discharge with ability and credit.'

On 29th June 1757, James Cook attended at Trinity House, Deptford, and passed the examination for Master Mariner. His Certificate qualified him 'to take charge as Master of any of His Majesty's ships from the Downs thro' the Channel to the Westwards and to Lisbon.'

Within two years of joining the Royal Navy he had raised his position, being promoted to Master Mariner, and more secure.

On 30th June he was discharged from *HMS Eagle* and entered as

Master of the 24 gun frigate, *Solebay,* under Captain Robert Craig, then patrolling the eastern coast of Scotland, as far as the Orkneys and Shetlands, to act against smuggling and 'treasonable intercourse' with France and Holland. *HMS Solebay* had just returned to base in Leith when Master Cook joined her there on 31st July. He had taken a month to travel north to Leith, so surely he had been to see his parents at Great Ayton.

HMS SOLEBAY[1]

HMS Dolphin man o'war, under Captain Marlow, was in charge of Leith anchorage, the wide stretch of water where a convoy was gathering to sail to London under Royal Navy protection.

On 27th June, the *Suffolk* East Indiaman, sailed in, laden with goods from China; she had come safely by way of Ireland and northern Scotland, to avoid conflict with the French. She saluted *HMS Dolphin* with 13 guns and moored, taking her bearings from Inchkeith and Edinburgh Castle. Next day her Captain William Wilson notes he 'received on board Captain Farquarson of the *HMS Prince of Orange* and entered several of our People into HM service.' The weather according to *Suffolk's* log was 'chiefly fine'. For *Suffolk's* men, who already had been at sea for three years, the outlook as pressed men was deadly.

HMS Hampshire came in, 13 guns from *Suffolk* were returned by 19, then *HMS Chesterfield* 11 for 15. On 24th July, Commander Marlow made the signal to sail. *Suffolk* was unable to make ready. Captain Farquarson had to lend Captain Wilson 4 midshipmen and 30 people to help sail the ship.

James Cook, watching from *HMS Solebay,* would see the convoy leave on 1st August with the Royal Navy escort of *HMS Hampshire* 50 guns, *HMS Chesterfield* 40 guns, and *HMS Dolphin* 70 guns, escorting the three East Indiamen *Houghton, Godolphin* and *Suffolk* in their company colours, along with '1 West India ship, 1 Virginian, 1 from Carolina, several coasters with the London traders'. By noon on the 5th August, the convoy was off Whitby, and would get to London in safety.

Captain Wilson of the *Suffolk,* Ralph's brother in law, had sent his purser by land, with letters and gifts to his wife Rachel's family. On 24th July, Mr. Ralph Ward received, says a pleased Ralph Jackson: 'One Quilted Satin morning gown with compliments, two pieces of gingham for Hannah and Dolly, and one dozen of neccloths for me.'

HMS Solebay with James Cook sailed from Leith on 2nd August, heading north to call at Stonehaven, past Buchan Ness, the easternmost part of the Aberdeenshire coast, to reach the Orkneys by the 9th, then Shetland and back to Stonehaven on 19th. She was back in Leith by the end of the month.

Vessels on patrol like *HMS Solebay* were part of the Navy's holding system, for men awaiting their next posting. It allowed them home leave, and to get paid for their last ship. For someone who had been in the thick of war, it was more like a holiday, except for one thing. The North Sea is notorious for producing freak waves, smashing vessels and men. There are often storms in August. James Cook would know it was just as easy to be drowned there.

His *HMS Solebay* log ends on 7th September. His next Master's warrant is dated 18th October, and on 27th he entered *HMS Pembroke,* 64guns, a 1250 ton, ship-of-the line, under Captain John Simcoe, which Thomas Bisset, his old Master from *HMS Eagle*, had left just two days before to go to the *HMS Stirling Castle.* There is a sense of forward planning, of recommendation.

HMS Pembroke had been launched on 2nd June and fitted out, she was almost ready to sail. Thomas Bisset was more than an ordinary ship's master. He appears more of a ship-builder, than most masters. We can sense the urgent planning in the Navy Office, to get the ships built, launched and manned. The war was going badly.

HMS PEMBROKE

Captain John Simcoe had become a captain at the early age of 23. He was now 43, an intellectual scientific man, interested in mathematics, navigation, surveying and military tactics. He had been unfortunate enough to be a member of Admiral Byng's court martial. So, at the least, he had been in the same room as George Jackson. If Simcoe had asked George to ensure a reliable Master for *HMS Pembroke* he had got one.

James Cook would serve under a captain who could develop his skills. A mentor to guide him in the direction of surveying. But first, there was a war, and these men were the front line.

Let us not mince words about these ships. They were designed and manned as killing machines. They were built as platforms for guns. So were the enemy's ships. *HMS Pembroke*, with her officers and crew, and Master James Cook, knew they were sailing out to die.

~~~

WILLIAM PITT
1708 - 1778

On 29th June, 1757, the same day James Cook took his Master's exam at Deptford, across the river another man took the seals of office from the King. This man ignored everyone's opinion, he was the only man single-minded, grim and clever enough to win the war.

William Pitt was 'an incendiary'. In 1755 his 'florid eloquence' in the House of Commons, his bitter speeches, the wide gestures, (which even the Shakespearean actor Garrick would be proud of said Horace Walpole), as he castigated those in government, cutting the air with the truth of their incompetence as Britain slid into war. Pitt accused them of ignoring French hostility since 1748. He had wanted to raise 500,000 seamen since 1751 He had been ridiculed. Now with the French encircling the English colonists in America, he accused the Duke of Newcastle of being a child in a go-cart on the edge of a precipice.

William Pitt was about to become the greatest War Minister Britain has had. Pitt's powerful words uplifted the British people.

Yet, unlike Winston Churchill in 1939, he had never fought as a soldier. Both had a clear vision of what was needed, but Churchill had the advantage of knowing about Pitt.

In 1757, at the crucial point of danger, the whole country swung behind Pitt's rhetoric. Ironically, he could only command this following because he was an outsider. His extreme patriotism attracted Tory support, although Pitt was a Whig; and he always put himself forward as a man uncorrupted by any consideration of self-interest, a man for the people 'out of doors'. His party political backing was in fact so weak, that he had no-one to please but himself. It did not have to be that way, he had great political connections, he chose that way, and did not mind offending anyone. Of his speeches, it was said, 'a greater rhapsody of violence could not be flung out.' He was persistent, bullying, brilliant, had huge bouts of gout which laid him low in bed, and was dogged by fits of manic depression which destroyed his health. Yet he rose to meet every danger. The country could not do without him.

William Pitt was the grandson of Mad 'Diamond' Pitt, an adventurous East India merchant of volcanic temper, unstoppable energy and self-belief, who had ended up as Governor of Fort St. George, Madras, and come home with a diamond almost beyond price. He said he was given it. He bought it.

His grandson William was the only person Diamond Pitt liked.

As an adult, William became a Whig politician who after the Jacobite rebellion in 1745 came into his own. He had a clear policy: supremacy at sea, domination of trade, and Down with the French! At the outbreak of the Seven Years War, William Pitt became Secretary of State with almost a free hand. The City of London merchants were his friends, the Tories backed him, his policies were in fact risky and took time - about three years to mature, but he succeeded, and put Britain on the road to the domination of world trade which would lead to the British Empire.

First, the British island Kingdom had to be protected from invasion. Militias, he said, were to be raised in every county to guard the home front. The Army chief, the Duke of Cumberland was furious; he wanted proper soldiers, a professional army. He asked if the amateur Pitt would go himself to meet the French at Dover? Pitt was adamant. He would have Militias.

To control the supply of money and the votes in Parliament, the Duke of Newcastle, master of detail, joined with Pitt. It was an odd pairing. The Duke gave everything, said the diarist Horace Walpole, and Pitt did everything. Competence was Pitt's requirement, the ability to 'do the business'. He appointed Lord Anson to lead at the Admiralty, and Lord Anson knew what was needed.

The outlook was terrible. The main theatre of war in Europe was reaching crisis point, The Prussian army, led by King George's nephew, Frederick, lost heavily, the Russians massed on his borders; the Duke of Cumberland's army was defeated, surrendered and, when he got home to London, his position was denied by his father the King. Forty battalions of French troops moved to the Channel coast. Invasion of Britain looked imminent. People in their homes were afraid to sleep.

The Deputy Lieutenants of the Counties (the King's representatives), the Justices of the Peace and the parish Constables, like Mr. Sanderson, had control of the parish guns. These were often ancient and kept in the church vestry. All these men, many of them old, expected to be killed by the invading French.

The Army was recruiting, but so were new local militias.

The Royal Navy had nearly 300 ships but not enough sailors to man them. The new 74 gun warships were still building.

LOUISBOURG 1757

William Pitt thought on a global scale. He put analysis above friends' feelings. He needed something to spur the spirit of the Nation. He calculated that he needed a trophy victory. He needed something crucial to lift the Nation's spirits. He decided to take Louisbourg.

Louisbourg was the only French harbour on the north coast of America able to hold the French fleet. It was easy to find. By simply sailing west between latitude 44 and 45 degrees North, looking out for Cape Breton island, there it was.

Unless there was fog.

On the Grand Banks, where the warm Gulf Stream met the cold Labrador current, fog created Louisbourg's best defence.

Otherwise it was indefensible. Built on a low spit of land at the harbour entrance, fortified with walls made with seasand cement, which crumbled in the constant rain, it was surrounded by hills, making it easy to lob shells into the town. Yet its harbour was safer than it sounds and could hold the French warships.

Louisbourg's value to the French was to defend their part of the cod fishery. The main current and winds carried the fish home quickly to Europe. But any attempt to hurry the French Navy to Louisbourg, met with the same head-on winds, heavy swell and long delays. Louisbourg, plentifully stocked, but always short of gunpowder, could never hold out long enough to be re-inforced when attacked, seven weeks was the average.

In the spring of 1757, France sent 43 ships and 3500 men to bolster their possessions in French Canada. They sailed by the southern circle route and arrived by 19th June. This was a clear threat to British America. The British response, of 14 ships of the line, with 50 transports carrying 5000 soldiers, was held up by strong westerly gales. They left only on 8th May. Reaching Halifax, Nova Scotia, the rendevous with the British Army in America, they found their Army had arrived from New York unprotected.

Among the British transports piloted into Halifax harbour between 16th July and 8th August, 1757, were Whitby ships and sailors who knew the North American coast.

The British had arrived too late in the summer season.

Fog covered the whole of Cape Breton island. Louisbourg was hidden, the French ships of the line lay safe in its large harbour. Royal Navy frigate captains came back to Halifax, time and again, saying no-one could see. Fog defeated the British. Admiral Holbourne was forced to advise postponing the attack until another year. In fog ships of the same side destroy each other, in collisions and with guns. And the rocky coast was jaggedly treacherous.

On 4th August, the order was given to return to New York.

The transports were sent back to Chivecto. The *True Briton* was paid for 80 days (15th August to 2nd Nov.) and her Master John Major, a Scarborough man, was paid an extra £10. *Ann & Mary* was paid for 76 days.[2]

The British Government was furious.

The war was going sour. The American colonists grumbled, especially those of New England, who wanted Louisbourg's trade.

Meanwhile in Britain, increased force and patriotism was building the Militia, the Army and the Royal Navy.

At Whitby, landsmen too were being impressed. There was fear for the alum workers.

On 25th June, Ralph Jackson left before 4am to ride to Whitby 'to get our Servant Jack and Peggy's Bro. clear, he being impressed the other day by the Tender's Men now in Whitby tho' he has never been at Sea'. Ralph was too late, the young man's name had already gone up to the Admiralty.

The Countrymen's Association prepared a Petition to the Admiralty 'they are alarmed.' This group of landholders in Yorkshire, not all gentry, were respected arbitrators, trusted and influential. They often settled disputes, preventing them from going to Court. Some were Quakers, who were excluded from civic life as they would not swear the Oath but were trusted for their honesty.

The alum trade was so dull and afraid that the owners lowered the price 'by cartel' from £14 to £12-10s per ton.

The Ward family had had a fright. In April George Jackson had taken ill, in danger of his life, with a London fever. He was at his cousin Captain Ward's in Mile End, away from his children in Fenchurch Street. Ralph and Rachel dashed to London. It was a fast journey taking only three days by coach. Then tragedy - at their Uncle Joshua's they heard their father had died at Richmond, in the middle of moving house. Ralph rode back 226 miles to Richmond, taking 2 days, and spending 28 hours on horseback.

George, the commanding son, could only retreat by sedan chair to Hackney, in the open countryside, to recover. He determined then always to have a country retreat. He acquired land at North End, next to that of his distant relative by marriage, a Mr. Charles Dingley, who had been secretary to Mr. William Pitt and, through him, met the great man, who would become George's patron for his next promotion.

LOUISBOURG 1758

In 1758, a new attempt was to be made on Louisbourg and Master James Cook on *HMS Pembroke* was going.

The British fleet, though again held up by contrary winds, beat across the Atlantic and gathered at Halifax on 24th May. Pitt had chosen Admiral Boscowen to lead 21 warships, 12 frigates, and 13,200 soldiers in transports. Gales had allowed the French fleet to arrive first at Louisbourg. The town was entrenched.

The British appeared off its rocky shore on 2nd June. The weather was appalling. Strong east winds pushed the ships too close to shore, anchors dragged, heavy surf smashed small boats. British soldiers in stiff red uniforms were clinging on. One of three young brigadiers, under General Amherst, was James Wolfe. The attack began so badly that Wolfe called off their landing as impossible, by waving his hat, but three ordinary soldiers had found a gap and were already landing in a tiny creek; 1000 men piled ashore, secured their footing and dried out their guns. The brigade had squeezed through. Wolfe was ordered to march them to the other side of the bay. British troops took command of the high ground. Louisbourg was surrounded. Though heavily defended, it was just a matter of time. The British burnt the great French ships in the harbour. On 26th July, the French Governor surrendered.

Next day, James Cook, Master of *HMS Pembroke,* was ashore at the cove where Wolfe had first landed. He stopped when he saw a man carrying a plane table on a tripod and making notes. Samuel Holland, was Dutch, the same age as Cook, a lieutenant and professional surveyor. James Cook was anxious to learn so, says Holland, they agreed on the next day. Captain Simcoe, being indisposed, asked Holland to dine on board, and the next day Cook and two 'young gentlemen', probably midshipmen, joined Holland for instruction in surveying. The lessons may have gone on for a month. Then *HMS Pembroke,* with five more ships of the line, was ordered to raid the mouth of the St. Lawrence, as a warning, creating fear in French settlements along the Gaspe. One result was a survey of Gaspe Bay and harbour 'by James Cook Master of his Majesty's Ship Pembroke taken in 1758 and published by Mount and Page of Tower Hill.' Meanwhile, James Cook was sent off in command of a schooner to get coals for the Navy.

By 19th November, *HMS Pembroke* was moored in Halifax harbour for a long and tedious winter, waiting for 1759 orders.

With Louisbourg taken the Gaspe subdued, the French city of Quebec was vulnerable. The city was the key approach to the centre of America. One value of Louisbourg to the French, was as a rendezvous for ships from Europe on their way up the St.Lawrence estuary to Quebec. With Louisbourg taken Quebec was at risk, but before British ships could attack, charts had to be made of the approach up the St. Lawrence estuary.

Sam Holland later described their activity. On board *HMS Pembroke* charts were being put together to make the best possible picture. As a military surveyor he seems to have been teaching James Cook about surveying from land, not just sea. Their charts were so comprehensive that Admiral Holmes sent over the charts he had accumulated. The accumulated result seems to be the chart dedicated to Sir Charles Saunders in 1763.

The ice was lifting, the mouth of the St. Lawrence River mapped, the Royal Navy was ready to attack Quebec.

12

WAR AND VICTORY

THE BATTLE FOR QUEBEC
1759

The city of Quebec was set on high cliffs. It stood where 350 miles of treacherous sea estuary was fed by a tidal river, the gateway to the interior of north America. Protected by three miles of mud flats to the north, the city was hurriedly building up its other fortifications.

Quebec's main protection was the water of the St. Lawrence estuary. In winter it was solid jagged ice. In summer, the sea estuary approach was divided by the large island of Isle d'Orleans into a north and south channel, the north difficult but buoyed, the south destructive and sinister. The French took up the buoys. They sank ships in the channels to block them but did not have enough.

The ice melted. Thirteen British war ships, under Admiral Durrell were advancing up the St. Lawrence estuary with the wind behind them, a fast sailing wind. So, leaving only a few ships at Bic, his ordered rendevous, he advanced to the Ile aux Coudres, a triangular island tucked into the north shore, and began to reconnoitre ahead, capturing small vessels with provisions and tricking the river pilots onboard by flying French colours.

The St. Lawrence estuary was vast and tidal, but underneath its salty surface the deep channel of the river flowed, providing the depth of water the approaching British fleet needed, to get past the islands. Ahead of them, from close to the north shore, the sinuous deep channel squeezed by the Ile aux Coudres, hugged the wooded Cape Torment, swinging out diagonally beneath the water to the Isle d'Orleans in a dangerous cross-over called the Traverse. It met the southern channel, which cut between the large isle and the tiny reefed Ile Madame, around the bare flat rock of d'Orleans to reach Quebec Basin. From there they could attack the city. The French had never brought a big ship through this dangerous south channel to Quebec. The French pilots simply took up the few buoys there, and hoped they were safe.

The dangerous Traverse would have to be surveyed. Four ships, including *HMS Pembroke,* and three transports were ordered up to the Isle d'Orleans. The population fled. For two days, all ships boats 'manned and armed' were out sounding the channel, so we know where James Cook was.

Between 8th and 10th June they marked out the rocks, shoals and depths. James Cook, Master of *HMS Pembroke* records: 'Retd, satisfied with being aquanted with ye Channel'. Their division sailed through and anchored at the other end, each ship sending a manned boat to the *Squirrel,* the ship nearest the enemy to guard against expected attack from the French and the Indians.

Behind them, Admiral Saunders, with his great fleet of nine ships of the line, thirteen frigates and 119 transports, was sailing up the lower St. Lawrence estuary. They anchored off Bic on 18th June, and within days were waiting at the head of the Traverse.

At 11 am on 25th June, James Cook, Master of *HMS Pembroke* logged 'a Sigl.for all Boats man'd & arm'd, in order to go & Lay in the Traverse, as Buoys for the Ships to come up'. The large fleet began to sail through. French pilots, under threat of death, guided some ships, but long experience of reading the water stood the British masters in good stead.

On board the transport *Goodwill,* 'old Killick' put his Mate at the helm and went forward carrying his speaking trumpet, taking Army Captain Knox[1] pointing out the channel to him. 'Shewing me, by the ripple and colour of the water, where there was any danger; and distinguishing the places where there were ledges of rocks (to me invisible) from banks of sand, mud or gravel. He gave his orders with great unconcern, joked with the sounding-boats who layoff on each side, with different coloured flags for our guidance; and, when any of them called to him, and pointed to the deepest water, he answered, "aye, aye, my dear, chalk it down, a d****d dangerous navigation eh, if you don't make a sputter about it, you'll get no credit in England." After we had cleared this remarkable place, where the channel forms a complete zig-zag, the Master called to his Mate to give the helm to somebody else, saying, "D*** me, if there are not a thousand places in the Thames fifty times more hazardous than this; I am ashamed that Englishmen should make such a rout about it".' Did James Cook in a boat, hear him and chuckle?

Within two days, the whole British fleet had anchored unscathed below Quebec, to the horror of the city. 'Next year', said the French General Montcalm, grimly, there was 'now hope of having a good chart of the river.' Only *HMS Neptune* the huge 90 gun British flagship had stayed behind, waiting for a special pilot. Lying below Quebec were over a hundred transports, Whitby ships some of them, sheltered by fast frigates like *HMS Leostoffe,* Durrell's 80 gun *HMS Princess Amelia,* the 84 gun *HMS Royal William,* the 70 gun *HMS Northumberland*, *HMS Stirling Castle* with Thomas Bisset her master, the old ship *HMS Centurion,* in all twelve men o'war, and sloops like the *Hunter.* It was a terrifying sight.

ADMIRAL SAUNDERS

Charles Saunders had been chosen by Lord Anson to lead the fleet. In 1740 he had gone on *HMS Centurion* with Anson, it is said at Anson's 'particular request' on a harrowing voyage around the world. Saunders had been at sea since the age of 14, fought through the war, and made his fortune of at least £30,000 from capturing a Spanish treasure ship. When the 1748 war ended he became MP for

Plymouth and, later, Hedon (Hull) in Yorkshire, treasurer of Greenwich Hospital, and Comptroller of the Navy. Back in fighting service, he sailed on 17th February 1759, as commander-in-chief of the fleet to attack Quebec. His portraits show a craggy altertness and endurance. He was a man of few words, Horace Walpole called him 'That brave statue' and 'no man said less and deserved more'. Calm and patient, he complimented the volatile Wolfe. At 46, to Wolfe's 32, he was a steadying influence. Lord Anson knew what to do to protect the Navy.

MAJOR-GENERAL WOLFE

James Wolfe had spark, impetuosity and flair. With an egotistical oddness, he took risks. At 32, he was chosen by Pitt to act as Major-General to command the attack on Quebec. Wolfe had two personal problems. Having been in the brutal army since the age of 16 he had tuberculosis and failing kidneys. But he was delighted with his promotion, as he had courted Catherine, the sister of Sir James Lowther for two years and was now important enough to be considered as her husband. His second problem was that the three young aristocrats, appointed as Brigadiers to serve under him, were not amused by Wolfe's promotion, especially the efficient malicious Townshend, the nephew of the Duke of Newcastle.

The British were faced with a fortress stiff with cannon, on a 300 feet high bluff, protected on all sides by miles of shore batteries, ravines, redoubts and wide mudflats. Time was short. They needed a speedy victory before the autumn ice closed in.

Soon after it anchored, the fleet was struck by a wild hurricane. Great seamanship saved them. Next day the French launched fireships and rafts, the nearest British ships had to cut their cables and run. Wood, tar and cordage could turn into torches in seconds. Ships' boats were out on the water towing away the flaming rafts, amid feats of seamanship, and unrecorded acts of heroism, the things men do when terrified. Admiral Saunders decided to move the fleet into the wider basin in front of Quebec. Batteries were set up on Isle d'Orleans and Point Levis facing Quebec. *HMS Pembroke* was anchored off Point Levis, James Cook was in charge of her boats helping to land artillery. For 10 weeks Point Levis guns pulverised Quebec across the river, destroying its houses and guns.

Montcalm sat tight. Wolfe's dilemma was obvious, especially to his critical Brigadiers. By its natural situation, its high cliffs and its fortifications, Quebec looked impregnable.

As night fell on the 18th July, seven British ships, including the frigates *HMS Squirrel* and *HMS Diana,* filtered up the narrows below Quebec's guns, moving upriver past the town. A sloop fouled *Diana,* which went aground, *HMS Richmond* went to her aid and, by 2 o'clock the next afternoon, the heavy *HMS Pembroke* was called up. James Cook logged 'Cut and Slipt pr order of the adml. and run up the river in order to cover the Richmond and Dianna wch was Attacked by a Number of Enemys Row boats, wch Row'd off as Soon as we got up ... Sent the Long boate and 30 Men on Bd the Dianna to assist in getting her guns out, at 4 fired a 24 pd Shot at the Enemys row boats going down the River.'

The fleet's ability to move upriver was to lead to Wolfe's answer, and victory.

Yet at first, Wolfe decided to invade downriver from Quebec, on the north shore of the sea estuary, by the Montmorency gorge, using Townshend and Murray's brigades. Wolfe went with them. Acting high-handed, he infuriated his Brigadiers. Wolfe thought he could attack the Beauport redoubts. Two armed transports of men were to be run aground, as close in as possible. 'The Master of the Pembroke,' wrote Wolfe to Brigadier Monkton on the 28th July, 'assures the Admiral that a Cat, can go within less than 100 yards of the Redoubt.' Of course it could. James Cook had learned that as a 16 year old, at Staithes, when Staithes sailors regularly beached a vessel in Hole Wyke at Boulby, on a narrow beach under a 200 foot cliff, on the high tide. Admiral Saunders despatched the 64 gun *HMS Centurion* to fire on the redoubts. The Cats grounded too far out, caught on a barrier of rocks, but only because the attack had taken place at low tide, the Army had forgotten about high tide.

The attack on 31st July failed. The Cats were smashed by enemy fire and burned. Admiral Saunders must have reproached Wolfe, who explained that 'Mr. Cook said he believed the cats could be carried within 40 or 50 yards of the redoubts, and that 'certain conditions.......did not at the critical moment present themselves.'

This failed assault had been launched against advice from the Brigadiers, particularly Townshend who drew a caricature of Wolfe and handed it round the mess. Wolfe took the insult calmly, 'If we live this shall be enquired into, but we must first beat the enemy.'

During the outward voyage, Wolfe had formed a sound if unlikely friendship with Admiral Saunders. The Army and Navy were co-operating. The ships began to move upriver. Saunders planned to attack above the town. Wolfe hesitated. He intended to land above the town, but where; how could he get enough men ashore before they were fallen on by the French? At that point a landing upriver was planned to be a feint, with the main attack back down the estuary, below the town once more. Admiral Holmes, nine miles upriver attacking the French farms, which were stiff with militiamen, was trying to lure Montcalm out of fortified Quebec.

It was harvestime. Food was short throughout Quebec province. The Indians fighting for him, informed Montcalm they were going home to their villages to harvest, or their families would starve. The French militia men started to go home too. Quebec's defences thinned. British Army re-inforcements were expected overland, from the south. Could this be Wolfe's chance?

On 4th August. Brigadier Monkton was sent miles upriver to find out where the British Army was, in its second prong of attack approaching Quebec overland. Eventually, he came back to say, Success! but they could not reach Quebec before winter ice forced the British fleet to leave the St. Lawrence. Wolfe's attack was failing.

What was it like to be there? John Hale can tell us. Listen to him.

JOHN HALE

On that same day 4th August, 31 year old Colonel John Hale was with his regiment based at the British camp on the north shore below Quebec, when he saw Brigadier Murray going further up the river with a detachment of about 1200 men. His own regiment were skirmishing on the north shore, near Montmorency, burning boats, and securing their position. John Hale was keeping a Journal; this is his account.[2]

On 8th August, an Indian of the Messasague tribe, crossed their defences and tried to scalp a sentry, 'he was stark naked except that he had a small woollen cloth which covers his posteriors and private parts' says the red uniformed, braided and buttoned Col. Hale. Next day he learned that Brigadier Murray had got upriver about 30 miles. A small schooner with some provisions got past the town's guns, but two frigates could not. The situation was nasty, the British were too scattered.

Their sailors were too thinly spread out on the water, their small boats in danger. It is said *(by Kippis[3])* that James Cook was out sounding or laying buoys, when a group of French and Indians in canoes tried to cut off his boat, which dashed for the Isle d'Orleans. Cook leapt out at the bow as the Indians leapt in at the stern, though they were driven off by the hospital guard. Thomas Bisset of the *Stirling Castle* was also having problems. Apparently *(see Kitson[4])* he **was** cut off while sounding between the island and Montmorency falls, lost his ship's barge and its equipment, and one man was killed.

The French were attacking, there was death on the water.

John Hale says: 'The enemy sent down a floating stage and when our boats crew touch'd it a number of musquets went off and wounded two or three of them'. The body of a sailor was found 'who had been killed some time, his head cut off and laid upon his back'.

161

The British soldiers began to retaliate. After one skirmish, says John Hale: 'One Indian Chief was left upon the field whom our people killed and Scalpt.' Wolfe eventually had to forbid 'the inhumane practice of scalping except when the enemy are Indians or Canadians dressed like Indians.'

Then, on 20th August Wolfe fell sick, so ill that he told his doctor he was incurable, asking him only to ensure he would be without pain for the few days needed to do his duty.

Struggling, he wrote to his three Brigadiers with three different plans. They rejected them all. They preferred a landing far upriver on the north shore, to cut Quebec's provision line from Montreal. Wolfe desperately wished to avoid 'torrents of blood' he told his mother in a letter. He discussed it with Saunders.

The season was advancing fast toward autumn and ice.

John Hale says, his men were 'drawing down 8 long 12 pounders and embarking them in the flat bottom boats to be sent to the batteries at Point Levi' the headland opposite Quebec which commanded both channels.

On 24th, he notes, seven sailors maurauding on the south shore were attacked by Indians, two were scalped, five wounded. Another skirmish saw the British scalping 14 enemy, 'among whom was Pere Portneuf the priest of the parish.'

The army upriver needed supplies and, with extra guns to cover them, at 9pm the 'Leostoffe frigate and Hunter sloop with three transports past the Town.'

In a nasty stalemate, the regiments regrouped - for strength.

Early in September, Wolfe withdrew his army from the north bank camp by the Montmorency Falls, to the southern shore.

On 1st September, says John Hale 'Last night and this morning all the Cannon and Stores sent off - last night the Seahorse frigate with 3 or 4 transports past by the town, the fire from the batteries was very great but no damage done'. Two days later the regiments retreated from Montmorency under the guns of the *Porcupine* sloop.

Otways, Braggs, Anstruthers and his own Lascelles Regiments made a new camp on the hill opposite Quebec.

Wolfe had formed his plan. It was astounding.

The three Brigadiers objected, as much as they dared.

Admiral Holmes was not sure the Navy could manage the wild difficulty of their orders but he knew what had happened to Admiral Byng. On 3rd September Holmes passed Quebec with his 22 ships, 3600 soldiers, and moved upriver, while Monkton and Townshend marched their own men westward upriver, along the south shore.

The French were watching. They had only 300 men stationed on the north shore between Cap Rouge and Pointe aux Trembles under their officer Bougainville. He was puzzled. Was this another effort to tempt Montcalm out of Quebec's defences? Was it an attack further up river?

Admiral Holmes moved upriver to Pointe aux Trembles, and began allowing his ships to slide downriver and upriver, on the outgoing and incoming tide; mirrored by Bougainville's small number of French soldiers marching backward and forward on shore, who soon grew exhausted.

Wolfe had decided to launch his assault using the Foulon Pass. It was an act of bravery, copying his men at Louisbourg, brash, brilliant and risky. His three Brigadiers protested. Admiral Holmes doubted his sailors could manage the currents at night. Later he said it was 'the most hazardous and difficult task I was ever engaged in'. The Brigadiers wanted to land further upriver. Murray later said the landing they achieved was 'almost impossible'. Wolfe's plan was either complete folly, or a stroke of genius.

The first wave was to be 26 boats with 1300 of Monkton and Murrays, and 400 Light Infantrymen. The second wave was to be 1910 soldiers of Townsend, with 1200 in reserve.

John Hale, waiting among his men, noted in his Journal on 5th September the regiments 'embarked in the transports laying above the Etchenin river about 6 miles from the town, under fire, but no-one hurt.' Next day Brigadiers Monkton and Townshend, with a detachment of 1200 men from Amhersts, Kennedys and the Highland Regiment, joined them aboard the transports. General Wolfe arrived among them in the evening, escorted by a company of Highlanders. Next day, the men o'war and transports 'stood up river as far as Cape Rouge, Leostoffe frigate fired upon.'

'At three this morning a cat, 2 sloops and a schooner past the town.' The weather began to blow up. Within hours it was so bad, with the troops 'excessively crowded on board', at last almost 1800 men had to be landed and billeted in captured houses. Would this be another failure? They kicked their heels nervously for three stormy days. The brigadiers squabbled. The delay allowed Wolfe to recover his health a little. During this build-up, James Cook's *HMS Pembroke* was stationed off Point Levis with other large ships; commanded by Durrell on *HMS Princess Amelia* among 11 ships off Ile Madame. Small boats patrolled the shores, pitching in wild waves, servicing the groaning ships and gun batteries.

Wolfe's audacious plan was ready.

A diversion was needed downriver to fool the French. John Hale notes: 'NB from 11 o'clock on the night of the 12th to 5 o'clock in the morning of the 13th, Admiral Saunders made a feint with a great number of the men of war and transport boats on the side of Beauport which keeping them in suspense as to our design and harrasing them much, contributed greatly to the success of our real attack.'

12th September, the eve of the battle:

That night, upriver from Quebec, 2000 men silently embarked in boats, hidden behind their large ships, which floated downriver on the tide, as usual, to Ance de Mer, just above Quebec town. Under the shade of the cliffs of the Heights of Abraham, the British waited unseen in the dark. As the tide turned they began to drift back upriver

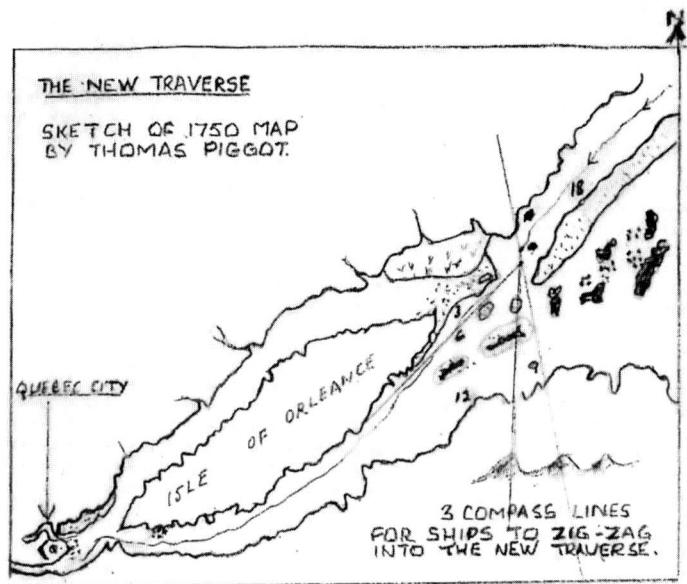

THE NEW TRAVERSE

SKETCH OF 1750 MAP
BY THOMAS PIGGOT.

QUEBEC CITY

ISLE OF ORLEANCE

18

3 COMPASS LINES
FOR SHIPS TO ZIG-ZAG
INTO THE NEW TRAVERSE.

St. Lawrence River the narrow Traverse approach.

*To make a huge sailing ship zig zag is a major task needing
brute strength and 'all hands'.*

Cliff path at Staithes like the Foulon Fault.

The shop where James Cook worked was on the beach shown.
It was washed away by the sea in 1812.
Salvaged, the shop was rebuilt in Church Street.

toward the fault in the cliff face. The *Hunter* sloop lying in midstream, in the dark, thought they were French provisioners and ran out her guns; she had to be scrambled into silence.

At 4 am in the darkness, the hidden boats pulled clear of the large ships, sailors rowing them to land under the 180 foot high cliff. There was only a lightly guarded zig zag path to the top of the Foulon fault. In silence they began to climb.

Col. John Hale, in the dark, climbed in the thick sweat of his men. 'About 5 this morning the troops landed and march'd up a hill which being allmost perpendicular the French had posted only 100 men at the top to defend it..........The Light Infantry were the first who mounted the hill, 2000 men having gained the summit the boats were dispatched for the rest on board.' In all the Navy landed over 4500 men up this fault in the cliff. Within two hours 4828 men had reached the top. Col. Hale implies that when the fighting started they only had two 6 pounder guns at the top. Montcalm's report confirms: there were only two pieces of cannon.

The Army was unprotected. The Royal Navy was busy hauling more guns up the 180 feet cliff fault, to the heights. But at the start of the main battle, at 10am only eight 24 pounders, six 6 pounders and four howitzers were at the top.

James Cook, out on the water below, would know the horrendous task facing the sailors hauling up the guns. The Foulon fault was just like the fault in the 200 foot cliff behind William Sanderson's grocer's shop, at Staithes, both with a narrow precipitous path.

As dawn broke on the morning of 15th September, British redcoats, on the plain at the top of the fault, were lining up for battle as the French awoke in Quebec town. James Cook, Master of *HMS Pembroke* was with the sailors. John Hale was on the heights with his regiment, the 47th Foot lined up with his soldiers. They were being picked off by snipers. General Wolfe ordered them to lie down. In the tense anxious moments before the battle began, Colonel Hale remonstrated with his friend the Commander in Chief,

James Wolfe, for wearing a plain new bright red uniform, thereby making himself more conspicuous to the French and Indian marksmen. He was proved fatally correct.

At 10 o'clock the main action began. Wolfe had already been shot in the wrist and groin when he ordered a bayonet charge, leading the men himself. Within minutes he was shot through the chest. James Wolfe lay dying, at the moment of his victory; struggling to say:

'I am aware that it is the aide de camp's privilege to carry the despatches home, but I beg .... as a favour .... to request that my old friend Colonel Hale, may have that honour.'

At 11 am as Wolfe's corpse was carried down the cliff to board *HMS Leostoffe,* troops and guns were still pushing past, up the fault.

You will not find Colonel Hale in the great portrait of the battle. His daughter said years later, he refused to pay the printer a monstrous £100 to be included, he protested that everyone in the country knew very well, he had been in the hottest part of the fighting, whether the printer recorded him or not!

Quebec signed the surrender on 18th September.

Master James Cook's log records: 18th Sept, 'at 6, every Ship in the fleet sent a Boat mand and Arm'd, under the Comd of Capt Palleser, who whent and took Poss'ion of the Lower Town.'

[Adm.52/978]

Four days later, the frigate *HMS Leostoffe* sailed express for England with news of a glorious victory, the defeat of French hopes to dominate north America, and John Hale aboard, escorting the body of his friend George Wolfe. Though they made a fast passage with continuing gales N to NW, and sighted the Scilly Isles on 21st October, the news had travelled ahead of them.

On 21st October in Guisborough, Ralph Jackson says: 'By this post we have an Extraordinary Gazette with the agreeable news of Quebec's having surrendered to us on the 18th ultimo. General Wolfe

Wolfe who commanded the Land Forces was killed .... Brigadeer Monkton was wounded by a ball that entered in his right breast and lungs but it is hoped he will recover. Admirals Saunders, Durrell and Homes commanded the Fleet.'

In England, Colonel John Hale was rewarded with £500 and the 'opportunity' to raise the 17th Light Dragoons, at his own expense. More to the point, within five years, he came to live at Guisborough, to enter the Skottowe/Wilson/Jackson social circle and add his experience and influence to theirs.

John Hale fought and lived to old age. He became a General. Viscount Downe aged 37, who owned the Esk valley between Whitby and Great Ayton, would die of wounds received in the war.

John Hall of Skelton Castle, had earlier lost his son. 'Mr. Hall of Skelton had on Friday advice of his Eldest Son's death who was a hopeful young man, and an officer in the Guards.'

All over Britain, villages and towns mourned the loss of their loved ones. At Great Ayton, his parents learned that James Cook had survived.

The people of Britain illuminated their houses in Victory celebrations. In Britain it was seen as a great and welcome victory. For William Pitt it was the vindication of his aggressive policies. It secured the interior of Canada for the British – or so they thought. Although there were further attempts by the French to retrieve Quebec and Newfoundland, they failed.

But the Ward family at Guisborough did not join in. They were suffering too much death and loss at home.

~~~

BATTLES FOUGHT AND LOST AT HOME

AUGUST 1759

As the battle raged in Quebec, Mr. John Jefferson died at home. Wednesday 22nd August. Staithes.

'Dr. Waine thought Mr. John Jefferson in a bad way'. So Ralph sat up with him until four o'clock. 'At Eight I got up and continued very ill of the toothache. Mr. Adam Boulby and Mr. Pease came from Whitby, and Mr. Fox from Gisbro'.... At Nine in the evening Mr. John Jefferson died of a Diarrhoea, or flux, which he has been subject to of near Thirty Year. He was 62 years old a few Months ago. He was at Church last Sunday twice, having dined at the Revrd Todd's at Hinderwell in seeming very good health, but at midnight was seizd as above, continued all day on Monday, sent for Apothecary Proddy on Tuesday morning, though Proddy bled him, and Mr. Waine prescribed Medicine without the least effect.'

Friday 24th.

'I spent at Staithes in assisting Mr.Fox to look over the deceased's papers. We compute him to have died worth about £8000.'

Saturday 25th.

'There was a cold Table provided which the Company dined at, and about Four the Corps was put out of the window* and carried to Hinderwell church, and burried close by his wife[5]..........The Bearers were Mr. Pease, Senior, Mr. Sanderson, Mr. John Holt, Mr. Wm. Skinner [both of Whitby], Mr. Wardell, Mr. Francis Fox, Mr. John Robinson and myself.' *still done

The childless John Jefferson had been fair. His will left money to his sisters, shares in his ships to his Jefferson nephews, Nat and Sam Campion, and John Gallilee. His brother Anthony got his share in the *Thomas and Richard*. Anthony's small boys were not forgotten. Ralph Jackson, George, and the younger relations on Elinnor Jefferson's side got cash gifts.

The large extended family had mourning scarves to wear, they were all very sad about losing jolly Mr. John Jefferson. In the empty house Ralph helped Mrs. Pease to pack the china and silver plate. Everyone waited for Thomas Spencer, executor of the will, to arrive from London. And then things began to go fearfully wrong.

Fifty-six year old Thomas Spencer arrived at Mr. Ward's with his servant in a chaise on 12th September, very late and 'a good deal fatigued' and promptly took seriously ill.

Young Dr. Askew was there but went home to Newcastle when he heard that his wife Dolly (Boulby) had given birth to their first living child. It was her third pregnancy. The baby died.

Thomas Spencer get worse, Alex Pulman set off to Newcastle to bring back old Dr. Askew, who prescribed Uncle Joshua's sweat to be given after a pint of old Hock whey, made about half and half.

Mr. Ward was lying ill in the parlour, failing, worried and in distress. A senior figure Adam Boulby arrived from Whitby. There was nothing to be done. Thomas Spencer, his brother-in-law, died just before noon in the presence of Oliver his servant and Ralph's mother.

'My uncle was vastly affected when she informed him of it,' says Ralph. 'I indeed apprehended his death would be the consequence.' Mr. Ward knew what needed to be done but was too old, too ill. In four weeks the family had lost two of its key figures. Richard Pulman was sent fast to Northallerton with a Packet directed to Mr. Spencer's partner in trade, George Clifford. The postmaster charged £2-18s-6d. for it would go express in 36 hours to London. Three days later, a copy of Thomas Spencer's will arrived by post from London. He had died worth about £100,000, a multi-millionaire in today's terms. And a vast amount of inheritance to be shared by his family.

He had left behind in the Guisborough house an 'annonymous book entitled the Present State of Europe', Ralph Jackson, bewildered by events began to read it.

On 21st October,at the height of their distress, the Extraordinary

Gazette had arrived with the news of the victory at Quebec. Ralph says that 'Some houses were illuminated in Guisborough on account of the news, but none of the principals did so' in respect. Their friends were too sad, the family too anxious. Old Ralph Ward was very sick and 'seems visibly to decline', thought Ralph.

Mr. Ward was still lying in bed in the parlour, with Jack lying on the couch. He struggled to deal properly with the business caused by the two unexpected deaths. On 22nd he signed his own new will. There was virulent fever in the town Ralph's sister Hannah was as sick as ever, he says the fever was being blamed on the very hazy weather.

Then came more awful news from Newcastle; 24 year old Bella Hudspeth had died, she for whom the boys had bought ribbons. Ralph wrote a kind letter of condolence to her uncle, his old master William Jefferson; Bella, he comments, had never been well since her brother Billy Hudspeth had died the previous year. 'Mrs. Hudspeth also has been inconsolable' he adds distressed. Not even a strong character or a good person could defeat fever.

Yet Ralph was to learn that old age and kidney stones were a test of mental make-up. In Guisborough on the 5th November, Dr. Proddy told them that Mr. Ward would not recover, but their Uncle Ralph Ward got up, though his urine, said Ralph, was 'thick and slimy', Next day Ralph thought his uncle seemed to baffle Mr. Proddy's judgement, making plentiful water and that a good colour. Grapes and cheeses arrived at Boulby by sea from Colonel Gansell.

Thomas Presswick and Alex Pulman were sitting up at night with Mr. Ward, who then decided he had a mind to take Dr. Wayne, the physician's advice and sent Thomey to get him. While Dr. Wayne said the patient was dying, the patient refused all medicine. On Tuesday he was weaker but would be up. Ralph got his uncle to take a little 'julep with some heart-burn cakes infused'. John Galillee turned up from Staithes, he was a beneficiary of John Jefferson's will, but there was no-one left to ask about it. Ralph writes solemnly:

'at a quarter past five in the evening Died my Unce Ra. Ward supposed to be sensible to the last, tho' he has not been able for near two days to speak so as to be understood.'

Next morning, reverently opened, Ralph Ward's will showed Ralph's mother to be the sole executor. Mr. Ward had loved his exasperating sister and trusted her sons. Ralph sent for his brother George Jackson and asked him to come north.

The funeral was 'conducted with the utmost regularity and Decorum,' says Ralph respectfully.

At 23 Ralph Jackson was now a rich young man. His uncle had tried his best to prepare him for the responsibility. Time would show that Mr. Ward had used his shrewd sense of character and chosen well. Ralph was nearly always conscientious. Still, for a very young man, there was a lot of money.

By their first count Ralph found his uncle had left £21,499 to be spread through the family, and more besides. Ralph was to have nearly all his property in Yorkshire.

George Jackson arrived on the 30th November, by Post Chaise to York then, catching up with his own horses which he had sent on ahead, he was met by Ralph at Thirsk. George found he had inherited Biddick colliery, and its law suit; old Mr. Ward had chosen wisely there too. George stayed for a month, there was a vast amount of business to attend to. For George, his inheritance was something to be developed. It gave him the financial backing to buy higher places in his Navy career.

For his mother, if she could be prevented from spending it, the money meant a marriage portion for Dolly, and security for her invalid daughter Hannah.

Ralph was young, rich and eligible, educated, trained. He had lightened his uncle's last three years with companionship, amusement and physical help. At first he worked carefully, as if in a businesslike dream.

By December, Ralph's mother had decided to move down the street to live with him at his uncle's house. She sublet her rented Winns House in Guisborough to Mr. Harrison the Attorney.

Ralph had lived independently of his mother for over ten years; he took the precaution of having John Price put some locks on the drawers in his library closet. John Price made him a little iron chest and, it seems, that this was the chest in which his journals were found 100 years later.

WILLIAM WHITE GETS LOFTUS GRAINGE FARM

Loftus Grainge farm gives an insight into farming at the time. William White had been a faithful steward to Mr. Ward at Loftus Grainge. Ralph Jackson, acting for his mother, felt it fair to offer William White the sub-tenancy, at an agreed price of course. So he was miffed when William White hesitated. William wished to consult first with his brother Thomas White of Seaton Hall farm.

6th Feb. 1760. Ralph and William White 'fixed the ardors of the tillage at Grainge' this was a husbandry lease, laying down what was to be grown or laid fallow, what lime and ashes to fertilise the land. George Mewburn of Ormesby visited the farm to value the horses and drank a dish of tea with Mrs. Jackson. They decided that William White should give Ralph's mother 4 guineas for 5 old horses. Says Ralph dumbfounded, 'the horses or guelding called Wagtale, Trenham, old Brown Mair (near blind) and 2 black mares. They are all broken winded, and there ages altogether amount to upwards of Ninety!'

On 18th February, Ralph went up to Mary Havelock's inn where Mr. Preston was drawing up the articles for letting Grainge Farm to William White for £126 p.a. for 9 years, excepting an outrent of £12 p.a. to Loftus. It was a very fair rent for such a valuable farm, and sounds as if Mrs. Jackson wanted money up-front, so Ralph had put on some corrective pressure against a high rent.

William White had become a substantial tenant farmer. If we ask why old Mr. Cook did not do the same at Airyholme farm in 1755 with Squire Thomas Skottowe, the answer seems to be he was the same age as the Squire, touching 65, too old to undertake a mortgage for a lease. William White was still quite young.

JAMES COOK Master of the *Northumberland*

On 23rd September, 1759, as Colonel Hale sailed home down the St. Lawrence, James Cook was appointed Master of *HMS Northumberland,* a 70 gun ship of the line, commanded by Alexander, Lord Colville. They too left the St. Lawrence, before the ice closed in, to spend the winter at Halifax, Nova Scotia.

Admiral Saunders returned home to London.

On 23rd April, 1760, as the ice broke in spring, *Northumberland* sailed back to Quebec, where the French were besieging the city, determined to retake it. But James Cook had been busy that winter.

That day, in London, Saunders wrote to the Secretary to the Admiralty, saying he had material ready for publishing a chart of the St. Lawrence river. This chart, dedicated to Sir Charles Saunders, was published by Jeffreys later that year. Among the materials must have been the two charts by Holland and Cook, done on *Pembroke* the previous two years, along with sailing directions, and with their south channel islands 'determined by triangles'. Holland, being a Military Surveyor, appears to have taught James Cook triangulation.

Some chart must have gone with *HMS Northumberland* back to Quebec, but it is not certain what this was. Meanwhile there was no reason why James Cook should stop mapping, sounding, sketching and recording sailing directions.

HMS Northumberland left the St. Lawrence before the ice formed, again to winter over 1760/1 in Halifax, during which he completed three manuscript copies of a survey of Halifax harbour. It must have helped the boredom, as the Navy remained on station, waiting out the last months of the war until August 1762.

On 10th July, 1762, a brig sailed in with news that St. Johns in Newfoundland had surrendered to the French! All sailors prefer a moving ship. *HMS Northumberland* and *HMS Gosport* hurriedly sailed out to join Captain Thomas Graves, the newly appointed Governor of Newfoundland, who was ready on *HMS Antelope,* with *HMS Syren,* and the troops on transports, to attack St. Johns.

Thick fog fell. The French army, finding themselves abandoned, surrendered.

The treacherous Newfoundland coast was no place to be rash. James Cook was deeply involved in surveying to keep the Royal Navy safe: mapping Placentia harbour, St. John's harbour, the coast to the south and the fishing grounds in Conception Bay.

Lord Colville wrote:[6] 'Mr. Cook who was particularly careful in sounding them has discovered that Ships of any size may lie in safety both in Harbour Grace and the bay of Carbonera'

25th October 1762.

The war had spent itself, fizzled out into deep resentment and enmity. Peace was a financial necessity. On 7th October *HMS Northumberland* sailed for home.

The Royal Navy was being stood down.

What would happen to James Cook now?

Could he have a future on half pay of £40 a year? Could he get married?

On 30th December, 1762, Lord Colville wrote again to the Secretary of the Admiralty, Philip Stevens:

'Mr. Cook late Master of the Northumberland acquaints me that he has laid before their Lordships all his Draughts and Observations, relating to the River St. Lawrence, Part of the Coast of Nova Scotia, and of Newfoundland.

On this Occasion, I beg to inform their Lordships, that from my Experience of Mr. Cook's Genius and Capacity, I think him well qualified for the work he has performed, and for greater Undertakings of the same kind....'

This is what the Royal Navy called a 'Good Testimony' but it was also a glowing reference for future employment.

~~~

176

THE WAR ENDS IN 1762 – 63

The expense of the war had created a frightening level of debt. Peace was a necessity. If only to save the Government from bankruptcy, the Army must be downsized. The Royal Navy had been stretched as far as it would go.

Ralph Jackson placed his money in the safety of land.

Mr. Sanderson was slandered.

And James Cook came home to get married.

RALPH BUYS NORMANBY

'Consett inadvertently says he does not mind his Credit,
what is that to him?' *Ralph Jackson..5th March, 1760.*

Matthew Consett was a soldier. He had inherited the Normanby estate and borrowed against it, almost all its value, mostly from Mr. Ralph Ward, who had let the debt ride on. Deliberately? Now the war was ending. Mr. Ward was dead and Ralph Jackson, to put his mother's money in order, was forced to demand payment.

Ralph needed an estate of his own, to invest his own inheritance. He had over-excitedly wanted to buy the £26,000 Marske estate - until his brother George, and William Wilson, squashed him. Now, they all saw a way of bailing out their mother, establishing Ralph and solving the Consett debt. It was February 1762 and the weather was treacherous.

'Friday 12th…… …… By this Post Mr. Preston tells me that Mr. Whitehead…. ….would not come lower than £4600 for Matthew Consett's Estate which being £150 more than I commissioned Mr. Preston too, the Sale broke off.

Saturday 13th…. We have had ten days hard frost with little intermission. Some snow, wind NW.
Monday 22nd…. ….befire Eight I mounted and took Jack with me

to Mr. Matthew Consett's at Normanby with young Mr. John [Preston] Present by appointment. Mr. Consett and I signed an article of Purchase agreement for his Estate that my Mother has in security for £3100 Principle and several hundred pounds interest due thereon .... The terms are these £4,400 to be paid on 12th May next, out of which my mother is to be paid her Principle, Interest and Costs of a Bill of Forecloser she has preferd in Chancery it amounting in the whole (I reckon) to £3,545. Ss, 6d, and the remaining £845.14s.6d. to be paid to said Mr. Bell in part of his Principle money etc. which he has upon [2nd] Mortgage of this Estate (after my Mother) and all others belonging to Mr. Consett. We dined at Gisbro. We were often obliged to ride off the Causways on account of the large drifts of Snow·'

'Tuesday 23rd The Post did not come in today.

Ash Wednesday 24th. Messrs. John Harrison and Augustine Skottowe dined with me. We then took Horse together drank Tea at Mr. Oldfield's at Lofthouse. I laid at Boulby and they went down to Stathes and laid at Mr. Sanderson's.'

MR. SANDERSON IN TROUBLE.

'Thursday 25th.

Mr. Wardell and I went down to Staiythes. There's a ship laying there that was blown up in last Sunday's Storm, and likely to become a wreck. Messrs. John Watson of Stockton, Oliver Preswick, Wm. Richardson of Ayton, and George Ward, a Countryman*, and myself were appointed 10 days ago to arbitrate (as this day) a difference between Mr. Wm. Sanderson and Richard Weatherell, the latter having (as appeared to us upon examination of several witnesses) utterd and taken a great deal of Pains to propagate reports to the discredit of the former, as that Mr. Sanderson was arrested by the late Revrd Mr. Marsden's Executors for £2000, and by Mr Francis Easterby for £5-600. It appeared to us that he had some slight information of the latter, but the former seemed to have sprung out of his own head. As Mr. Sanderson is a Merchant at Staiths this reports were likely to become very detrimental to him, and had in consequence prepard to have the Affair tried at this Lent Assizes at York, but was prevailed to accept of our decision, which was this, that Richard Weatherell shoud pay to Mr. Sanderson 50 Guineas (10 of which he laid down, and gave his Note for 40 to be paid next May day) and acknowledge in writing that he had been a very great aggressor in spreading reports which he found were without the least foundation, that Mr. Sanderson shoud pay the Law charges on both sides, and the expences of this day amounting in the whole to near £30, and that both parties shoud give reciprocal discharges for all Damages and demands, which was agreed to. Mr. Matthews was employed by Richard Weatherell, and Mr. John Harrison for Mr. Sanderson.'

*The Countrymens' Association was an Arbitration group of local respected men, some of whom were Quakers.

A snowy February was followed by a very hot summer, the crops did not grow. With not enough fodder for the winter, animals would have to be killed. That meant no fresh meat for the ships' next spring, and salted beef brought on Scurvy. High corn prices meant poor people could not afford bread nor to keep their animals. Discontent would cause violence. Prices and taxes were rising.

TAXING THE BETTER OFF

One method of increasing government income was the Window Tax. Details of its collection partly depended upon owning a Cow. Ralph Jackson describes how it worked:

Wednesday 8th September. 1762.

'Messrs. Wm. Turner, Thos Skottowe & Roger Beckwith, Justices of the Peace, and Michael Smith, Commisioner of the Land Tax, met at the Cock to Grant Licences to Alehouses etc. and hear the appeals on account of the Window Tax. My tenants Wm. White, Wm. Taylor, Chr.Dale, John Mason & Robert Corner of Grainge & Upton appealed,

… the former on having his Bakehouse window charged.'

'His appeal was not heard, nor was Taylor's, Dale's or Mason's ......their appeal was on account of being Poor Cottagers, which was Corner's appeal also,

....but it appearing that (tho' Taylor, Dale & Mason paid only 15s per annum for their House, yet) as they each had a Cow they could not properly be called Paupers, and that I let them as much Ground as grew hay only for that Cow, they were also dismissed,

....but Corner only paying 15s per annum for a House, had not a Cow, nor any Ground, his appeal was admitted.'

The preliminary peace Treaty of Paris was signed on 3rd November, 1762, and passed through Parliament - after a rumpus caused by a furious William Pitt in the House of Commons, and inept opposition in the House of Lords. The young King wanted peace.

The completed Treaty followed in February. It re-shuffled ownership of distant lands, including restoring French rights to fish off Newfoundland, which was now British, but giving France three small islands off its southern coast, to dry their fish.

Petitions began to be received for grants of land in Newfoundland. One joint petition was from the Navy men, Augustus Keppel, Sir Charles Saunders, Hugh Palliser, and Philip Stevens the Admiralty 1st Secretary. But how did they know what they were getting? A land of fog and bog and mosquitoes? Or decent farm land?

Master James Cook, being more lowly, was discharged from his ship in the middle of November, with five years back pay, about £300. What next? Well there was one young lady waiting anxiously for his return.

JAMES COOK'S MARRIAGE

The war was over. He was alive. He must have thought he had good prospects. It was time to marry.

James Cook had chosen for his wife, Elisabeth Batts aged 21. He may have known her for some time. It appears he already had work to do for the Royal Navy which would take him away for months. In Elisabeth, he would have a wife whose step-father was a Master Mariner, and whose family would know the rules.

Elisabeth was the daughter of Samuel Batts, licensee, since 1722, of the Bell Alehouse at Wapping. It stood on a corner, where Brewhouse Lane met the High Street, and opposite the entrance to Execution Dock Stairs. In late middle age, the widower Samuel had married Mary Smith. She was probably 17. Elizabeth, baptised in 1741, was only a baby when her father died in 1742. He left her young mother generously provided for.

Like many people at the time, he did not live in property he owned: a freehold property in Kingshead Court, Booth Lane, in the parish of St. Giles Cripplegate; six leasehold properties in the parish of St. Paul's Shadwell on Corkhill; another in the Raggfair in the parish of St. Georges; another in Broom Walk in the parish of Christchurch Surrey. All property and rents would go to his beloved wife Mary for her natural life, except for a tiny annuity to his married daughter Sarah Fforde (from an earlier marriage).

He left no provision for baby Elisabeth. First babies were expected to die. His will had not been altered from the time of his marriage to Mary. If the younger Mary died before the 26 year old Sarah, Sarah and her heirs got all the property. Yet a remarriage restriction was not included in the will.[7] Mary could take her property and rents with her into another marriage. Within three years she married John Blackburn, Mariner and now landlord of the Bell. So Elisabeth her little daughter had no marriage portion from her father, only the kindness of John Blackburn to rely on.

The Vicar General's Licence for the marriage of James Cook and Elisabeth Batts is dated 16th December 1762 It is kept at Lambeth Palace Library.

There were a number of reasons for a Licence. It had status. It allowed the parties to be married outside their own parish: in his case now Shadwell. It avoided the delay of three consecutive weeks of reading the 'banns' in Elisabeth's church in Wapping. It allowed the couple to find a qualified vicar, many of them being absentees, especially at Christmas.

Elisabeth had been 'evacuated' as a child to Barking, after her father's death, taking her one year old self away from the raucous Bell Tavern. The Quaker, Mrs. Shepherd of Wapping had relatives at Barking and so did the clergyman who married them. Elisabeth remembered walking over the fields to church.

The modern idea of a honeymoon did not apply, though a newly wed couple usually spent a week when they sat in state in their home, receiving 'Bride Visits', with their bride's maid and groom's man in attendance. Then they had a wedding feast possibly in James and Elisabeth's case, Christmas Day.

The Certificate of marriage for James Cook and Elisabeth Batts at St. Margaret's church Barking, is entered in the Church Register on 21st Dec 1762. The two witnesses were John Richardson and Sarah Brown: he may have been James' Whitby sailing friend and she may have been linked to Brown's public house at Wapping.

The Certificate is held by National Library of Australia MS7.

The couple set up their home at 126 Upper Shadwell, on the Ratcliffe Highway. Standing near open fields, the house was previously held by Elisabeth's step-father, John Blackburn. He and her mother now lived in Starr Street, nearby. While James Cook was away for months at sea, Elisabeth would be among familiar faces. She must also have visited Great Ayton, where, in the cottage near the green, there would have been softly spoken Northumbrian, straight-talking Yorkshire, and a jaunty Cockney accent! It may have been then, that they took back to London with them, Frances Wardale, a family friend from Thornaby.

Frances, at age 6, had been placed in the Bluecoat School at Kirthleatham by her father, after her mother's death. In yellow and blue uniform, white pinafore, she would have learned to read, write, cook and sew. At 17 she was ready to take a decent place in the world. More a companion than a servant, she would go eventually to America and become Mrs. MacAllister.

As for James Cook, he was fortunate in not being put on the beach. What appeared decisive, was his surveying skill.

19th April, 1763, he was ordered to sail on *HMS Antelope* to Newfoundland, appointed King's Surveyor to the Governor, Captain Thomas Graves. In 1764 some financial juggling with the Navy regulations by Captain Palliser gave him 10 shillings a day.

It is doubtful if James Cook would have married without prospects. It must have had something to do with his patrons. Was it through Palliser, or Simcoe's connection to Graves? Cook had plenty of patrons to ask. It would be to their advantage to have their own man in Newfoundland, establishing the extent of the lucrative fisheries and valuable and strategic harbours.

THE WILSONS MOVE TO AYTON

Mr. Scottowe now lived in the old Manor House at Great Ayton. His mansion Ayton Hall, next door, had been mortgaged to Mr. Ralph Ward and now Mrs. Jackson inherited it.

Tuesday 7th September, 1762. 'This Post brought a
Letter from (Capt) my Brother Wilson to my Mother
telling her that he willingly embraces her offer of
being made Purchaser of the Mansion House &
Ground at Ayton ....'

The Wilsons moved north, their furniture and maid coming from London by ship, unloaded in the rain on the banks of the Tees, it took the help of carts owned by all neighbours from Guisborough and Ayton to bring their goods to the Mansion house on the Low Green. They arrived themselves by coach, chaise and horseback, Rachel Wilson riding behind Jack, and Captain Wilson on the grey which Ralph had brought to meet them at Entercommon. Esther Jackson busy on duty in the empty Mansion house, was trying to create order for their arrival. Ralph had bought them a clock.

The Wilsons became his bedrock. With George in London, he no longer felt so alone, their children delighted him. He became more secure. His sisters thought he should find a wife. They failed.

PART II

EXPANDING WORLD

A Surveyor measures a feature from

different angles.

We can measure James Cook

by looking at him from the angle of

Britain's other Navy,

the East India Company Navy captains.

He had never been to the Pacific.

They had the experience.

We can put him in his true context,

of Exploration, Surveying and Scurvy.

13

THE HONOURABLE
EAST INDIA
COMPANY

INTRODUCTION

The Company, as people called it, was one of the greatest trading companies ever established by British business men. Its whole purpose was to bring back to London high-value goods from India, China, and the East Indies. The huge profits to be made gave shipping agents, clerical staff, accountants, engineers and sailors an opportunity of a lifetime, to become unshakably rich.

The Company was so powerful it had twice the wealth of the Government.

To protect their own trading ships, the Company had set up its own Navy and called it the Bombay Marine. Its first naval office seems to have been at the Elephant and Castle, near the docks.

We can meet the men who were involved in its sea-power. And we begin to see how their experience across the world, their skill and adventure on distant oceans, must have affected Captain Cook's attitude and the development of his career.

BRITAIN's OTHER NAVY

We are entering a new circle of influence. At first, the best way to see the East India Company's importance to Captain James Cook, is to leap forward in time, and look at the *Endeavour* voyage from his own viewpoint in 1768.

James Cook's appointment to command the *Endeavour* had one glaring fault. He had no experience of far eastern oceans. Being a careful man it must have worried him.

He would know that captains of the East India Company ships had to build up experience over 15 to 20 years. The dangers were clear. There was the Monsoon, a severe wind-and-rain weather system, against which it was impossible to sail for months. There were pirates, the real danger of capture and slavery. There was the practical problem of repairing the ship; problems of unusual local customs, of food supply, of money. The known ports for re-fitting in the far east were Macao in China, or Batavia in Java. Could James Cook find a way through what was thought a barrier of unmapped land, to reach Batavia from the south Pacific?

He was lucky. With a vast amount of experience available to him from the East India Company captains. There was one outstanding man in a perfect position to help; Commodore William Wilson had all the right knowledge, and he was living in retirement in exactly the right place, Great Ayton.

William Wilson was a famous sailor, having discovered, in 1758, a passage through the East Indies which defeated the seasonal head- on Monsoon winds in the China sea. His passage, to enter and leave the Pacific, had opened up a fast route to China. Known as Pitt's Track, this route could be used at all times of year. Ten years later in 1768 it was still very new. Charts were extremely rare. Yet Pitt's Track could be the answer to James Cook's way out of the Pacific, and *Endeavour's* safe journey home. Commodore Wilson would have the chart, and the sailing instructions in his own private log. It would be odd if James Cook never saw them.

William Wilson was Mr. Ralph Ward's nephew (by marriage), and brother-in-law of George Jackson, 2nd Secretary to the Admiralty, having married Rachel, George and Ralph Jackson's sister. He lived at Great Ayton, in the Mansion House recently vacated by old Thomas Skottowe, Esq. who had moved next door. A house well known to James Cook and his father who now lived only a few hundred yards away across the Low Green.

James Cook's orders to take *Endeavour* to the Pacific meant he needed help. Why not from that great extended family, the East India Company captains? Now we know why we are entering their circle, we need to go back ten years to 1757, and meet them.

~~~

COMMODORE WILLIAM WILSON
1715-1795

'The English have a right to navigate,
wherever it has pleased God to send water.'
William Wilson.... to the Dutch Governor of Batavia. 1759.

William Wilson came from a respectable Yorkshire family. His father Henry Wilson ran a large glassworks in London and, like many of those involved in early industry, lost his money. He had a son Henry, and William was born in 1715. The boys had to make their own way in life.

William entered the East India Company at the age of 13, working his way up through the ranks of seamanship, until in 1744 he was appointed captain of a private Ship-of-War, the *Great Britain,* a vessel of 30 guns and 250 crew. He was 29.

ENGAGEMENT BETWEEN THREE INDIAMEN AND TWO FRENCH FRIGATES, 1757

With Britain at war, Captain Wilson took her to sea and frightened off a large Spanish frigate. He captured a Spanish sloop with £10,000 on board, taking enough in prize money to start off his fortune. He engaged in battle three French West Indiamen who carried letters of marque, private ships licensed to attack 'enemy' vessels. Each had 20 to 24 guns. He captured two. The daring young captain was on his way to promotion.

In 1748 he re-entered the East India merchant service as captain of the *Suffolk*. He chose trade as his path to riches. William Wilson was brave, amiable and shrewd, with a robust appetite for life. He was capable, he always brought his ship back. He was lucky, he did not die of tropical fever. He was a relaxed man but careful. His favourite sayings were 'I would suppose .. ' or 'I imagine ... ' Writing in *Suffolk's* Log he says, 'Being in liquor Immagine he fell overboard,' of the ship's caulker.

The *Suffolk*[1] made three voyages under his command:

> Oct. 1748 - July 1750 to Batavia in Java.
> Oct. 1752 - May 1754 to Madras and China.
> Oct. 1755 - Sept 1757 to Madras and China.

As they returned from China in 1757, *Suffolk* came across a French ship of the line *Compte de Provence* of 74 guns, with a frigate *Sylphide* 36 guns. Britain and France were at war. The *Suffolk* 499 tons, the *Houghton*, under Captain Walpole, and the *Godolphin*, under Captain Hutchinson, had about 72 guns between them. Outclassed, and heavily laden, each held a fortune in cargo, in tea, silk and fragile china. The sinister enemy frigate was a fast war machine, the French ship-o'-the-line a terrifying wall of blazing death. William Wilson, after sending a boat to the *Godolphin* to discuss their action, led the English merchantmen in broadsides on the enemy.

'9th March, 1757.   (from *Suffolk's* Log)
At 3 pm saw two sail made all the necessary Precautions
for Engaging but if possible to avoid them for which
we agreed to steer N ......they showed no colours
till the[y] bore down and fir'd which was not till
after 8 in the morning when the Engagement began

& ended about half past 11 one was a small ship about
26 or 30 guns the other a 60-70 gun ship.
Our people behaved well and we have no great damage.'

For his courage William Wilson received the thanks of the Lords of the Admiralty, as well as the East India Company's Court of Directors, who presented him with a silver tray. As we study the formal battle plan it seems so stylised, so lacking in imagination that we long for the future, for Lord Nelson and his flexible tactics. Captain Wilson would probably laugh at that remark, knowing he had actually won the day and that no battle is tidy for long.[2]

To avoid the French warships in the Channel, the three British ships arrived back via Ireland, sailing around the north of Scotland, waiting in Leith to join a Royal Navy convoy for a safe passage to London. The three ships were surrounded by rumours of bravery and medals.

Suffolk was anchored at Leith with her expensive cargo, waiting for the convoy to form. Her officers wore their Company uniforms, blue with black velvet lapels and cuffs, lion buttons and gold embroidery. The year is 1757. That is the sight James Cook saw when he arrived on 31st July, to enter *HMS Solebay* for the first time as a ship's Master in the Royal Navy.

William Wilson came home to sadness. His first child, called Harry had died. Captain Wilson was home for only 5 months. His next voyage would bring him fame. In 1768 James Cook needed to know about the Pacific. William Wilson's experience was available. to him.

Suffolk's measurement in China shows her as 98 feet long and 26 feet 5" on the beam, about the same as the *Endeavour*?

In order to understand the knowledge James Cook needed and the   expertise available we can sail with them on the East India Ship *Pitt*.

~~~

PITT's VOYAGE TO THE PACIFIC
1758 – 1760

In October 1757, with the nights drawing in and a cold sharp wind off the sea, the herring fleet made its way back to Staithes for the winter. Ralph Jackson writes:

'4th October. Jack from Steaths with Read[3] Herrings, Yarmouth biscuits and Pease, the Herring or five-man boats being returned from Yarmouth.'

Sharp John Gallilee was deciding to wait until mid December before laying up the *Mary & Jane* at Shields. He was short of loose cash, maybe to pay the crew. Mrs. Gallilee sent an urgent note requesting coin to Guisborough, where Messrs. Jacksons the grocers were able to promise £120 in a fortnight's time. The North Sea sailing season was ending.

For the East India deep ocean sailors it was just beginning.

On 12th October Ralph received a letter from his mother:

'which informs us of My Brother Wilson's again going to China, but in another Ship (not the Suffolk of 24 guns and 90 men, but the Pitt, called after the Secretary of State of that name of 50 guns and 250 men.) I suppose his advantages will be encreased as also his Reputation for tho' she is a Merchant Ship she is to be as Convoy to a fleet, vid. about Christmas next (if all be well) that being the time appointed for his leaving England.'

Christmas came, and cold wet days. Ralph read 'Thompsons Travels through Asia.' Rachel Wilson was again expecting the Captain's child, due in May. The ship had not sailed.

Ralph Jackson's mother had a row with her unwell brother Ralph Ward. She wanted to visit London leaving her invalid daughter Hannah at Guisborough. Mr. Ward decided she just wanted to gallivant. Provoked, he told her 'he supposed there was a necessity for her going on Sister Wilson's account…..... otherwise her family at home required her presence.' By the day of the row, *Pitt* had left:

'13th February, 1758. Brother Wilson took leave of his wife about a week since and I saw by last Post's papers had got to Portsmouth,' says Ralph, trying hard to stay on neutral territory.

Pitt was one of the biggest ships to have sailed for the Company. She was a huge responsibility for William Wilson. Named after the Secretary of State William Pitt, the ship *Pitt* was privately owned, but chartered by the East India Company, as shown in the records of the Company's agents in China. These men, called Supra-Cargoes, were British merchants who bought and sold all the cargoes. At that date they were still travelling the world with the Company ships. In port they grouped together in 'Councils' to trade. The Canton Council later noted:

'Captain Wilson inform'd us he wanted 1800 Spanish dollars for the use of the Ship Pitt, we accordingly paid him Taels 1296 or 1800 Spanish Dollars at 7s/6 PER Dollar at £ St[erlin]g 675 for which he has given us his Respondentia Bond on the Owners of the Ship Pitt payable to the Hon'ble Company.'

Silver and gold bullion were being sucked out of Europe in order to support the growing trade to China. Sometimes Ralph Jackson's journals show, there is simply no cash to be had. This dearth of coin helped to spur on a new British banking system based upon notes. The East India Company normally chartered ships at around 499 tonnage: *Pitt* was entered at 600. She was measured on arrival by the Chinese authorities for harbour dues, at 201.8 units; the average being 178-188 units. *Pitt* was big, she needed to be, she was going out not just as a merchantman, she was taking soldiers to war.

The voyage of the *Pitt* in 1758-60 is one of those adventures which become a turning point. *Pitt* under Captain Wilson took British troops to save Madras, and so save India from French domination. Captain Wilson then sailed on to discover a new route to China by entering the Pacific. A route which took the China tea trade outside the limitation of the Monsoon, it doubled the trading season, and the profits. This one voyage, provided the East India Company with security in India, and commercial edge at home

James Cook was a truthful man; he has been regarded as a reticent, modest man. Maybe he was just sensible of the facts. When he was chosen for the *Endeavour* in 1768, he would be aware of blunt comparisons being made at home in Yorkshire, by the sea-going fraternity; and he would know there were Yorkshiremen who had themselves been to the Pacific on their own voyage of discovery ten years earlier. The crew list of the *Pitt* begins:

William Wilson	Commander
Joseph Jackson	1st Mate
Jeffrey Jackson	2nd Mate

Jeffrey was married at Great Ayton, James Cook's home village.

There were six Mates in all on the *Pitt.* Her officers included a Purser, a Surgeon and the Gunner John Pemberton, and these men all had their own mates and servants. It was common to take a very young member of the family to sea as a servant; Nelson himself first went to sea as Captain's servant to his uncle. Jeffrey Jackson's servant on *Pitt* was his young brother William Jackson, and we can see both men in later ships' logs, working their way up in the East India Company's service. Ten years later in 1768, as James Cook was rounding the Horn in the *Endeavour* to enter the Pacific, William Jackson, as 4th Mate of the East Indiaman *Speke,* was making ready in the Thames to sail to China under the command of the above Captain Jeffrey Jackson, who was by then married to Ralph Jackson's tomboy sister Dolly. But William Wilson and Jeffrey Jackson were not unusual. Other East India captains and crews were scattered all over Cleveland.

Cleveland is a landscape painted in fields of soft lime green, smoky grey trees, smudgy browns, misty blue skies. Yet in Cleveland lived men who carried in their minds' eyes crystal sharp turquoise seas, aching white sands, brilliant pinks, yellows, purples, of profusions of flowers, of pungent spices, and dark-skinned people, jewelled sultans, bright silks, dark green jungles, myriad coloured fishes off white coral reefs. A tantalising vision, the excitement of distant lands leaking out through the steady conversation of seagoing men. James Cook must have met them, heard them; his imagination must have been caught, his horizons widened, years before he was chosen to command *Endeavour.*

Why is this relevant? In 1768, James Cook did not have their experience but he needed to match their quality. He badly needed their information. One way for us to understand their world, to see with him their vast expertise and knowledge, is to sail with them on the *Pitt,* into the Pacific, 10 years before Captain Cook did.

PITT OUTWARD TO CHINA 1758 – 1759[4]

The Log of the *Pitt* begins on 27th November 1757, in London river, when Captain William Wilson writes 'Fair weather, wind northerly, came out of the Dock and took in the Moorings.'

At Guisborough in the north the weather was cold. There was a miniature corn riot by hungry poor people. They had no bread. No export of corn was allowed from the kingdom due to the war with France. Tobias Taylor of Skelton was found out, shipping corn to smugglers. Young Thomas Presswick, nephew of Mr. Ralph Ward's secretary Thomey, had returned from ten months in a French prison to his father's hemp mill at Waterfall. The local constables, like Mr. Sanderson of Staithes, and Mr. Sparnell of Guisborough, had listed all the men of 18 to 50 liable to serve in a local Militia, as ordered by Parliament. England had to raise 32,000 men. There was urgency and anxiety in the air. The Justices who met at the Cock Inn found 'a great number of people mostly inferior, assembled from Lyth, Egton, Danby and all the little country towns thereabout' who demanded to see the Constables' lists. They grabbed them - it is unspoken that they altered them - before Mr. Michael Smith of Marske, the Chief Constable of the Langbaurgh Division could summon the Petty Court to hand in the names.

In London *Pitt,* the huge new ship, resplendent in the Company's colours, was fitting out to take troops to India to protect the main trading port of Madras. In an atmosphere of war she began to take on Kentlidges (ballast), plus 200 pigs of lead, as men levelled the hold. From 7th-9th December they stepped the Main and Foremasts and Bowsprit. Christmas Day was cloudy with rain as the last puncheons of beef, hogsheads of pork, barrels of suet and lard, casks of potatoes swung on board. On 26th December 'The Pilot came on board and prepared for sailing... but the wind Dying away prevented our moving,' says Captain Wilson. *Pitt* being new, no-one knew how she would handle when fully, or over loaded. They had to find out.

In view of what happened some years later, in 1772, during the contention about Captain Cook's ship *Resolution,* it is helpful to see William Wilson's problems with the *Pitt.*

Sailing ships need to be balanced. If not, they slop about sickly and corkscrew, at worst they overturn. Correctly trimmed they are both safer and faster. The *Pitt,* while large, about 600 tons, with a crew of 250, had yet to take on board Lieut.CoI. William Draper's company of 85 soldiers and Major Cholmondley Brereton's company of 79. The method of accommodating the troops was the same as used later with the *Resolution,* that is the poop was extended by being built upwards. This extra deck weighed down the ship, tilted her backwards and altered her balance.

On 2nd January 1758, Captain Wilson moved some casks of dry and wet provisions to bring the ship up by the stem. On 11th *Pitt* sailed downriver to Gravesend to take on her guns: 24 x 9-pound cannon for the upper deck, 6 x 4-pounders for the Quarter deck, 35 chests of silver for the Honourable Company, 3 chests of gold, 48 bundles of stockfish. It was all weight to be distributed. On 21st January the two companies of soldiers arrived, 20 officers, 164 men, all with their baggage and equipment. Next day Captain Wilson took on some private trade and stores of his own. The day after that, the ammunition arrived: 2 chests of small arms for the ship's use, 1440 x 9 lbs round shot (weighing about 6 tons), 240 x Double-headed shot, 360 x 4 1b shot, 60 x Double-headed shot, 6 cwt of musket balls, 2 cwt of pistol balls and some bird shot, plus iron for the forge.

The wooden ship was grossly heavy. Could she handle it?

Pitt weighed anchor on the ebb on 2nd February, tried again at 5.30 and anchored downriver to take on grenade shells and gunners stores. Gunpowder was kept well outside London. Six passengers, who were merchants and soldiers, joined the ship at East Tilbury. By 8th February, *Pitt* had lumbered further downriver to the Sunfleet anchorage. The outlook was bad. Fully loaded, with her extra poop deck, the ship would not steer.

Only experience could give a Captain the assurance of knowing how dangerous was his stowage of men, munitions, stores and cargo. There was still the important Ship's brandy and 32 chests of Company treasure to come aboard at Spithead, from where *Pitt* was due to sail in convoy on 19th February. Captain Wilson did the best he could. But the new, unfamiliar ship, possibly overloaded, delicately balanced with her high extra poop, continued to wallow sickly all the seven months it took them to reach India. As the soldiers disembarked at Madras, the pragmatic Captain Wilson had already dismantled the extra deck around them. They anchored on the 15th September; on 16th he notes with relief: 'Cut down the remainder of the Poop.'

~~~

Now we can indulge in a small privilege of historians and leap forward in time for a moment, to compare Captain Cook's trouble with the bark *Resolution* in 1772. With her extra poop she was so bad she did not even leave the Thames estuary. She fell over on her side, then, as the men were leaping from her for their lives, righted herself without warning. She was ordered into Sheerness dock. The Lieutenant, who had taken her downriver with the pilot on trials, reported she was a bitch.

Her extra raised poop deck had to be removed altogether, losing her the spacious accommodation for the 'gentlemen' as Captain Cook called them, which is the main reason Joseph Banks did not join the *Resolution's* voyage of discovery. That he acted petulantly, which Lord Sandwich told him he did, must be measured against the fact that poop extensions were normal at the time. Captain Cook kept a low profile during the whole affair. The *Resolution* was a Whitby Cat. He must have known fine well she might not be able to cope.

Now return to 1758. In the crowded conditions of the ungainly *Pitt,* on her outward journey to Madras, in the lurching rolling ship they had disease on board, said to be typhus brought by lice. As well as nearly 450 men, their guns and baggage, they were carrying live animals and poultry. Thomas Hammon the poulterer, would die on the voyage. Thomas Ker the cooper, would be one of the few men to drown. There were surgeon's mates, gunners' mates, Thomas Jones the armourer, Daniel Locker the Master at Arms, carpenters, caulkers, Michael Stenton the Quarter-master. Captain Wilson had his own cook, Benjamin Drinkwater, his own steward Richard Williams, and two servants, John Barton and Thomas Driver. There were 20 young midshipmen on board. Of the crew of about 250, 53 would die (21.3%). Of the 164 soldiers, 30 died before they reached Madras (15.4%). The numbers were average for that date. But disease, wreck and survival, was every man's question.

Pitt's death rate can be found in later chapters on Scurvy. Here, we see the urgent need to fix longitude.

Pitt bore away from Madeira, picking up the north-east trade wind heading for the 'elbow' of South America. It is about then in the ship's Log that it dawns on a modern sailor, with a fearful horror, that they are navigating in a wide surly ocean mainly on latitude. Longitude was too vague. The officers could try to find it using tables based on our moon, or Jupiter's satellite moons, but these were complex and faulty, and could take three hours to work out. There is still no accurate clock chronometer to fix longitude.

They are sailing an erratic ocean in an awkward 600 ton ship, possibly overloaded, with only William Wilson's experience to keep them safe. The sailors on board are reading the running of the waves, flotsam, clouds, colour of the sun, smell of the wind, the officers taking noon sights, star sights, listening to the sounds in the rigging as the big ship plunges through the great Atlantic swell. It is the land which is dangerous.

Even latitude could be wrong. No-one knows where they are. *Pitt's* officers are looking out for the islands of Fernando de Noronha, lying off the jutting elbow of South America, without luck. Maps of the land are wrong too.

'As to the Island of Ferdinando Loronha we were at a loss for the certain Latitude of it,' says Captain Wilson in his log. With latitude fixed for the ship but not for the land, sailing is hair raising.

MADRAS to CHINA
The discovery of the Pitt Strait

In later years Pitt's Track came to mean any path through the Moluccas, but Captain Wilson knew precisely which strait he meant. It was details James Cook needed to know. What follows is what Captain Wilson could tell him at Great Ayton

Pitt left Madras on 26th September 1758, accompanied by the *Success,* a small two-and-a-half masted vessel called a Snow, which Captain Wilson had bought at Anjengo, in tropical south west India. He says, she cost £345 and was solidly built of Mauritius teak. He was clearly concerned about safety, both in navigating badly-known channels in a huge ungainly ship, and in case *Pitt* foundered and sank during the coming Monsoon. He must have decided that safety in strange waters depended on an extra vessel.

Three days out, in the Bay of Bengal, they came upon a foreign ship. This incident has been portrayed as a Brave British Encounter, it reads more like a farce, a naval dance of avoidance. Both ships pretended to be someone else then, each admitting their true colours, they exchanged one broadside. Captain Wilson was then told that the

Pitt had taken some water through her lower gunports, which was common enough, but darkness was falling, giving both ships an honourable chance to slip away. With discretion, *Pitt* and her enemy lost each other in the night.

October passed. The crew sighted Bouton and Quedah and the ship was reaching for the Straits of Malacca, the main bottleneck to enter the China Sea, a place so vulnerable to enemy blockade, they could face attack, capture and death. On 1st November Captain Wilson writes:

'Sent Mr. Jeffy. Jackson to Salengore in the Pinnace for Intelligence and if possible to procure a piece of Teak timber sufficient to fish our Main Yard which will hardly hang together.' He sent the *Success* snow to look at the Inner Passage through the Straights. The boats returned after two days without the teak, but talking of an English snow from Bengal, and her Captain Thornton, being there with news that the passage was free from the French. Using her ship's boats to sound the bottom, *Pitt* sailed safely through and anchored on 10th November at Malacca.

It is always surprising how many European trading ships could be found in these far eastern waters. The East India Company had the monopoly of the out-and-back trade but 'Country' ships, small merchant vessels from all over Europe, were growing rich on the far-east inter-port trade. *Pitt* at that point was not heading for an empty ocean, there were thousands of small boats, huge Chinese junks, Philippine prohas, Russian traders, Indian vessels, pirates, adventurers, free merchants, and slave traders stinking downwind. But all these sailing ships were at the mercy of the weather, whose main event was the seasonal Monsoon.

This fierce wind, is drawn in by the land heating up in summer, and air rising over the landmass of China and India. Wet air rushes in from the southern oceans to fill the vacuum. In autumn, as the northern land mass cools, the southern ocean holds its heat, air rises there and wet warm air rushes back. This happens in a seasonal three to five month pattern. It can destroy a sailing ship.

Captain Wilson had arrived at Malacca too late. He could not confront the head-on Monsoon in the China sea. It was impossible for him to sail northwards to Canton, but he had known it would happen and he had a plan.

Two months earlier, in Madras, in spite of the anxiety of the French seige, Captain Wilson had talked to his young acquaintance Alexander Dalrymple, who showed him the Log of John Saris. In 1616 Saris had sailed from Bantam (in Java) to Hirado (Japan) in the winter, by heading for the Moluccas, then north across the Pacific to Okinawa. Saris had apparently circled around the Monsoon. Circle sailing was now a great point of discussion, quite fashionable. Palliser had used it in the Atlantic to take troops to Virginia. William James had recently brought news to India of the outbreak of the Seven Years War, by sailing a circular track through the Indian Ocean. Young Dalrymple whose interest was academic, and Captain Wilson with experience, thought it possible to circle through the East Indies to reach China. George Pigot, President of the Madras Council agreed. Captain Wilson who had some charts, including the details of Dampier's voyage, may have taken other historic charts from young Dalrymple.

The East Indian Company Commodore William James had circled round the Monsoon in the Indian Ocean, by sailing to 10 degrees below the Equator. With this in mind, William Wilson left Malacca and headed away from China, east to Batavia (modern Djakarta) in Java, 6 degrees South. He was in well-known waters. *Pitt* sailed past the Cardamons and the straits of Banca, anchoring in Batavia roads on 15th December, among several Dutch ships and small vessels.

Batavia was built around a swamp of decaying canals. It was rife with tropical fever. Only the Dutch, whose own country was built on low levels and canals, would have kept Batavia as the major Freeport in the far-east. They were well established. They had no intention of encouraging British trade in what they saw as their monopoly of the East Indies. The Dutch Governor was difficult. On 23rd December, Commodore William Wilson sent a message to ask, would the Dutch Commodore return gun for gun in salute, or not? Next day, boats coming out to provision the Pitt were stopped on Dutch orders.

Commodore Wilson protested:

'Believing it my Duty not to put up with this affront offered to the British Colours, I immediately wrote to the Governor to acquaint him with what had happened Demanding such satisfaction as would acquit me to my King my Country and the Honourable East India Company,' he reported the insult in letters to his superiors back home.

On Christmas day, the Pinnace returned with an answer from the tricky Governor. 'Mr. Jeffy Jackson who was in her,' said he had delivered the letter in spite of it being first refused. The Governor had said the action was to prevent his own people deserting. It was a plausible excuse; the *Pitt's* caulkers mate, Oloff Gunnerson, had run away three days earlier. He probably felt no need to die for Britain, and they were heading away into the unknown. Batavia was so unhealthy, men were glad to get away, on any ship.

Short on provisions, *Pitt* left Batavia, sailing east along the north coast of Java, shadowed by the Dutch. William Wilson wrote in his log: 'Shaped our course to run within or to the S'ward of Carimon Java' [Kariminjawa] a large high island; at noon that day it was NW by W.

On 1st January 1759 they saw the island of Salombo [MaselemboBesar] and were headed for a myriad of islands and straits, shallow seas with too little depth for the heavy *Pitt.* So they stopped a passing sloop to ask the best way, giving her Master a present of beer and he 'being pleased' offered advice. In 'a moderate Monsoon and hazy weather' and very warm, they crept eastwards past the Isles of Tanakere to the straits of Salayer SW of Celebes, a maze of islands. Captain Wilson found there was 'an error in the chart difficult to account for', it was unsafe to sail at night: he logs a recommendation to future sailors to anchor at night. By the 8th January the Island of Cabyna [Kabaena] was N7 degrees W and 3 leagues off. In two days they had eased round to Bocton [Butung] where they anchored and bought goats, fowl and fish, by permission of the local King. The Dutch were there first, watching.

It was time to turn north. It was Captain Wilson's intention to sail north-west if he could, past the volcanic island of Ternate, famous for cloves, to enter the Pacific near the Philippines. It proved impossible. There was a tidal bore in the Sulla strait.

As they approached, Captain Wilson 'kept the snow ahead and the pinnace and yawl on each bow.' After five days, Jeffrey Jackson in the Pinnace boat found a 'good watering river and wood'. The weather was humid and oppressive and Captain Wilson writes:

'The confin'd air in these narrow straits does not seem to agree with our People, some complaining of the Flux, some want of Appetite and others waisting without any sensible complaint.'

It proved too difficult to get through the strait. The tidal bore ran too strongly against them, the outlying boats were in danger, in the turbulence one was overset. *Pitt,* spinning, bucking and sliding backwards, was making no headway north toward China.

Captain Wilson called together the officers to consult them. It was agreed to 'bear away for some of the straits of New Guinea in which Tract we may expect Leading winds appealing to the crew.'

For two heavy hot days they were becalmed off Sulla, but light airs at last sprang up to take them to within sight of the large islands, Obi Latta and Obi Major; Gomono was 1 degree 50' South. By 14th February they were off the SW end of Popa island. Could they find a channel into the Pacific? They scoured the old maps, the sea and the islands.

They would try the channel between Mixoul and Popa:

'The opening of the straights appeared very fair between Prince of Wales island and King George island but the bearings differing much from the chart, stood in to Discover the land, and observe that Pitt's Straits shut in when it Bore N63° 30'E by bringing the Noermost land of King George's island and the Somost land of the P of Wales Island in one, at the same time the Round Hummock on Popa W6°So, Cape Raymond (which is the Cape Mabro of Dampier) N13W, the entrance to Pitts Straits N48°E, the Body of K.George's Island E20^{0}N distance about 5 leagues & the So'most of the Dene Islands S° distance about

4 leagues. And from Cape Raymond about 5 leagues.' Captain Wilson logs:

Latt. of Medium of our Observation	1°06' South
By which I make Cape Raymond * to lay in	0°51 "
The entrance to the Pitt's Straights	0°55 "
And Point Pegou * in	1°01 "

He was fixing the land by compass bearings from a moving ship.

'NB'adds Captain Wilson: 'Capt. Dampier in his Voyage for the discovery of the coast of New Guineau mentions seeing this opening which forms Pitt's Straits, but passing Cape Mabro which he calls the NW Point of New Guineau, went thro' a Straits to the No'ward of it.'

He adds, 'As it is probable these Straights have never been passed by any ship before, I have taken the Traveller's Licence of giving it and the Adjacent Islands & headlands such names as I thought proper.'

* The names were of officials of the East India Company.

Jeffrey Jackson had an island named after him too. On 17th February, going through the Strait passing Patriot island, they 'saw several Canoes near the isle with Woolly Headed people in them strikeing of fish.' The current was in their favour, the weather fair with light winds, they passed Cumberland isle, took bearings of the land, and saw 'coral rocks seen plain through the water.' Six natives paddling canoes appeared from King George's island. Captain Wilson 'Sent the Pinnace with Mr. Jeffrey Jackson in her to Endeavour to speke to them.' Jeffrey Jackson hurriedly took with him presents of rings, rice and knives. The natives ran away. Jeffrey landed on Jackson island and left the presents for them to find.

Next day *Pitt* was in the middle reaches of the strait, the crew continued to work through, anchoring at night, in difficult light and

Map of Eastern Sulawesi and Halmahera, with : view of Ternate; line engraving with later colouring from the *Atlas* of chans accompanying J. van den Bc[c]h's *Nederlandsche bezittingen in Azie, Amerika entfrika* van Cleef, The Hague 1818..

variable winds, sailing eastward from New Guinea towards the Cape already named by Dampier, Good Hope.

'22nd February, 1759, We find ourselves much at a loss to ascertain the opening of the Straits of New Guineau, having made two openings, but as we ran to the E'ward there did not appear to be a passage thro' either, neither does either of them appear to be near so large as Represented in the chart.

Yet within two days they had found a way through. There is a quality to their seamanship which is rare now. Boats out taking soundings, lookouts high in the rigging reading the colour of the water, the least ripple and swirl speaking of rocks below. The big gilded wooden ship easing along a newly marked channel. It reminds us of James Cook and other ships' masters, laying the channel up the St. Lawrence that same year.

The corkscrewing *Pitt* crept steadily on. '25th February: Kept a good look out in the night for three small Islands seen by the St. John in their passage this way from America, Anno. 1705'.

Next day there was cloudy weather with frequent showers of rain and a large swell from the NE, a sign of deep wide ocean. They 'saw a great many fish and several Birds .... Kept the snow ahead in the night to look out for the three islands mentioned before .... Several of our People have Symptoms of the Scurvy.'

They were in the Pacific!

Early March Saw *Pitt* staggering northwards through the Pacific Ocean east of the Philippines. There was a confused swell, light winds and baffling calms. In hindsight it become obvious that *Pitt* was lucky in the weather. While the Log complains 'Sails flapping and wet weather has almost destroyed all the sails above the yards', it was much better than being dismasted in a typhoon. On 8th March, William Wilson was looking for the Isles of St. Andrew 'layd down in the French Neptune[5] in Latt 5°00'N which I suppose to be those called Johannes in the English charts and lay'd down in the Latt. 6°00'N.'

A week later they were east of Samal in the Philippines but 'Our People Daily complain of Scorbutic symptoms, and some are taken with the Flux'. More of *Pitt's* crew began to die.

The ship lurched on, sails in rags, men failing. Thomas Kerr was drowned.

Their voyage was now longer than a year.

By the end of March they had reached the Bashe Islands, and turned west for China, and on 13th April they picked up the Lima Pilot and reached Macao, the gateway to Canton. For anyone on board, who had never been to China, there were some amazing rules to greet them.

CHINA!

The Celestial Empire of China was a civilised country, and had been since 210 BC, almost two thousand years. It was bigger than Europe, and divided into country-sized Provinces, each ruled by a Viceroy, called a Tsongchuck. Chinese life was based on a completely different set of ideas, expressed in a complicated language, deeply formal manners, ancient customs, strict law and ornate military order. The arts, theatre and medicine were highly developed, well in advance of Europe. As was the manufacture of porcelain, silk and paper, which was why the ships went there to buy them. The effect on China of European ships arriving at Canton, was as if a few flies had settled on an elephant; their presence was noted, but it would be best if they went away.

CUSTOMS, OFFICIALS & LITTLE WHITE LIES

The European ships arrived first at Macao, a warm southern port, an enclave run by the Portuguese. There the ships waited for permission to sail up the Pearl river delta, to Canton to load. As all power centred on the Emperor of China in Peking, over a thousand

Miles away to the north, this huge country was kept under control by an attitude of respect and obedience, and by an over-powering bereaucracy, whose civil servants operated a complex and mathematical system of government. Their customs duties alone were worked out to 9 decimal points. It was the Mandarins who were responsible for law and order. To them the Europeans were a dangerous nuisance.

Looked at from the Chinese officials' point of view, fifty or so foreign ships, each armed with 24 to 74 guns, arrived during a short season. Over 5,000 sailors, many of them French and English and so sworn enemies, had to be kept apart, they brought trouble. The Mandarins were not amused. The Europeans were not allowed inside the city of Canton. They were told to unload their guns and store them on land. To pleas that the crews had been at sea for two years, the officials unbent enough to allow the sailors an island in the river for recreation. The French had to have a separate island in the river otherwise fighting began. The Chinese insisted: all the usual Chinese customs and harbour dues were to be paid, all the usual presents given. No European was to learn the language. Official Chinese agents were appointed as Hong Merchants to control trade. Everything was to be conducted through proper channels, there was to be no appeal to higher authority. No opium was to enter the country. All rules and laws were to be obeyed. Any Chinese who co-operated with foreigners to break the system were tried and beheaded.

The Chinese began their control far out to sea. As the European ships approached, war junks met them at sea, demanding an account of their guns, ammunition and gunpowder. The East India captains answered with a standard fib. The ships then waited at Macao until measured for harbour dues, which is why we know so much about them. The official Present cost about £650 per ship, nearly six times James Cook's wages. Unofficial trade by the sailors attracted Chinese criminals. There was theft from the boat's chests. There was the occasional murder. Prices shot up and down drastically for the home market; shopkeepers were tempted into chicanery. The Mandarins were fierce and determined to keep law and order. But they too had their official perks.

CLOCKS, CURIOSITIES AND SINGSONGS

By rule of law, all trinkets, jewels of a certain type, watches, clocks and singsongs (musical boxes!) belonged to the Emperor, and went to the Mandarins as an exclusive purchase. It was a firm rule, waiting to be broken. The sailors set up a wicked little trade of their own. The Mandarins, relying on their official monopoly, offered the Hong Merchants less than the items cost, the merchants forced to make up the difference appealed to the Company SupraCargoes. The Mandarins were fiercely prepared to use their soldiers to enforce their monopoly. Trouble flared up all the time.

The Canton SupraCargoes issued an order - but Commodore Wilson on *Pitt* had anticipated the problem. He wrote from Macao, before entering the Pearl river:

'As it had always been my Endeavour to avoid giving Trouble I have not brought either clock, watch or trinket of any Sort, and on enquiry I have the pleasure to inform you that there is not any thing of that sort in the ship.' With a crew of 200? Could he be sure?

Pitt was allowed to move up the Pearl River to Whampoa roads, before the old city of Canton. They moored against the Middle Banksall island on the 15th April, to the surprise of the captains and crews of the European ships already loading there. It was the wrong season to arrive. Commodore Wilson would have to explain himself to the SupraCargoes, to the Company captains and to the suspiciously wary Chinese, who could arrest him.

The shipping roads were full of vessels loading. Prices were high, fresh provisions would be short, on board *Pitt* more men were dying. So many European ships were jostling for room, that the Company Council of SupraCargoes was extremely anxious, fearing that an inadequate gun salute could trigger a fire -fight, particularly with the

French, and start up the war in China.

The Company's Regulations of Salutes sent to Commodore Fisher 'desired Him as Commodore of the Road to make them known to the Rest of the Captains'.

There would be no conflict between the two Commodores. Captain Fisher was William Wilson's newest cousin by marriage. It behoved them to be polite. Their wives were best friends.

~~~

CAPTAIN FISHER

Ralph Jackson writes:

'23rd February, 1758. Cousin Bett Ward I saw by last Post's Papers had been married to Captain Fisher of the Drake Indiaman, a few days before.'

It was a last minute wedding. Captain Fisher was about to sail on *Drake,* headed to China for three years.

The Jacksons were close to their Ward cousins. Benjamin Ward visited the boy apprentice Ralph Jackson at Newcastle in 1749. Edward Ward junior, commanding the East India Company ship *York* to China, would write to him. Their sister Bett Ward was a livewire. With Dolly Jackson, her best friend, Bett was always ready to join in the fun. On 6th August 1757, Ralph writes 'Saturday. Sister Dolly at West Auckland to see Capt. Ward, his Lady and sister Bett there.' They were visiting their sister Mrs. James.

Captain Ward lived from 1757 in the hamlet of Mile End.

Bett continued to visit her Staithes cousins, and then the Sandersons, for years, riding home on the double horse behind Ralph Jackson. We could expect Edward Ward to visit Staithes too. Both Edward and Bett may have known and talked to James Cook.

In Canton, on board the anchored Pitt, his men were dying, so William Wilson decided to make a quick turnaround. The Monsoon would soon reverse, to blow once more against them. So they would go back the way they had come, the circular route by Pitt's Track, it could be the fastest voyage ever, *Pitt*'s men would stand a better chance. A cargo had to be bought and loaded quickly.

LOADING THE SHIP

Safety of a ship depends on a high level of skill in loading her. A shifting cargo can make a ship turn over, even in the lightest breeze. Too much load forward and she can plough under in full sail. While *Pitt* was a 'wallower', *Endeavour* at first had a tendency to 'swim by the head' says James Cook. He altered her ballast then, her men agreed, she was a trim little ship.

Endeavour, heading for the Pacific, was to carry stores and fragile scientific specimens, and around 100 men, for 2 or 3 years. James Cook only had experience of Navy stores, coal and timber, and troops. An East India Company captain was an expert in sailing long distances with fragile cargo. To gauge the expertise needed, let us load a ship.

No ship under canvas can sail safely without ballast. And in China, ballast caused problems. About 40 tons of 'Kentlidges', iron scrap from a ballast shore of the Thames, was needed for a ship chartered at 499 tons, such as the *Drake.* Shovelled out at Canton, in order to repair her hull, the Chinese officials decided to charge *Drake* iron export duty to shovel it back in. Afterall it was iron. Which caused a furore. Was it the same bits of iron? *Endeavour* was to carry normal iron ballast. *Pitt* carried lead as part ballast, which was sold to the Chinese merchant Chetqua: 1677 Peculs at 3 Taels per Pecul raised 5031 (£1638), exchanged for Chinaware and singlo tea. When *Drake* arrived from Bombay with 'only half her proper amount of Kentlidge and, as shingle would take up too much cargo space, her commander asked to have a quantity of tutenague put in to her.' Tutenague was a metal alloy of copper, zinc and nickel. 'We determined to purchase forty Tons of tutenague which by the last Price Current from England will turn to good account, if we procure it about 5 Taels per Picul', which they did. The clear message to the

the Captain of the *Endeavour*, James Cook, was that iron ballast caused trouble. The secret was to use something else.

Dunnage, often sand, levelled off the ballast. Then the ships were floored with chests of china, full sized and half sized chests, to fit the shape of the ship, and make a dry floor, for the tea. A special arrangement for mutual convenience was made with the commander of the *Pitt*: 'In order to expedite the Dispatch of Captn. Wilson we agreed to make over to Him 10 whole & 90 half Chests of china Ware, cost Tas 1459, which he informs us will be sufficient to floor the ship, so that we shall not send any on Board for account of the Company.' The holds were now ready for the China tea.

Tea as we know has its own fragrance. The tea chests, lined and tarred, holding about 67 lbs each, were loaded above the china, the Bohea went in first, it was the cheapest. This was the dry way to load fragile plant specimens! They were loading teas with wonderful names, such as:

The Black Teas: Bohea, 1st Congo, Souchong, and Pekoe.

The Green Teas: Hyson, Singlo, and its varieties Hyson

Skins & Twankay.

(Hence Widow Twankey in the Pantomine Aladdin. The Sultan of Aceh in Sumatra, at that time, was actually called Ala-uddin).

Above the tea they packed the delicate silk, raw silk for weaving in huge amounts and, in the 1750s, woven silk, silks of all kinds, silks of all colours - except yellow, that was the Emperor's colour and its export was forbidden. They were loading bales of lustrous Taffeties, plain, checked or flowered, striped or brocaded; Paduasouy, smooth rich and black; Grogram, stout corded and durable; Bed Damasks, those heavy large-patterned brocades for bed hangings, we can sometimes still see in stately homes; then there was Goshee, maybe a watered silk; Poisee a plain black silk; and Satins, and thousands of silk handkerchiefs. We can see them gleaming in 18th century portraits.

In the ship's holds, above the silks, accessible for unloading were stores for the island of St. Helena, tea, sugar and chinaware. While stacked wherever possible in every nook and cranny of the dark holds were small amounts of Anniseed, Turmeric, Quicksilver, Rhubarb, but no Musk was allowed on board as it tainted the tea with its scent. To pack all this, there were wedged hundreds of bundles of Rattan canes, used in Europe to make cane furniture.

As for the chinaware, anyone interested in antiques could consider the list for one ship alone. Take the *Prince George* in 1755. She was floored with 120 chests of china and 1 chest of Musters (documented lists). Most of the china was blue and white, some octagonal with details of plants, some white and flowered, some blue and white scalloped. There were 25,531 single plates, 477 eight-piece table sets, 200 teasets, 6728 halfpint basins, 1626 coffee cups, 226,171 cups and saucers, with 437 spare cups, 1596 pint basins, 878 three-bowl sets, and 675 five inch bowls ... and in two of the chests were 800 lbs of sago for use of the crew.

The East India ships were vessels of plenty, hardly anything they brought home was vital to Britain. Silk, china and tea were consumer goods. It has been argued that easily washed china and Indian cottons improved cleanliness. That tea was a healthier drink than ale or bad water, because the water had to be boiled. That the resulting better survival rate of children gave Britain the necessary people for trade expansion and development. The truth is, people involved in the East India Company were using ships to make money for themselves. China, silk and tea were fashionable. Demand was high, profits enormous. The private trade of the captains alone made them rich; many of them were younger sons of the aristocracy, out to make new fortunes. The company allowed all the sea officers a set amount of private trade. In 1764 Captain Hooke of the *Pocock* was allowed 110 chests of tea and 284 of china, Captain Webber of the *Lord Clive* 90 of tea, 111 of china, Captain John Mitford of the *Northumberland* 60 tea, 104 china, and the lesser officers amounts on a sliding scale. They brought home to Britain lacquered ware, china, silks, wallpaper, jade, mother-of-pearl. Some found their way into Cleveland houses and in some, may be there still. Chinese wallpaper was found quite recently at Ayton Hall, and is now in a London museum.

On 26th January, 1759, Ralph Jackson says, 'Yesterday my uncle had a box of china sent from Sister Wilson', probably from the *Suffolk.* And when Mr. Jefferson died in August, 1759, Ralph helped to pack the china 'of which there is a great quantity on', (on being used for of, in Cleveland speech.)

The main problem of the far-east was cash. This could come in Spanish dollars, Indian rupees, pagodas, German crowns, sterling silver. It was assayed by the Chinese, weighed, and exchanged for its silver content. Sometimes silver and gold were the goods for sale.

Imagine the ships arriving at Canton after a year and a half at sea, to find there were no goods to load, because the SupraCargoes had run out of silver to buy them. On this point, Pitt's Track could save a whole trading season at Canton. *HMS Argo* was sent that way, in 1765, for just that reason, with an emergency cargo of £96,651. The Chinese insisted her guns were unloaded. Her captain refused, saying His Majesty's Royal Navy did not surrender His Majesty's arms to a foreign power! It took ornate negotiation before a compromise could be reached, and the silver unloaded.

One unexpected effect of Pitt's Track was that the shipping season did not come to an end so the SupraCargoes began to stay on in China, buying all year round. They were able to gather cargoes in advance, and smooth out the prices. The Honourable Company knew this would offend the Chinese. They ordered the SupraCargoes to leave, year after year. Some made excuses, or ignored instructions, pleaded a broken leg, or went free-lance, and stayed.

PITT HOMEWARD FROM CHINA

At Canton, in the warm spring days of April 1759, as *Pitt* loaded, there was trouble. The Chinese Viceroy had been controlling the shipping trade to his own lucrative advantage. Things had got so bad, the Company decided to appeal to the Emperor of China, a thousand miles away in Peking. The man they chose for this known forbidden journey was Flint. An abandoned child of British parents, he had been raised by Chinese in Macao, and was one of those people who had a foot in both worlds.

Pitt left China on the 14th May 1759, accompanied by the *Success* snow commanded by James Evans, 5th mate of the *Pitt,* with Midshipman Matthew Hood and 15 crew. *Success* was carrying Mr. Flint on what was to become an historical, and circular, attempt to reach the Emperor by landing at Tientsin. The plan failed. For insulting the Emperor by daring to approach him, Mr. Flint was punished by being imprisoned for three years. His Chinese translator was ritually strangled. The *Success* and her crew left Tientsin in July and were never seen again.

Meanwhile *Pitt* was heading east out into the Pacific, with more of her men dying. At 5 o'clock one morning they 'Felt a severe shock of an Earthquake, the trembling of the ship and noise occasioned by it made it sccm as if she was grating over some rocks. It much surprise'd our People some running one way some another.' The crew thought the ship was on fire. The quake lasted three minutes. 'It was,' says Captain Wilson, 'some time before they could be Pacified.' With sick and frightened men they sailed on through the great Pacific ocean. Peter Cloiss the Sailmaker died, then Thomas Jones the armourer, the coopers were both dead, they had only 14 Midshipmen left. In moderate breezes and light airs they drifted southwards until at last on 31st July they were once more approaching Pitt's Passage. 'At 11 am entered the Mouth of the Straits,' writes William Wilson.

◄─────── *North*

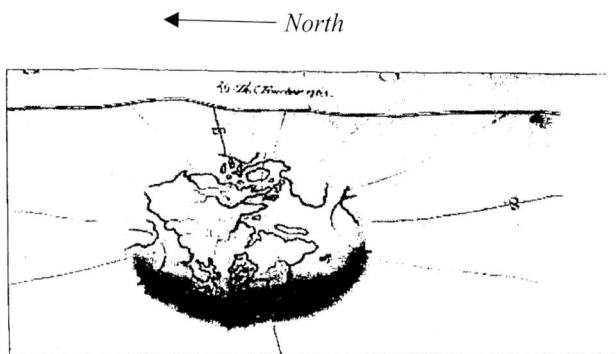

They were leaving the Pacific, and the chance of an easy passage west to leave it, looked good.

The winds were variable between south and east. 'The land on both sides of these Straits are covered with Trees and rise with a very Quick Ascent from the Water's Edge to a moderate height so as to be seen 12 or 14 leagues.' Captain Wilson logs the directions needed to find this exit from the Pacific by future mariners. 'About 4 miles within the Straits coming from the E'ward on the starboard side there is a Deep Cove where several canoes went in there is no Ground to be found in the Mid Channel with 120 fathoms of Line.' The channel was deep enough for the largest ship.

Pitt's Log holds a detailed description of the Pitt Straits.

They were using Hadley's Quadrant, allowing for the difference of the Declination and 'As we observe, and take our bearings with one of Morgan's Azimuth Compasses with the Horizontal Motion .... we have no reason to doubt the truth of our observations,' and he refers to Dampier returning from discovering New Britain.

Pitt's crew was interested in the local people. The ship's boats visited a village and 'Council house and ten houses all on pillars in the Malay fashion,' says Commodore Wilson, adding 'Their poverty was extreme.' *Pitt* sailed on, laden with chests of expensive china, she carried tea, silks, luxury, wealth. Yet full or empty it made little difference to her discomfort, 'She still in general…..labours in a heavy swell,' he says resignedly. *Pitt* it seems was a 'wallower' by nature. They were used to her foibles, her wobbles and lurches, and after two years they were on their way home. It was a matter of how many of them could survive.

Four months later, by Sunday, 9th December, 1759, *Pitt* had crossed the Indian ocean, sailed into the southern Atlantic and berthed at the island of St. Helena. They were unloading, careening and scrubbing the ship, moving 'Tea, Chinaware and pepper to Batton and secure the ceiling to prevent the pepper getting to the Timbers.' The *Warren,* Captain Scott, was there on a round trip to Madras. Four of *Pitt s* men went on shore without leave, and were caught. Next day they were Court Martialled on the *Warren.* Two days later, Captain Wilson consulted his officers about punishment for the prisoners, who all said the men needed flogging. So they were 'taken out of irons and given a dozen stripes each man with a Cat-'o'NineTails, except Wm. Cockerill who was released, it being adjudged he was not so riotous as the others, who were ordered back to their confinement.'

By 3rd February 1760, *Pitt* was standing in towards Kinsale in southern Ireland, contaminated and torn, one third of her crew dead.

Pitt sailed the English Channel and came up the Thames to Woolwich by 14th April 1760.

There was a new passage through to the Pacific! The voyage was a triumph, talked about for the rest of their lives, for William Wilson, Jeffrey Jackson, young William his brother, for their relatives in Yorkshire and for the East India Company Directors who awarded William Wilson a Gold Medal, showing Hercules astride the world.[6] For seagoing men, in Stepney and Wapping, in Deptford docks and Woolwich, and in coasting colliers, little coastal towns, dockside inns, it was something to wonder at. On Wapping quays the collier Cats of Whitby were arriving day in day out, passing the great battered ship *Pitt* as they came up river. Of course John Walker of Whitby would know about it. Did he write of it in letters to James Cook, who at that date was with the Royal Navy in north America?

Over tea in Great Ayton between old Mr. Skottowe, whose son Nicholas was an East India captain, and Augustine Skottowe, his wife Ann and her sister and brother-in-law, Mr. & Mrs. Sanderson of Staithes, it was something to amaze.

Commodore Wilson had found a new route to China, a new way through to, and out of, the Pacific!

William Wilson came home to his own private delight. His wife Rachel had presented him with his first living children, twin girls. He had never seen them. Hannah and Rachel were almost two years old. He left his ship on 28th April, four days before their second birthday party. He was never to command a great ship again. He retired from the sea, with fame and fortune. He was 44 years old.

We know William Wilson crewed on one later voyage in 1773, when he visited Staithes on a seaside holiday and the children, and their Uncle Ralph Jackson, went out in a coble with Mrs. Sanderson and her son John, sailing it to Runswick Bay for a picnic.

By 1762, William Wilson had given up his house at Maze Hill near Greenwich, and moved to live at Great Ayton, where he bought the mansion house lately vacated by old Thomas Skottowe. Commodore Wilson settled down to farming, neighbourliness and enjoying his children. He was one of those people whose energy was catching. He invented a seed drill, opened a colliery, burnt himself putting out a fire in the washhouse and, deciding Ralph Jackson was too slow to move the books into his new library, spent two days doing it himself. From 1762, William Wilson was a constant force in Ralph's daily life, and in constant touch with George Jackson. He and Rachel, looked after George's girls each summer, at Great Ayton.

William Wilson's fame lay in the discovery of Pitt's Strait.
George Jackson would certainly have seen the map and charts.
And from 1762, the people of Great Ayton, like James Cook's father, would know of the Commodore's reason for fame, that it rested on a route through to, and from, the Pacific. By 1768 it would look like vital knowledge for James Cook.

Yet Pitt's Strait was not easy. Ship's captains were not enamoured of it. During 1761, nine Company ships arrived in China. Two, the *Princess Augusta* and the *Caenarvon* were despatched home on 8th July, and had set out to sail by Pitt's Strait, but put back dismasted to Macao in mid October, with three months lost.

Even by 1771 the eastern Pacific route operating by Pitt's Strait, though in use, was not taken lightly. The *British King* arriving in March had come that way, but when the Council wished to send her, against the south-west Monsoon, by the same way home, her commander objected:

'Having duly weigh'd the great wear and tear of Sails Cables and loss of anchors the Ship has sustain'd in her Navigation of the Eastern Passage, I think it not for the Interest of the Hon'ble company she should return that way.'

Part of the problem was the lack of copies of the chart:

The *Bute* was despatched from Madras, 18th September, 1770 and the Council wished she should proceed by the Eastern Passage or Pitt's Track; her commander demurred, as he had been provided no charts for that route; she arrived in Canton on 13th July, 1771. The same reason was given why the *Stafford* should not take that route. In consequence the Canton Council sent to Madras a set of the charts.

Before his later voyages, Captain Cook searched for up-to-date charts, visiting the Tower military surveyors and London bookshops. Surely, in 1768 such a careful navigator would do the same. Master Cook would undoubtedly know of the chart of Pitt's Track. George Jackson was efficient enough not to withhold the knowledge, and William Wilson was of the practical, open nature to offer to show it to him.

If and when James Cook visited Great Ayton, it could be he had seen the detailed chart of Pitt's Strait, a certain way out of the Pacific to Batavia. James Cook's mother died in 1765. His father was 70 in 1768. It would be surprising if he did not come to Great Ayton before leaving on a three year journey into the unknown.

Doubts and fears must have been old Mr. Cook's. Of two men he could consult, each had had an opposite experience: his old employer Squire Thomas Skottowe, and his son's old employer, William Sanderson. The East India experience, was very different for these two fathers: one of success, one of loss and sadness.

To get a true picture of James Cook we must place him in his local context, among The East India Company families of Cleveland: the Skottowes, the Wards, the Jacksons, the Wilsons and the Sandersons. Most of them had seen triumph and wealth, some had suffered loss.

~~~

THE EAST INDIA COMPANY FAMILIES

ENVOY TO THE CELESTIAL EMPEROR OF CHINA

The *Success* with William Wilson's crew had disappeared.

The worried Honourable East India Company was forced to act, to try to free their envoy Mr. Flint, embarrassingly imprisoned at Macao, caged in view for all of the arriving European ships. The Company drew up a new Petition to the Emperor and entrusted it to a fast ship. Her captain was to put himself forward 'as brother to an Under-Secretary of State', he was Captain Nicholas Skottowe, son of Thomas Skottowe of Great Ayton.

His ship the *Royal George*[7] sailed up the Pearl river to Canton on 12th August, 1761. His Petiton was sent off to the Celestial Emperor. No answer came. No request by Europeans had any effect. Mr. Flint remained in prison. Captain Skottowe remained outside Canton. Officials kept him hanging about so long the Company's Council decided it was hopeless; they decided to send him away to Madras and home. He left on 17th December. They probably saved his life.

An answer refusing to free Mr. Flint arrived one month later.

In Britain there had been a political overturn. Early on the morning of 25th October 1760, 78 year old King George II died, on the lavatory, poor old man. The English, at least, had settled for this German born monarch, whose main fault seemed to be that he wanted them to protect his ancestral province of Hanover. The heir was his grandson, a tall fair and shy young man of 22, devoted to his tutor Lord Bute, both of them were determined he would rule over Britain as a true King. Neither liked Mr. Pitt. There were to be new ministers, new policies, bringing uncertainty perhaps with the war not yet over but, underneath that, a feeling of hope and dreams of future prosperity ran through the country. Canada had been grabbed, there were great gains in India, the Royal Navy felt they could rule the seas. There was much to celebrate.

It took nearly a year for news of a new King to reach China. Their celebrations at Canton were a shade late. But they were just in time for Captain Nicholas Skottowe to take part.

Oct. 31st 1761. 'This day we set apart for the observation of his Majesty's Accession and invit'd all the foreigners, except the french, the Comm's of ours and their Ships & the China Merch's'.

On Nov. 9th they got the bill.

'The Compradore brought us an Account of the Expence of this Entertainment given to about 60 Gentlemen on his Majesty's Accession Viz.

For provision & Utensils for ye Table	Taels	85
For ornaments for the Hall & Veranda Lanthoms		
Commedians & Fireworks		143
For Wine Clarret 8 Doz		69
	Taels	297
	[about	£99]

CAPTAIN NICHOLAS SKOTTOWE
of the *Royal George*

Three years later, on 12th December, 1764, Captain Nicholas Skottowe, son of Thomas Skottowe Esq. of Great Ayton, again entered his ship the *Royal George* in London river. A smaller and faster East India merchant ship, of around 400 tons, she was making ready for sea. This new commercial voyage would last three years, to 'Bencoolen, Banjar, Batavia, Bally, Balambovang, Moco Moco,' trading in spices and cottons, pepper and pearls. The trip would take them into debilitating humidity, virulent disease, tropical storms, danger and death. The financial rewards were great, both for the Company and for the ship's captain. His private trade could set up Nicholas Skottowe for life.

As he walked the deck in the winter cold, the raw wind off the Thames scouring the faces of the dock workers, now 34 year old

Nicholas Skottowe could be reassured by his previous two voyages as her captain. His first had been the dash as envoy to China via Madras and Calcutta, his second to Calcutta and back and, of course, there had been all the voyages before that as he worked his way up to captain the *Royal George,* the only ship actually owned by the East India Company, which was why he was entrusted with important and secret tasks.

On this voyage the *Royal George* carried a crew of 77 and 15 Lascars; of these Indian seamen 1 would die, 2 run away, and 2 be discharged at Bencoolen in Sumatra. Of the main crew 24 were to die on the voyage, in other words a death rate of 'the normal third'.

On board were four mates, Chief Mate John Tolme would die at Bencoolen in August 1766. There was Thomas Barnes 'cook to the slaves' discharged there. And there was the captain's relative by marriage, William Sanderson, aged 20, Ship's Surgeon, son of Mr. William Sanderson of Staithes.

The ship warped out of her dock and moored downriver to take on ballast, stores, coals, oil, pitch, water butts, hogsheads of salt beef and pork. She had to be self-sufficient, there would be passengers to entertain, important officers coming aboard; the captain would need his silver, his personal servants, his clerk. Administration of such a long trading voyage demanded hard work and vigilance, and stubborn bravery.

It took them a year to reach their destinations, bright seas, clusters of islands, difficult channels. The climate was humid and overwhelming, the ports foetid, the islands heavy with mysterious jungle. Slight dark-skinned people seemed immune to the fevers which brought to the ship's unprotected Europeans, sickness and death. Passengers came on board island-hopping. At Bencoolen on 7th October 1765, the family of four of J. Darvell Esq.* joined the ship with their six native servants, for its voyage to Moco Moco. The Sultan's son and his five servants came aboard too, and important agents of the East India company with their own servants, and three Malay linguists, and a group of soldiers

* *Darvell Bay can be found today in north-east Borneo.*

Leaving Bencoolen on the homeward leg on 9th September 1766, Captain Skottowe took on more soldiers 'to assist working ye ship,' the Chief mate and too many crew had died. At Batavia, that malarial port and notorious fever hole, they had taken on two seamen, Thomas Faie and John Brennan. The ship's surgeon William Sanderson was faced with the problems, in contact with the risk of dysentry, unknown tropical diseases, fevers, ulcerous scurvy At 5pm on 8th February, Gehard Mearns, the Captain's servant died, at 10 pm the next day Thomas Faie died. On 17th February, 1767 Captain Nicholas Skottowe wrote:

'At 3 am died Mr. William Sanderson Surgeon at S[ea] Committed the body to the deep.'

Two days later John Brennan died. The young Surgeon may have caught what had killed them, the small neat handwriting of Nicholas Skottowe does not say.

William Sanderson had been 22 years old; he was the baby who had been born in Staithes, when James Cook worked for his father in the shop.

On his return to England, a Company captain was responsible for 'dead men's effects'. As a relative by marriage it was Captain Skottowe's duty to visit Staithes to pay his sad condolences to William's parents, Mr. and Mrs. Sanderson. William's name is entered on their tombstone in the parish churchyard.

So, just before James Cook was appointed to the *Endeavour* in 1768, the Sandersons learned they had lost their son William. James Cook's father, at Great Ayton, was bound to know. Mrs. Sanderson's sister was married to Augustine Skottowe, living at Great Ayton.

By contrast, the Squire's son, Captain Nicholas Skottowe had returned to Great Ayton rich. He had completed the magical three voyages in command of an East Indiaman. There appears to have been an unspoken idea that three was the necessary number to secure a man's name and fortune. Perhaps this attitude affected James Cook's decision to make his third voyage of discovery which proved fatal? None of us are totally free of the conventions of our time.

Captain Skottowe stayed at home for two years, living probably in Hertfordshire, but regularly at Great Ayton. He was visiting there in October 1768 but we do not know if he had met James Cook.

Nicholas then offered the Company the ship *Bridgewater* sailing it twice more to China and once to Madras. He must have doubled his wealth. He retired from sea aged 45: another convention?

His elder brother John Skottowe, by 1767 had established himself in the Company's service, on the island of St. Helena. He was Deputy Governor when he entertained Captain Cook there in 1773, and Governor of the Island 1780-1782.

So, the Skottowes, Wards, Wilsons and the Sandersons were more East India navy families, than Royal Navy families. They knew riches and fame came at great risk. They had high connections, with those at the top level of the Company in London, influential men, whose power and experienced voices could back their choices for voyages to the Pacific. And they were all linked to George Jackson.

The Honorable Company was led by its Directors. George Jackson's cousin Captain Edward Ward had been a Director, and there were others up and coming to back James Cook. Men like the Lascelles brothers and William James.

CAPTAIN PETER 'BOMBAY' LASCELLES

'June 25, [1767] In a course of continual visits
and Invitations here *[Skelton Castle in Cleveland]*-
Bombay Lascelles dined here today - (his Wife
yesterday brought to bed) - (he is a poor sorry soul)
but has taken a house two miles from Crasy Castle-
What a stupid, selfish, unsentimental set of Beings are
the Bulk of our Sex! ... '
.... *said Lawrence Sterne writing in his 'Journal to Eliza*[8]

The late Captain Edward Ward, had commanded the *York* East Indiaman as early as 1754, and taken soldiers to Madras.

Peter Lascelles was then his Chief Mate. At the end of that voyage, Peter Lascelles took over. He was *York's* Captain for her next three voyages, in 1757, 1760 and 1764 sailing as far as Mocha, Bombay, Telicherry and China.

During these years, he often stayed with his brother, the Reverend Robert Lascelles at Skelton Castle. Mr. Ward met them, late in 1756, going to Stockton Races. Peter Lascelles' last voyage ended officially on 20th August, 1766.

On August 9th 1766, Ralph Jackson visiting London says, that he and his brother George Jackson, Messrs. Masterman & Duck[from Marske] 'went down to Deptford with the Rev. Mr. Lascelles and dined aboard the York Indiaman.'

By November, Peter Lascelles had moved into his house at Marske, with his pregnant wife, ready to take part in Cleveland life, hunting and shooting with his brother Robert, and dining with the sophisticated 'Demoniacs' literary club at Skelton Castle.

Rev. Robert 'Panty' Lascelles,* was nicknamed, it is said, from Rabelais' story of the giant Pantagruel, who voyaged with the hero Xenomanes 'the great traveler across perilous routes' who 'had mapped out…… in his great universal hydrography, the route they would take' in his mock-heroic sea-going adventures. It implies that Captain Peter was a popular raconteur, interested in maps, ocean hydrography and exploring.

He became a Director of the East India Company. With his home in Cleveland, he lived partly in London, and was closely associated with the Director William James. Both men were friends of George Jackson.

'I breakfasted with Rev. Mr. Lascelles and his Bro. the Captain at their Chambers in the Temple', says Ralph Jackson:

London. August, 1766.
* In northern England 'Pant' is the name for a drinking fountain.

Peter Lascelles was popular in the Company, and supported by family links in the chartering of Company ships, such as the *York,* even before he became a Director. He and William James could give powerful weight to William Wilson's patronage of James Cook, and strong advice to George Jackson about the proposed *Endeavour* voyage.

It is William James who links together the East India and Royal Navy men in Captain Cook's story.

SIR WILLIAM JAMES
1721 – 1783

Commodore William James had been commander of the Bombay Marine, the private fighting navy of the East India Company.

His portrait by Reynolds gives him a watchful but agreeable face. He had no formal education but great ability. By temperament, he was both affable and audacious. The tales of his origins are highly decorative, and we begin to think he encouraged them. Even his best friend Wraxall was baffled. They ranged from, being born a Welsh ploughboy, Royal Navy service in the West Indies, command of a brig trading to Virginia, capture by pirates, shipwreck, and a marriage to the landlady of the Red Cow at Wapping. All tall tales?

James Cook of course was a farmboy, and did marry the daughter of the landlady of the Bell Tavern at Wapping.

William James surfaces in reality as Chief Mate to Captain William Wilson on the *Suffolk* East Indiaman, in 1748. He could not have received a better induction to the needs of the India service. Whereas William Wilson exchanged the positive dangers of a ship of war, for the more certain rewards of the merchant service, William James saw his future in prize money, gained from the Company's fighting ships, and Captain Wilson recommended him for this appointment.

In 1750 William James commanded the *Guardian* leading a small squadron to protect East India ships and country traders, from the Angria 'pirates' along the west coast of India. To the British, all the

Company ships were a piece of Britain. The frigate-like Indian gurabhs of the Indian rulers were trying to assert control over their own territorial waters, but even to the Indian princes, the 'pirates' were not exactly legitimate. The new song 'Rule Britannia', sung by sailors, defying slavery, was apt and necessary off the Indian coast. Britain, and William James, decided to rule the waves.

The Angria 'pirates' were completely out of hand. They would sail up the wake of a Company ship, avoiding a broadside, swarming up between the guns. Commodore James determined to beat them, make his own fortune, and secure the west coast of India for British shipping.

On the *Protector* with 44 guns, he sailed into their strongholds and demolished their forts. A less pragmatic man would not have dared. His bravery cannot be in doubt. He was a first rate pilot who, by blowing up the supposedly impregnable fort at Severndroog, exploded the idea that any Indian ruler could escape retribution. The Angria's power was broken, the Indian princes flustered.

Early in 1757, news of the French Declaration of War reached Bombay on the west coast. To protect Madras on the east coast of India, the news had to reach Admiral Watson, whose Royal Navy squadron was at Calcutta. But at that season of the year, sailing against the Monsoon wind, a voyage around the "V" of India was thought impossible. Commodore James volunteered to try. He had studied the seasonal Monsoon wind patterns. He ran south to 10° below the Equator, sailed due east to Sumatra and, having circled the obstinate Monsoon in the Bay of Bengal, ran north to Calcutta in record time, to inform Watson and Clive.

He was hailed as a hero.

In 1759 Commodore James returned to England basking in prize money and rewards. He bought a country estate near Eltham, and a handsome town house in Gerrard Street, Soho, and married Anne Goddard, a beautiful and 'interesting' woman with a sentimental heart. When he died in 1783 she erected a Tower in his memory on Shooters Hill, near Eltham. It is still there.

Severndroog Castle, as it was named, was dubbed 'Lady James Folly'. The original Severndroog 'castle', shown in Robert Orme's painting, was a fortress built deep into the domed rock of an island in the middle of a cove. The Folly, very much of its romantic time, set up at a high point on Shooters Hill to provide a 'vista', is an unlikely three-sided Norman castle keep. Yet three sides are very appropriate. Lady James, stood at the centre of three great romances.

Firstly, her own. Secondly, George Jackson's happy marriage to his second wife, whose family owned the next door estate to Lady James' family in Hertfordshire. Thirdly, Lady James facilitated a renowned literary love affair: that between Eliza Draper, an entrancing young married English woman from Bombay, and the famous comic author Laurence Sterne, a lascivious long-married Yorkshire vicar, who was dying of TB. Eliza Draper provided the stimulus for him to write 'Sentimental Education', an erotic work of perfect prose. It was probably Lady James who provided the sentiment.

The realistic Eliza left them all to return to India, to a morose unfaithful husband, worried about her debts.

She left England on a company ship[9] on 3rd April 1767, Laurence Sterne was to join the James's to visit her at Deal. Eliza played the piano and guitar, Sterne sent her a hammer to tune her wires, brass hooks for her cabin, to hang her 'necessaries' upon, iron screws for the globes, and asked the Deal pilot to provide her an armchair. By 18th the ship had gone, and he was writing to her. Lady James instructed him how to send letters overland by Venice and Bussorah (Basra). He pestered Lady James with his languishing love, writing to Eliza:

'Was with our faithful friend this morning and dined with her and James. What is the Cause, that I can never talk about my Eliza to her, but I am rent in pieces? I burst into tears a dozen different times after dinner, (amid such affectionate gusts of passion, that she was ready to leave the room, and sympathise in private for us. I weep for you both, said she in a whisper).......... James was occupied in reading a pamphlet upon the East India affairs.'

Who can blame him? And was Lady James trying not to laugh?

Laurence Sterne was famous for his comic talent. It is April, and he has already started writing his sentimental and maudlin, 'Journal to Eliza.' Yet the title for 'Sentimental Journey' had been chosen two months earlier, in February 1767. Was he writing to Eliza to speed himself up, for his real work?

'Sentimental Journey' was published in February 1768, and proved another publishing sensation. There may have been a copy on board *Endeavour.* Lieut. Gore may have had one, for a Miss Gore (who may have been the Miss Gore, a beauty Sterne met at Bath) was one of the subscribers. Perhaps there was also on board, a copy of Sterne's famous comic novel 'Tristram Shandy' with its comment on travel to make Captain Cook and the gentlemen laugh:

'I think it very much amiss - that a man cannot go quietly through a town and let it alone, when it does not meddle with him.'

For 'through a town' read 'around the world'.

Tristram Shandy Vol VII Ch. iv.

William James, became a Director of the East India Company in 1768. As a close friend of William Wilson (Ralph Jackson called him 'Brother Wilson's shipmate'), William James often dined with George Jackson. He had the power to command the East India men to help Captain Cook, anywhere from London, St. Helena, India, to China.

And it was William James, who had earlier linked George Jackson to Alexander Dalrymple.

14

NEW LIMITS?
ALEXANDER DALRYMPLE
1737 - 1808

From 1762 to 1768, James Cook was not living in a vacuum. The world around him was changing. Other people were surging forward for position. Ideas on surveying, navigation, exploration and science were expanding. One of them with expanded ideas was Alexander Dalrymple.[1]

There are three ways of thinking of Alexander Dalrymple. One is to treat him as the fly in the ointment of Captain Cook's fame. The opposite, is to believe the knowledgeable, but hot-tempered Alexander who thought he had been robbed of command of the *Endeavour* voyage. And, to be fair, we must ask the question, was he? The third way is to balance the facts, to seek the truth of what happened and, perhaps, find both these views compatible?

Sir James and Lady Dalrymple were part of Edinburgh society. They produced 16 living children in 20 years, of whom Sandy was the 11th child and 7th son. The Dalrymples were a loving, outspoken family; their mother was a stickler for truth and family arguments were based on evidence. The Dalrymples were fiercely clannish. Most were pushy. Sandy added to the mix his own abrasive temper, generosity, and friends; many kept for life.

Alexander (Sandy) was born in 1737 and would expect to be educated as a gentleman of Scots society but, aged 8, the whole family fled south during the 1745 Jacobite Rebellion.

As a seventh son, in spite of being grandson to an Earl, Sandy had to make his own fortune. The heir, his eldest brother David, Eton and Cambridge educated, was a scholarly quiet Scots lawyer, a friend on the legal circuit of James Boswell, but inclined to be shy. Sandy abrasively informed David that he refused to attend the French school in Edinburgh to learn the language of his King's enemies! So David kindly brought him south to London to learn accountancy, in the hope of becoming a writer in the East India Company. They sent him to India at age 15, the Company reckoning that, if he survived the voyage, he would be 16, and old enough for their service when he got there.

The year was 1752. The *Suffolk,* bound for India under Captain William Wilson, was loading at Gravesend when young Sandy Dalrymple asked to come aboard. Immediately, Captain Wilson refused to take him, his passenger list was full. William James, Captain Wilson's ex-chief mate, being acquainted with Sandy's uncle, General St. Clair, persuaded Captain Wilson to find room for the boy. Knowing the practical William Wilson, he probably put Sandy to good use, in this first experience of ocean sailing.

The *Suffolk* left England at the end of December, arriving at Madras in May. Sandy, a boy alone in a strange country, faced social disaster; all those to whom he had letters of introduction were dead, apart from one who was a drunkard. Captain Wilson had taken a house ashore for a month, when he heard of Sandy's predicament. In his cheerful way he took pity on his youth and gave him lodgings.

We can picture the delicious breeze of a hot Madras afternoon, 38 year old William Wilson, pouring over a collection of old charts and sailing directions, planning his onward voyage to China, while outside on the brilliant dark sea, across the white sand, ships of all kinds, from all parts of the east, rode at anchor; and the imaginative Sandy looking from one to the other. Maybe the sailor laughed and said, 'Come and see,' and the intelligent boy realised at first hand that the Pacific was a blank, that there were no complete maps of the Indies and beyond. Perhaps it was there in May 1753, he first wondered what lay far out in the Pacific on that side of the world?

Captain Wilson and the *Suffolk* sailed away from Madras leaving Sandy behind, to sink or swim. The lonely boy started his clerical work, but his writing was so bad that, with no-one to support him, he was quickly demoted to work in a storeroom; and there he might have been forgotten and died of fever, had not a new Governor of Madras, George Pigot, arrived in 1755 and rescued him. Sandy was told to learn to write precisely. He did, a perfect copy of George Pigot's handwriting. Slowly, the boy recovered from his fear and despair and began to take an interest in the old records of Madras which he was copying. Robert Orme, the Madras Accountant, a refined older man with academic leanings who was later to become famous for his History of Hindustan, allowed Sandy the full use of his library. Two years passed and, by May 1757 Sandy, newly promoted to Deputy Secretary and with fresh hope of succeeding one day, began a slow systematic record of the vast number of Company documents at Madras. He was neat, he was orderly, he was listing them faithfully but their contents fascinated him. He used his time well, though the task could take years.

But the French were restless. War was declared in Europe. William James, now Commodore of the Company's fighting ships, arrived on the coast with news that the Seven Years War had finally broken out. The French attacked in India. Madras came under siege. Day after day their guns poured destruction into the fortified town. One killed William Roberts, who had been a Company SuperCargo on discrete voyages to Manila. With speed in their extreme plight, his effects were sold off. Sandy bought some Spanish histories of the Philippines.

His ideas were beginning to crystalise. If he could survive the bombardment, the war and the fever, there were great adventures, great projects to take on. His ideas were in fact the seeds of the future British Empire, which shows the breadth of his young imagination. He was now nearly 21, grown up, so politeness required the use of his proper name, Alexander. If he survived in India, he could make his fortune ten times over. Hope, adventure, the unlimited visions of youth exhilarated him.

The siege lifted, largely due to the extra troops brought by Colonel William Draper. When the huge ship *Pitt* commanded by Commodore William Wilson anchored with the rest of Draper's soldiers, the French left in a hurry. Once more there were meetings ashore. Commodore Wilson was anxious to be off, he had missed the season to sail north through the China Sea. Once more there was great discussion by the men and leaning over charts. Could the Monsoon winds be defeated? Commodore James had circled around them, to bring the news of the war. Alexander Dalrymple produced for William Wilson the work of John Saris (1616) who had taken a circular route through the Indies to Japan. Was it possible to sail around the head-on Monsoon wind in the China Sea, at that season of the year? We can imagine the young Alexander, head bent over the charts, alongside the three professional sailors, Joseph and Jeffrey Jackson, *Pitt's* 1st and 2nd Mate, with William Wilson weatherbeaten and longsighted, weighing up his responsibility for the Company's largest ever new ship. Sir George Pigot was consulted. They decided to give circle sailing a try.

William Wilson sailed *Pitt* off into fame, solving the problem of access all year round to China. Alexander stayed behind pondering that other stumbling block to China trade, the strangle-hold of the Hong merchants at Canton. What was needed was a British freeport, free of the Chinese, free of the Dutch at Batavia, of the Spanish at Manila, a freeport where ships of the Company could meet ships of any nation to unload and load without import/export duties. Alexander's vision was the early version of Sir Stamford Raffles vision, which would later create Singapore.

Alexander thought the right place for his freeport would be Mindanao in the South Philippines. He was young and no longer content with book learning. He asked Governor George Pigot's permission to follow *Pitt* to chart the islands. One night at dinner, Captain Thomas Howe of the Company ship W*inchelsea,* heard the young man's theories and invited Alexander to join his ship as far as Malacca; there he could pick up the smaller *Cuddalore* for a surveying adventure.

Colonel Draper was also leaving on *Winchelsea.* His health had declined during the siege. He intended to return slowly to England, via China. Perhaps catching Alexander's enthusiasm, he set himself to study the Philippines.

During the voyage to Malacca, Captain Thomas Howe who was brother to Lord Howe of the Admiralty, taught Alexander the fundamentals of seamanship. By the time he joined Captain George Baker on the *Cuddalore* he was able to put it to use. They spent over two years among the islands. He returned to Madras in 1762, triumphant in his own eyes, with hundreds of details, surveys, maps, charts, depth soundings and a chosen place for a new freeport, a much better place - Sulu.

Others were impressed too, including the objective intelligent Kempenfelt,[2] who said, 'Mr. Pigot was very happy in his choice of this young Gentleman for such a Service, as he is a person of Good Education Quick parts and Talents naturally adapted for such an Employ'. Kempenfelt also remarked upon Alexander's depth of enquiry and attention to the Company's interest. The plan grew, pushed by Alexander, to send him back to the islands to establish a trading centre on the Company's behalf. He planned to sail with Captain Nicholas Skottowe on the *Royal George,* who was anchored at Madras.

But Captain Skottowe was headed directly for China as fast as he could, to plead for the release of Mr. Flint from prison in Macao. At the last minute Alexander switched to a small ship the *London* paquet, which called at many harbours.

He sailed away from India, from positive promotion and wealth. He was only 24 and filled with fiery enthusiasm for a developing, expanding world. Accompanied by James Rennel, who was to become a lifelong friend as well as Surveyor General of Bengal, they searched, surveyed, negotiated treaties, and finally took possession of a superbly situated island, Balambangan off the northern tip of Borneo. They could proceed no further; this was an acquisition of territory for which approval of the British Government was needed, for it would have to be defended, by both the Army and Royal Navy. In 1764, Alexander Dalrymple, who hoped to make Balambangan his permanent home, sailed home to England to argue his case.

He had spent seven years surveying, navigating, and laying the foundation of seamanship which would eventually, after many other plans went awry, lead him to become the first great Hydrographer of the Navy, who would map the seas, and so bring eternal gratitude from generations of sailors.

He landed in England in the following July, with his future uncertain, yet filled with fervour for his great idea. By September 1765 he was at Great Ayton visiting Commodore Wilson.

George Jackson was also there, on his holidays.

Alexander Dalrymple was three weeks too late. Already, his great idea had been undermined. George Jackson and William Wilson had just learned the truth, first hand, about Manila, in the Philippines. And what had happened there at the end of the Seven Years War in 1762. The lesson of Manila is a reason Alexander Dalrymple failed.

~~~

MANILA[3]
1762

Britain's two-pronged attack, on Manila in the East Indies and Havana in the West Indies, was meant to give Spain a warning punch on the nose. To stop her joining France in the war against Britain. Lord Anson was nearing the end of his life. He attacked to win the Peace.

At first glance, the Manila attack seems have nothing to do with Captain James Cook. Yet the Manila expedition in 1762 shaped his voyage on the *Endeavour* in 1768. In spite of public jubilation, at British ability to take Manila, on the other side of the world, it showed the Royal Navy they would be over-extended, to protect a vast new continent in far-eastern oceans. Captain Cook's future voyages would cause the Admiralty to heave a sigh of relief, when he showed the Pacific to be largely empty.

But in 1762 many people believed in a great Southern Continent. Its possible existence horrified the Government. Were it to fall into the hands of France or Spain, its wealth could pour into those countries, fund another Spanish Armada, bring invasion or commercial ruin to Britain.

Fears arose early in 1761, when France and Spain signed the Third Family Compact, their thrones being occupied by members of the same family. If Spain were to join France in her war against Britain, then the American colonies, India, and the China trade, all so recently secured by victories in the war, would be under threat once more.

The 1st Lord of the Admiralty, the old sea dog Lord Anson, determined on action even before the Spanish showed their colours. He would demonstrate to them that the British Navy could attack Spanish wealth anywhere in the world. He would capture Havana, which was central to Spanish America, the fulcrum port of their treasure trade. And British troops would conquer Manila, central to Spain's 'South Sea' interests: it was the silver bullion port of the far east, the funding centre for the spice trade and trade with China.

Nowhere, was to be outside the Royal Navy's reach.

On 30th December, 1761, the Directors of the East India Company gathered in London. Their Chairman reported that he 'had yesterday a conference with Lord Anson, when His Lordship was pleased to say that the government had an intention to order an attack to be made upon Manila and desired to know what assistance the Company could give therein ....'

On Wednesday, 4th January, war was declared with Spain.

In the wintry days of 8th to 15th, the Secret Committee of the East India Company and Lord Anson, settled on a war plan to shock Spain back into peace. The Secret Committee approved Lord Anson's project of attacking Havana. It was the Secretary of State, Lord Egremont, who introduced the plan of his own protege, Colonel Draper, for taking Manila. This was also approved.

William Draper MA was 41 years old, his family long involved with the East India Company. He was a scholar, educated at Bristol Grammar School, Eton, and King's College Cambridge, where he became a fellow until 1756, when he married.

In 1757, it was the same William Draper who had raised a regiment of 1000 foot soldiers to sail to the rescue of Madras on the *Pitt*, under Commodore Wilson. During the spirited defence of Madras, William Draper grew well acquainted with the Governor George Pigot, and young Alexander Dalrymple. After the siege, William Draper's health broke. He knew the odds: most newly arrived Europeans died within three years of reaching India. He sailed for home, via China, on the *Winchelsea*, along with Alexander Dalrymple, who was going to join the *Cuddalore* to survey the islands. Colonel Draper spent much of his own voyage studying the Philippines, finding them perfectly placed strategically, but weakly defended. In 1761, and war with Spain imminent, Colonel Draper back in England, felt obliged to give this information to the King's Ministers; the King was impressed by his suggested plan.

Draper's plan was in two stages. Firstly, to capture Manila to cut off all trade 'betwixt the E.Indies and the Spanish America provinces'. A Governor from the East India Company would take over Manila from Colonel Draper's troops. Half of the invading troops would be supplied by the army in India.

Secondly, the plan was to found a base on another Philippine island (Mindano say the King's orders) which would become a major port on the China route, to rival the Dutch freeport of Batavia on Java, and break the Chinese merchant's monopoly at Canton. It sounds like pure Dalrymple.

The whole plan was too neat, maybe too intellectual.

Even before he sailed on 21st January, part of Colonel Draper's orders were obsolete. No-one appears to have told him that Mindanao, which had been suggested to the King by the Secret Committee, had already been surveyed by Alexander Dalrymple, who had found the harbours too shallow. Jolo was now the centre of Dalrymple's passion. The Minutes of the Directors of the East India Company for 19th January, two days before Draper sailed, show that 'a treaty having been made by Mr. Dalrymple of the Fort of St. George [Madras] establishment, employed from thence on discoveries, with the Sultan of Xolo [Jolo]'; the Madras Governor, George Pigot, was ordered to follow up this advantage.

The conquest of Manila would be a victory yet fated. For the British Army it was a fiasco. Nearly everyone involved, intended it to be temporary. Yet it made Spain hesitate. It exposed the over-stretched British forces. It put large amounts of treasure in the wrong pockets. And, incidentally, it provided the Royal Navy with details of the difficult Embrocadero passage out of the Pacific which, six years later, would make Pitt's Track even more attractive to Captain Cook

The Manila Plan began to go wrong as soon as William Draper, now a Brigadier-General, arrived in India to collect the promised other half of this troops. In a vast country seething with disease, there were hardly any soldiers. The figures shocked him, they were he said 'mortifying'. Of only 1,567 rank and file at Madras, 898 were sick. Two-thirds of the men were French deserters 'impossible to trust'. The 7000 Seapoys, he reported 'are ill disciplined'. As troops, 'such banditti had never been seen since the time of Spartacus.'

It ought not to have surprised him. He had been in Madras before. The greed and deceit of many East India Company officials was beyond belief. Of the troops who had saved them from the French in 1759, most could not get home to Britain unless they paid the Company's agents £100 for a passage. An Army captain earned about £60 a year. Many of the troops headed for Manila, had no hope of ever getting back to Europe.

Neither did the Company officials in India want the Manila expedition to succeed. They had a lucrative private trade with the Spanish at Manila and, at that very moment, had at sea a ship worth £70,000 hidden, reported General Draper 'under Moorish colours'. The merchants, secretly, had been buying Spanish silver from Manila to ease their own currency crisis in the China trade. The Manila expedition became a struggle as to who ended up with the Spanish silver.

There was a fatal error in the orders from London. They were ambiguous regarding treasure and booty; they said 'a moiety' (a part) was to go to the troops and to the Company. William Draper found himself defending his right to decide on one-third each to the Army, Royal Navy and Company. Governor Pigot said half to the Company, half to the invasion forces. In this tussle he allowed the Council to send as prospective Governor of Manila, Dawson Drake, one of the most venal greedy treacherous men the Company had ever employed. Any honourable behaviour by the King's officers was thwarted before they acted.

There was anxiety in George Pigot. He needed fit men to protect Madras and east India. He agreed to co-operate on General Draper's 'assurances you give us that the greatest part of the squadron and land forces will be brought back by the end of January.'

On this basis, the invasion force sailed. For eight weeks, they sped eastward on 'an agreeable passage', said Admiral Sam Cornish, who led the Royal Navy fleet. His thirteen ships, included the 60 gun *HMS Elizabeth*, the 50 gun *HMS Falmouth,* and the frigate *HMS Seaford,* whose Captain John Peighin we will meet later. They hove over the horizon before Manila on 23rd September 1762, just as the Monsoon rains broke. Manila town was surprised, puzzled, indignant, as the British warships sailed into the bay to attack. Manila merchants could not believe it.

Military conquest of the town was completed, in pouring rain, and squelching mud, within 13 days. There were a few awful atrocities but no large loss of life. It was only six weeks before General Draper handed over to the venal Dawson Drake Esq. He did not consult Admiral Cornish, who was loud in protest that the island had not been secured. But William Draper was a gentleman who had given his word to return to India by the end of January with most of his troops. So he ransomed Manila for £1 million, a sum impossible to achieve in the town. Richly decorated Roman Catholic churches were stripped, private fortunes confiscated, rings torn from wealthy ladies, merchant's wharehouses emptied, anything and everything grabbed. Finally admitting there was not enough, General Draper was forced to accept the equivalent of a cheque, payable in Madrid. Of course, there was hope in the silver bullion ship, now due from the Americas, when it arrived, if it arrived.

Dawson Drake Esq. had been quick to undermine His Majesty's forces. The surrender guaranteed the defeated Spanish Governor his furniture and personal effects. General Draper stormed into the house when he found these had been packed in chests marked 'Rice for Governor Drake'; but they still ended up with Drake in India.

Admiral Cornish was unable to intervene. He was under his own orders from the Admiralty, to seek out the treasure ship.

Each year, two Spanish treasure galleons crossed the Pacific from Mexico to Manila, laden with silver. Controlling the coinage, fixed Spain's power in the Far East and China. To capture the galleons was to cut out Spain. The Spanish treasure would pay for the British expedition, and make prize money for the men.

On the other side of the world in London, Lord Anson had a cold eye on those galleons. As a young man, he had made his own name and fortune by capturing one off the Philippines, when he had led a courageous crossing of the Pacific in 1740-44, a crossing so dreadful that the lessons bit deep, and those men who survived it, like Anson, Charles Saunders, Augustus Keppel and Hyde Parker, were seamen to the bone.

Now October 1762 in Manila, Admiral Cornish sent the warship *HMS Panther* under Captain Hyde Parker, and the frigate *HMS Argo*, under Captain King, to look for the treasure galleon due from Acapulco. The two ships waited at the exit of the Embrocadero, the channel by which the treasure galleons entered the islands from the Pacific. 'Just as the day closed', they saw a sail, and stood to northward of it, but around 8 in the evening *HMS Panther* was caught in a dangerous counter current. *HMS Argo* attacked alone, to little effect, it was daylight before *HMS Panther* could come up. The Spanish galleon was so huge and strong, even *HMS Panther's* guns could not penetrate her hull. Yet the galleon struck to the British, because only 13 of her 60 guns were mounted and able to fire. Then, says Captain Hyde Parker he 'was no less disappointed than surprised' to find he had taken a near empty galleon the *Santissima Trinidada* which had left Manila on 1st August, and was returning dismasted for repairs after a Pacific storm. She was the wrong ship!

All the same, she was one of the largest ships the British had ever seen, which says something for Captain King's courage. A prize now, at over 2000 tons, she drew 28 feet of water. They brought her in to Manila. General Draper reported excitedly to the Secretary of War on 22nd November 1762: 'PS. We have taken a galeon worth four hundred thousand pounds.' She arrived in England as a prize, to amaze Plymouth on 9th June, 1763.

Captain Hyde Parker meanwhile had informed Admiral Sam Cornish about the Embrocadero, that 'the navigation is very dangerous for large ships', like his. Sam Cornish despatched the *Argo* and the small *Seaford,* under Captain John Peighin, to find the correct treasure galleon *Phillipina.* And it was Captain Peighin who would, early on his return to Britain, visit Great Ayton.

General Draper had his promise as a gentleman to fulfil. In mid November he left Manila with many of the troops, leaving behind a scattered weak soldiery, an insecure peace, a horribly traitorous Governor Drake. Admiral Cornish could see anarchy breaking out all around him on land, but he had to follow his Admiralty orders and find the treasure ship with its cargo of silver. He reported: 'On 15th February the Argo and Seaford joined me in the Bay of Manila after being absent above three months in quest of the patache [bullion ship] Phillipina. The NE Monsoon setting in so strong that after several fruitless attempts to enter the Embrocadero they were obliged to return without being able to perform the service they were sent on.'

Admiral Cornish, struggling to repair his ships, was making ready to leave on 2nd March; he had orders to leave behind two ships to support the remaining troops. 'I have therefore given orders to Captain Brereton of the 50 gun Falmouth and Captain Peighin of the Seaford,' to wait for a change in the season then preceed to Palapa to get possession of the *Phillipina* 'and her treasures agreeable to the capitulation'.

Unknown to the British, the *Phillipina,* and her cargo of silver, had already arrived on the island's east coast months earlier. Her officers had buried half the silver at a nearby monastery, half was dispersed to the guerillas in the hills, whose growing strength was actively helped by Dawson Drake. He too wanted that silver.

A disgusted Admiral Cornish wrote to the Secretary of the Navy on 14th March, 1763: 'I ... cannot but consider it my peculiar misfortune that by the nature of my instructions I am connected with a set of men who having no other views than to accumulate immense wealth for themselves too frequently bring discredit on His Majesty's arms.' Of the Indian troops, 400 had been bribed to join the enemy, Dawson Drake freed crucial enemy prisoners, imposed tax and forced labour on the Chinese population against

General Draper's express orders and told every secret transaction to the enemy. After Admiral Cornish sailed away, the ships meant to return for the troops left behind, did not turn up. Chaos resulted. Dawson Drake sold their food supplies to China, the abandoned soldiers starving, under attack, were murdered, units and men disintegrated. Today, some of their descendants still live in Manila.

In the jungle was a certain Captain Thomas Backhouse. With 80 men he had set out overland for Palapa to prevent the guerilla leader getting the silver. 'I marched some hundreds of miles, drove about 6000 of the enemy from their strong posts .... intercepted a convoy, beat them, took part of their treasure all their guns.' Arriving within one day's march of where the silver was lodged he 'prepared for a merry push' when 'to dash all my hopes, I received a preremtory order from the Governor and Major Fell to ' return directly to Manila'

Thomas Backhouse was adamant. 'Had our forces been properly employed immediately after the departure of General Draper, the whole island would soon have been at peace. 200 men well conducted would have been sufficient to have made everything quiet.'

Amid the anarchy, he reported that his commanding officer, Major Fell, who had 'taken violent measures against Governor Drake' in October 1763, had now fled 'leaving the garrison with their arms in their hands'. The Major defected, but he was cheated; Governor Drake imprisoned him, and sent him to India for Court Martial. Thomas Backhouse suddenly found himself in charge. The guerillas had the *Phillipina* treasure and 'the many deserters drawn from us'. The Declaration of Peace, which had arrived in 1763 was disregarded, 'the numerous and insolent enemy seem every day more determined'. The strained Captain Backhouse reported to General Draper, who was comfortably back in England:

'February 10th 1764. You will see by the returns how much our numbers are decreased by desertion death etc .... The situation of His Majesty's troops exceeds all description. No hell that human nature ever experienced can equal it......... The Governor daily does things inconsistent with our public safety and honour, and indeed inconsistent with everything but his own avarice ....

In England, the honourable gentleman William Draper forwarded Capt. Backhouse's report to a W. Ellis* of the Government, complaining 'my poor regiment have neither clothing or pay they are brave fellows and deserve a better fate'.

*Mr. Weborne Ellis, Secretary of War.

Many surviving British soldiers were taken off Manila on 12th April 1764. Others were left behind.

An East India official Mr. Horne summed up the mess: 'with respect to us, except the admiral and general and a few captains of Men of War I don't know a person but what are considerable sufferers, indeed chiefly oweing to the misconduct of our chiefs (who if they have their deserts all deserve the gallows)' it had cost the Company enormous expense, [£201,101-9s-6d was the final bill] and put India at risk by lack of troops. 'Happy for the company the French have neglected such an opertunity. You will imagine I am very happy in being returned from so disagreeable an expedition.'

[IOR Orme MSS 27fo 137]

Dawson Drake returned to India grossly wealthy, but probably not beyond his own wild dreams.

Spain did not honour the cheque; it was decided in 1928 that, legally, the sum was still due.

In default of anyone else, the man obliged to arrange the handing back of Manila to Spain, was Alexander Dalrymple, who had been in Jolo during the attack.

In Britain, things had changed. Lord Anson had died in June 1763. The Secretary to the Admiralty died too, being replaced by Philip Stevens. George Jackson had risen to the important post of Assistant Clerk of Acts at the Navy Board. He was 40.

In the early autumn of 1765, both Captain Peighin and Alexander Dalrymple turned up as visitors at Great Ayton. George Jackson was staying with his brother Ralph for his summer holiday, to see his mother and collect his daughters to take them back to London.

On 27th August, Ralph noted in his Journal:

'Bro. Jackson went early this morning to meet Capt. Peighin of the Seaford (Man of War) who is at Ayton, and returned to dinner. Messrs. Wardell and Smith sat an hour in the forenoon .... Mr. Skottowe his daughters Wood and Skottowe and granddaughter Wood with Capt. Peighin, Bro. & Sister Wilson drank tea with us.' A courtesy call by a Royal Navy Captain was due to George Jackson, but why would the second most important administrator at the Navy Board hurry to meet a frigate captain? What was discussed that morning? It sounds like a meeting of the pragmatists. We can almost reconstruct their conversation.

Whatever was discussed at Great Ayton, and something of the Manila fiasco must have been said, both George Jackson and William Wilson would have been aware of the hard reality of supporting an East India freeport, before Alexander Dalrymple turned up three weeks later.

George and Ralph were enjoying fresh air, the dogs and country sports, in fine September weather. William Allen, once Gentleman usher to the Queen, came from Richmond to join them. Ralph was having his usual poor success.

'Wednesday 11th after breakfast my Bro. Jackson (his servant) Mr. Allen (his servant Beaujolais, a French man) myself (& John) road upon Roseberry Topping we returned by the Moors but could not meet with one hare.'

'Thursday 12th…………… While we were breakfasting at Ayton, Mr. Dalrymple, an acquaintance of Bro. Wilson in East India came.'

The gentlemen were joined by Mr. Augustine Skottowe, and their dogs. They spent the morning hare coursing.

'Friday 13th, after breakfasting at Ayton, my Brothers Jackson & Wilson & Messrs. Allen & Dalrymple, with myself, rode over Barnabymoor by Mordale Beck and came into Guisbro' by

Northoutgate to diner, we found the ladys from Ayton. Dr. Wayne drank tea with us.' It was Ralph's turn to be host. The formal pattern of visiting, not used nowadays, except in old Cathedral cities, meant everyone knew, who to expect when.

The morning after, saw George and Ralph down at Loftus Grainge farm, in a party of nine or so local friends, Mr. Wardell, Mr. Harrison, Augustine Skottowe included, where 'some Shott and some coursed; at two we retired to a cold diner there, Sat four chearful hours.'

It was George's sporting farewell. The next day, Sunday, the family party split up. Mr. Allen went home to Richmond. 'So did my Bro. Jackson to London`, taking with him his three daughters who had been with their grandmother since 14th June, and his sister Dolly.

'Mr. Dalrymple intending to stay till Tuesday with Bro. Wilson, he could not set my Bro. Jackson, so I did not go.' It would have been impolite, for a host to leave a guest, so Alexander Dalrymple was likely visiting Ralph. 'Setting', is a north of England politeness, where a guest is accompanied the first part of his journey, one third of the way if near, to the bus stop now, in those days to the nearest coaching inn. 'Meeting', was riding out to the boundary to greet important guests, such as when Whitby men rode out to meet Captain Cook in 1771.

Ralph Jackson was 29, Alexander Dalrymple 28, the two young gentlemen were left to entertain each other and talk of the wider world.

We can imagine too, the conversation during the earlier shooting parties; Alexander's enthusiastic promotion of the strategic value of a base at Balambagan to George Jackson; George's shrewd questioning about the Philippines after what he had learned three weeks earlier from Captain Peighin; George's scepticism of Alexander's project, knowing the Royal Navy would be over-extended. Then the value of a freeport discussed with Commodore Wilson, the rustling of maps in the Ayton Hall library. The choice of Balambagan? Could the Royal Navy protect it? Could the East India

Company Navy? Then there were Alexander's wider ideas, exploration of the Pacific, finding the lost Southern Continent. Surely, this would be an occasion when a chart of Pitt's Track was produced?

George Jackson must have been aware of the chart, the problems, the idea of south Pacific exploration. There was growing political pressure to explore. The French must not gain dominance.

Ralph Jackson was always interested to learn of anything exciting, as long as he did not take risks; there was a romantic streak to his imagination. We can be sure that he questioned Alexander Dalrymple enthusiastically about his experiences.

In the Jackson/Wilson/Skottowe circle, Dalrymple's ideas of exploring the Pacific would be the hot topic. Would Augustine Skottowe talk about it to his brother in law, Mr. Sanderson of Staithes? And did the talk spill out further in Great Ayton?

Yorkshire gossip is usually straightforward and blunt: Who is he? Where's he come from? What's he got to say?

Family stewards, when retired, are apt to help out when there are visitors, extra horses to be seen to, hay provided. I wonder if old Mr. Cook, pottering about at Mr. Skottowe's met Dalrymple himself? And told his son?

'Exploring the Pacific eh?

What d'ye think about that, James?'

A Southern Continent, eh?'

~~~

HAVANA[4]
1762

Lord Anson's second prong of attack on Spain in 1762 was aimed at Havana in Cuba.

This campaign brought to the foreground, points which echo in James Cook's career. The Royal Navy had it brought home to them that a good chart meant the difference between failure and success. It made clear, that disease could wipe out even a victorious army and navy. And it brought to Cleveland, into the Great Ayton circle, an eminent soldier, a man linked directly to the great war minister, William Pitt.

Lord Anson's plan was to take Spain's main port in the West Indies, Havana, a cosmopolitan city, with a fine harbour on the north shore of Cuba. A freeport teeming with merchant ships, Spain's treasure galleons collected there each year to cross the Atlantic in convoy. Cuba was a luscious popular island, with all types of people: white settlers with small farms, sugar millers, tobacco growers, ranchers, slaves. Small villages with churches served the largest towns, mostly Havana, where the merchants, ship builders and administrators lived, and were unacceptably rich. The Royal Navy's main task was to block this trade.

Havana felt protected by the treacherous northern Bahama Channel, which shipping avoided in favour of the sea to the south of

Cuba, choosing instead the Jamaica passage. If the Royal Navy was not in Jamaica, then Havana felt safe. Unknown to them, Lord Anson had an ancient Spanish chart of the Bahama Channel, kept from his youth.

Admiral Pocock, commanding the fleet had Commodore Augustus Keppel, a tiny man, as his second-in-command. They arrived at Martinique in April, with the Royal Navy fleet and 30[5] transports.

On one of the ships was Colonel John Hale, who had fought at Quebec. He was there partly as an observer, at the instigation of William Pitt. And he began to write his reports to his mentor:

'April 28th, 1762 from Martinique.

My Dear Sir,

Our expedition being necessarily detain'd a few days at this
Island ..… I have double pleasure in finding that my worthy friend Genl. Monkton has gallantly executed those spirited orders which my Best Friend and Patron dictates. This island is the Key to all the Carribeen …..We are proceeding to Havana…. for my part I should be more confident of Success had we set out under your Auspices and had the climate and Season been considered as what it certainly is, the most 249ormidable Enemy we have to Cope with …'
He signs himself 'sincerely and affectionately …'

Colonel Hale was right to have doubts. The army was led by two more Keppel brothers, neither knew the tropical climate. In the Carribean, yellow fever usually took six weeks to kill new arrivals, and preferred to choose young adults, among whom the death rate was 80%. It would have to be a very short campaign, to succeed.

John Hale next wrote from on board *HMS* N*amur* off Cape St. Nicholas on the west end of Hispaniola[6] on May 27th 1762, reporting that they were proceeding with the expedition 'in which I am a Volunteer'. After 19 days waiting, they had 'at last assembled 19 sail of the line and half a dozen frigates' to attack Havana. There were 9,700 fit troops in transports and they carried 1,241 sick with them. They were expecting 2,000 men to arrive from New York.

Admiral Pocock decided on surprise. They would use the treacherous northern passage through the Bahama channel, 'a very dangerous Navigation' reported John Hale, but that they would 'Drive an Expedition as far as it will go', was determined by Sir George Pocock, Commodore Keppel and his brother the Earl of Albemarle leading the Army.

The frigate *HMS Richmond,* under Captain Elphinstone, ranged ahead of the fleet of 200 ships, using Anson's chart, buoying the Old Bahama Channel, lighting fires on jagged reefs to guide the ships at night. The attacking force, the Royal Navy at its most brilliant, rose over the horizon to shock Havana on 6th June.

Whatever the Royal Navy had gained, the Army then lost by incompetence; by engaging in a slow European tactic of siege, while yellow fever incubated fast in the men. Havana's wonderful harbour was protected by Morro Castle at its entrance. With feats of valour, a small Spanish garrison held the whole British force at bay. The British Army, by besieging the castle for six weeks, gave yellow fever its chance. John Hale wrote to Pitt from Cuba HQ on July 16th that, although 600 men were killed or missing, the number of sick was 300 and daily increasing. When the promised troops arrived, they found the British army too weak to further an attack. It was an old ruse of Havana, to hold out in a siege until the invading forces died.

John Hale told Pitt, Sir George Pocock was 'one of the bravest and best men living, seconded by the gallant active (little) Commodore Keppel.' The Royal Navy took over, the sailors landed naval guns on shore. They astonished the British soldiers, by using the naval system of firing. Not for them the 80 or 90 cannonballs in 24 hours. The sailors fired quickly, 149 times in 16 hours and, not having a rolling deck, their aim was deadly. It took three weeks. Havana fell. 1,800 British soldiers and sailors had died in the fighting, 560 afterwards, nearly 5,000 died of disease.

The rewards for the living were breathtaking.

A hundred merchant ships and their cargoes were captured in the harbour, nine Spanish warships and warehouses full of booty. Prize money for the troops alone amounted to £750,000. The Admirals and Generals received between £50,000 and £100,000 each, every soldier £4 -14s -9. ¾d. Col. John Hale's share was £10,000.

He had survived war and fever. He had money. It was time to marry.

By May 1763, he was home and writing to Pitt from Pall Mall, sending him 'sweetmeats' and adding 'I am, going out of town, not to return again for a long time. I shall take the liberty of waiting on you at Hayes to take my leave. Yours truly your faithful and affect, humble servant, John Hale.'

On 11th June, 1763, at St. George's, Hanover Square, London, John Hale married Mary, 2nd daughter of Mrs. Chaloner of Guisborough.

'Polly' Chaloner was a young girl, John Hale was 36. She received for her marriage portion the Guisborough farm at Tocketts, known as Plantation, it had a distinct West Indian style. They retired to the countryside of Cleveland, to live on the farm, though he was forced to build a larger mansion house. They produced 21 children. Some were twins. By the eighth daughter they had run out of names, so called her Octavia. The 20th child they named Vicesimus (twenty) which Ralph Jackson thought remarkable.

Colonel, later General, John Hale, became part of life in Guisborough, in constant company with the Jacksons and Wilsons. Deeply aware of the disabling effect of disease on the Army and Navy, he would be an excellent sounding board for George Jackson. From 1763. Both men now had a direct link back to William Pitt.

William Pitt wanted to continue the war to a decisive end.

The new King George III did not.

The King did not like William Pitt. Lord Bute settled the treaty with France, conceding too much. The Royal Navy was furious. Officers and men were unemployed. Would James Cook find work?

15

THE SURVEYORS

We have to set James Cook's surveying within the context of what other surveyors were doing in the mid 1760s.

Surveying was becoming the essential work of land owners. Land Enclosure awards were being granted, arguments arose with farmers over boundaries and loss of grazing rights on common land. The local Overseers of the Parish, a changing rota of local officials, had always ridden the boundaries of their parish to reaffirm them. In fact this is still done at Richmond in Yorkshire led by the Mayor (often the Mayor is thrown in the river as a celebratory finale).

In the 1760s surveying had become more serious. Landowners believed that rivers ought to be controlled. Canals were being built.

Across the Atlantic, the newly acquired territory of Newfoundland needed to be mapped, its dangerous coasts and harbours surveyed. James Cook had already surveyed some of those anchorages. It was suggested in 1763 that he be employed again to survey three islands due to be given back to the French under the terms of the Peace Treaty.

ST. PIERRE et MIQUELON

Newfoundland is a huge island, a rough triangle with 6000 miles of rocky coast, hundreds of inlets and nasty currents. Its climate is cool, rainy and mosquito-ridden in summer, icebound on all but the south shore in winter. In 1763 its foggy sea teemed with cod.

Lying 15 miles off the south coast, three foggy and cold islands, St. Pierre and the Miquelons, were barely touched by winter ice; it made their harbours valuable. To the anger of almost everyone involved, these islands were given back to the French in the hasty Treaty to end the war. But before they were handed back, the Royal Navy insisted on surveying them, in case of future conflict.

St.Pierre, a small hump of an island, had a fine harbour.

Petit Miquelon (called Langlade), a treacherously flat separate island, is now joined to Miquelon by a seven mile sandspit. There were so many wrecks in the channel it silted up, helped, it is said, by inhabitants combining farming with wrecking, they hung misleading lanterns on the horns of their cows.

James Cook re-appointed to continue mapping Newfoundland was

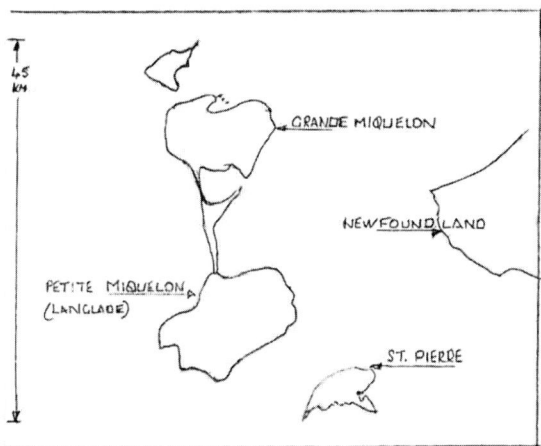

ordered to survey the three islands, St. Pierre and the two Michelons.

On 12th November 1764, the Admiralty ordered 'Instruments and other necessaries for taking Plans and Surveys of the conquered and ceded islands £94 to be paid across to the Navy Board.'

On 18th April 1765, 'Mr. Cook, who is employed in making Surveys at Newfoundland, is to be allowed the expense he has been at in providing Stationery, and for the repairing and cleaning of his instruments, amounting to £37.10s. 0d.'

That winter Master Cook had been to the Tower, to the Military Surveyors, having asked for a Theodolite – a land surveying instrument. Mapping a coast had usually been done by compass from a moving ship. James Cook was using triangulation, to fix the land features from a base line, much more accurate. He would call his finished survey 'A Geometrical Plan.'

James Cook sailed on *HMS Antelope*, under Thomas Graves and arrived at Trepassy harbour, 150 miles away on the eastern tip of Newfoundland, on 13th June, 1765 on his way to survey the three islands. These ought to have been handed over to the French on the 10th June. The situation was delicate, time had to be stolen. Safe ice-free, winter harbours, strategically placed, were what the Royal Navy insisted on knowing about.

They decided to survey St. Pierre first. The climate was, said James Cook, 'foggy and unfavourable'. He managed to finish surveying St. Pierre by 4th July, and went on to Langlade, then to the boat harbour of Dunne (now called Great Barachios).

Captain Dongley of *HMS Tweed,* James Cook's superior officer, was hiding his nerves; the delay could have sparked another war. 'I procured him all the time I could', Captain Dongley writes anxiously. Master Cook was by then at Miquelon, a large lonely island, while Captain Dongley, to entertain the French, kept the wine flowing: the cost to him was £50. To his great relief, the quiet Cook returned in time to hand over Miquelon on 31st July. The French were all smiles.

Master Cook's Plan was on a scale of three and a half inches to the mile, and measured 7' 8" x 2' 5."

On his return to London, Master Cook wrote to Graves, reporting that he had handed in his survey of the islands, and saying he had been offered the chance to survey the equally contentious Natral Islands, by Mr. Whatley of the Treasury, but had been obliged to decline.[1] The ownership of the Natral Islands in the West Indies had been in official dispute since the war of 1748. It was old business, to be tidied up. James Cook had his eye on future developments and was sticking to his mentors and patrons, especially Palliser.

Commodore Palliser was appointed to Newfoundland in 1765, 1766, 1767, 1768. On April 12th 1765 the Admiralty Ordered 'The Lark to proceed to Newfoundland to protect the fishery and cruise between Cape Bonavista and St. Quen'port and follow Commodore Palliser's orders.'[2] His other ships included the *Zephyr* and the *Pearl.* Orders for the Newfoundland ships usually went out 1st April. They sailed as soon as they could.

Palliser's fleet was to protect and assess trade. Their work was considered commercial.

Newfoundland was now British. The Government suffered a fling of offers for the whole island. No! they said. Not more than 20,000 acres to any one person! By 1767, of 66 grants of 20,000 acres parcelled out, 17 were to MPs, 8 to merchants, and 5 to Navy men: Keppel, Palliser, Rodney, Sir Charles Saunders, and Philip Stevens, 1st Secretary to the Admiralty.

Charles Saunders became the new Governor of Newfoundland

James Cook was following his patrons.

Yet he was not the only Royal Navy Surveyor working in Newfoundland. Another was Lieutenant Constantine Phipps.

~~~

LIEUT. the HONORABLE CONSTANTINE PHIPPS
(Lord Mulgrave)
1744 – 1792

Constantine Phipps had a voice like a foghorn and, said Dr Johnson's friend Mrs. Thrale, 'such boisterous Merriment and a laugh so like a Post Horn' that his friends enjoyed his enthusiasm with a wince. He was a sailor with salt water in his blood, he would swear, 'and that', said Mrs. Thrale, 'was bringing the Quarter-Deck to dinner rather too completely'.

Phipps was interested in everything. He had a talent for botany, which he shared with his Eton schoolfriend Joseph Banks, and a leaning toward archaeology, which led him to dig up chunks of Mulgrave Castle estate. A loud amiable disposition, with bursts of abrasive attack, framed Constantine Phipps' happy fault of enthusiasm. Underneath, he was scholarly. He was so fascinated by the law, he was nicknamed 'The Marine Lawyer'. He was someone George Jackson would be well aware of, indeed wary of.

Constantine Phipps was an aristocrat. In 1743, his father, a descendant of the Duchess of Buckingham, became Lord Mulgrave, so lord of the manor which held the village of Staithes. At that date, James Cook was working at Staithes, as a grocer's boy.

Leaving Eton at 16, Phipps served on the 94 gun *HMS Dragon* with his uncle, and fought throughout the Seven Years war. At 18 he was a new Lieutenant. His quick rise through the Royal Navy was due to courage, ability and family influence. By 1762 he was with the fleet in the attack on Havana, by 1763 had command of the sloop *Diligence,* then posted to the *HMS Terpsichore* in June 1765.

Constantine Phipps had mathematical genius, education, and a talent in map-making which would interest him in James Cook - eventually. It is doubtful that they met before 1766, the social gulf between them was too wide. Yet their careers were to match, in many points, not just in a link to Staithes. They were both to become Royal Navy captains, members of the Royal Society, friends of Joseph Banks, and both go on important voyages of exploration. But, against the steady reserve of James Cook, Constantine Phipps was a hearty joker. 'His mirth,' warned Mrs. Thrale, 'puts an end to that of many People …for my Part I am not so much afraid of any Man living …. he will stop at nothing for a joke.' She feared that conversation in mixed company suffered, for want of security, when he was about.

Larger than life, in 1766 Constantine Phipps was 'on the beach', one of many Lieutenants on half-pay, when he was given a Royal Navy mission to Newfoundland, sailing on the *HMS Niger,* a 32 gun frigate commanded by Sir Thomas Adams. She was one of the ships appointed, under Commodore Hugh Palliser, on 1st April that year, to patrol and defend the fishery of Newfoundland. The *Zephyr,* under Captain Omtiny was another. Together with small boats and a cutter under Captain Wells, they were ordered to make landings on the rocky coast. They found the French everywhere; their job was to survey while keeping the peace.

As a guest of Lieut. Constantine Phipps, Joseph Banks sailed on *HMS Niger.* It was probably arranged through his fishing friend, Lord Sandwich's, influence at the Admiralty. For Banks and his schoolfriend Phipps, the botany would be intriguing. Details of fish would be valuable. Could the land support a ship's company, or a colony? In the Admiralty records the Newfoundland fleet lies under the title 'Commercial.'

Joseph Banks soon discovered he was constantly sea-sick. Phipps probably guffawed. Yet on the voyage out, they caught seaweed, measured jellyfish, counted and stratified icebergs and, on arrival at St. John's after 20 rough days, they went ashore and classified fir trees; noting that Black Spruce made 'a liquor Called Spruce Beer'; they collected the recipe. Mosses, lobsters, birds, starfish, all were recorded, and trees; the Larch they noted 'which is said to make better timber for shipping especially masts than any tree this Countrey affords.' Four feet of snow fell, then rain and fog, and it was late, the 11th June, before they set off as ordered, to a lonely place on the North West corner of Newfoundland called Croc, where Lieutenant Phipps was to set up a building for over-wintering fishermen. He also set up a garden, as an experiment, then dubbed the whole effort 'Crusoe Hall'.

The weather was hot. 'Give him his due,' said Joseph Banks, 'he works night and day & Lets the Mosquetos eat more of him than he does of any Kind of food all through Eagerness.' Banks left him to it and caught a shallop[3] whose master was going south to inspect harbours. Banks was able to botanise in a way he thought wonderful, sleeping in his clothes for days, in and out of small open boats. The French were everywhere, in larger and numerous ships. Lone English fishermen were complaining of interference with their seine nets and fishing grounds, and one master warned that as muskets were being carried by the French bait boats, if proper precautions were not taken, mischief would certainly ensue. Banks caught a fever, which laid him low for all of July, recovering just in time as *HMS Niger* sailed for Chateaux Bay on the Labrador coast, where they were to build a blockhouse to leave 20 men and a lieutenant, to guard the overwintering fishermen and their stores from the Indians. Joseph Banks' seasickness had left him.

The 22 year old Banks grew interested in the Indians, especially their method of scalping, which took off the face, down to the upper lip. He collected a scalp, to demonstrate the method, that of one Sam Frye, a British fisherman, who had been killed trying to swim in terror back to his ship. Sam was, noted Banks, so well preserved that his friends recognised him. Then Banks tells of the Whobby bird, which whoops and dives at night. In 1765, Commodore Palliser on *HMS Guernsey,* in harbour in thick fog, was informed that the Indians were coming, so cleared the decks and called all hands to man the guns, marines formed up, when a flock of Whobbies appeared out of the night. *Niger's* people coming aboard *Guernsey* next day, or next year, did not let anyone forget.

The weather turned nasty, starting to blow wild; so Sir Thomas

Adams confined small boats to the ship. Thwarted, Banks was brought a live porcupine, which sulked for four days until he persuaded it to eat. By the beginning of October they had left Labrador, and sailed back to Croc to see the garden. The beans had bolted, the salads thrived, the turnips sweet, the onions small but tasty. The poultry had survived, the ship had fresh food. But insects blew in clouds, and made life a misery, Banks and Captain Adams took ill, they were all glad to sail on the 10th October, and in three days sailed into St. John's, where they found Commodore Palliser and *HMS Guernsey.* They were just in time for St.John's' annual Coronation Ball.

St. John's was a filthy town, the houses surrounded by fish flakes. Fish offal was strewn everywhere, rotting, even the cow's milk tasted of fish. There were too few women. Banks was startled to find even his washerwoman and her sister were official guests at the Governor's Ball. The dancing was robust, the supper surprisingly elegant. Everyone ate and drank fine wine to excess. Outside in the murky harbour, *HMS Guernsey* was dressed with flags and favours; she looked like 'A Peddlar's Basket at a Horse Race', with ribbons flying in the wind, thought Banks.

James Cook missed the Ball. He sailed in to St. Johns harbour two days later on the morning of Monday 27th October, in the *Grenville.* He would be bound to report to Palliser, as Commodore of the Road, and Governor of Newfoundland, apart from personal friendship from their days together on *HMS Eagle.* He would also, as a matter of courtesy, have to acknowledge in some way, Captain Sir Thomas Adams of the *Niger.* Would Phipps' enthusiasm with navigation and mapping alone, force him to burst upon the scene, though within the bounds of Navy discipline? Phipps would want to see Cook's recent maps and calculations, Banks would be curious about the plants in the land surveys Cook had made, of areas in which *HMS Niger* had not been (a farmer's son ought to know). And Master James Cook would be interested to hear how they had found the harbours of Croc and Chateaux, two of the four harbours he had himself surveyed in 1763 and mapped. It is almost certain *HMS Niger* was carrying his sailing directions, if not his charts. They were probably the reason *Niger* had been directed there in the first place; the coast was notoriously difficult and being wrecked a constant danger. A reliable chart was vital.

HMS Niger was due to sail on the Wednesday.[4] There would be formal dining in *HMS Guernsey's* great cabin, with officers in uniform. James Cook, in command of the *Grenville,* would likely attend, wearing the uniform of a ship's Master. Perhaps, he was able to take the measure of young Mr. Banks, see his intense interest in nature and exploration, and his sunny temperament. Phipps, under the eye of his Commodore, the blunt, irascible Palliser, would no doubt be merry, loud, but disciplined. One wonders if that is why his family sent him into the Navy in the first place.

HMS Niger sailed home via Portugal. Joseph Banks arrived in London in January. He had been made a member of the Royal Society, in his absence. Maybe the Newfoundland trip was in aid of securing his acceptance.

Almost certainly, Joseph Banks, and Lieutenant Constantine Phipps, had met James Cook. We have to wonder if Lord Sandwich took an opinion of James Cook from these two men.

In Newfoundland, Master Cook was establishing himself as a Royal Navy surveyor. The theodolite he asked for in 1765 was for land surveying. If he were to be put on the beach on half pay, there was plenty of other surveying to be done, even at home in Cleveland.

Land surveying had always been used for military fortifications and trench warfare. Now it was being used for civil engineering, in land reclamation and canals. James Cook was building his skills to secure his future. Yet he was not the only surveyor from or in Cleveland.

JAMES COOK/Isaac Smith
1.10 **A Sketch of Part of the Bay of Rio de Ianeiro** [Nov–Dec 1768]

A Scale of [4] Miles [= 4 in.] (1:72,960), ink and wash, 436 × 490 mm, w/m LVG with fleur-de-lis in shield and crown = 1 PORTAL

Inscribed in ink 'A Sketch of Part of the Bay of Rio de Ianeiro situated on the Coast of Brasil. L: 22° 50'. Long 42° 15' W' from Greenwich. By Lieut' I. Cook Dec': 1768' (u.r.), and 'N.B. A Bay runs in here to the Northward, the head of which is said to extend within a few miles of the back part of the Town.' (l.l.). Also inscribed in ink a topographical key (c.l.) corresponding to letters adjacent to features on the chart:

References
A. Viceroy's Pallace.
B. Bishop's Pallace.
C. Castle of St Sebastian.
D. Benedictine Convent.

Cook's Admiralty MS (PRO, Adm 55/40) carries a reference to this chart in a marginal note on f. 21' 'See Sketch N° 2'.

'The few days delay we met with in geting out of of Rio de Janeira gave me an oppertunity to draw a Plot or Sketch of great part of the Bay, but the strict watch that was kept over us during our whole stay hinderd me from takeing so accurate a Survey as I wished to have done and as all the observations I could make was taken from on board the Ship, the Plan hath no pretentions to accuracy, yet it will give a very good Idea of the place, difering not much from the truth in what is essential.', Cook *Journals* I, p. 29; 7th December 1768.

Reproduced in Skelton (1955), pl. II.

BL, Add MS 7085, f. 2

Rio De Janeiro
James Cook 1768
showing the sea approach[6]

WILLIAM STEVENS

William Stevens, the mathematical boy genius from Stokesley in Cleveland, who had been educated by Mr. Ralph Ward, trained as a surveyor. He came to Guisborough 3 months before Mr. Ward's death in 1759, to visit his patron, and see Ralph Jackson his voluntary assistant in astronomy. His tutor Robert Harrison, the Newcastle Trinity School master arrived too. William was clearly ready for the working world. But where did he go between 1759 and 1763 when he turned up again at Ralph Jackson's? It was South America.

William Stevens' sketchmap of Rio de Janeiro harbour, is dated 1763. It marks the anchorages, but concentrates on Rio's fortifications, and numbers of guns. Of great interest to the Admiralty, this map easily could have been available to James Cook.

When *Endeavour* reached Rio de Janeiro in 1768 Captain Cook needed a map to enter the harbour. He had an outline map, like a tracing, with no details on it, and later made another sailing map, based upon that. But whose map did he use, to sail in to Rio's fortified anchorage? Was it the 1763 map by William Stevens?

In 1763, Ralph Jackson returned home one Saturday in March, to find William Stevens had arrived from London. Ralph was busy surveying his newly bought Normanby estate. He commandeered 20 year old William Stevens to help.

The estate had a big variation of land types, from tidal salt meadows along the river Tees, rising through pasture and arable, up to the steep fellside and gorse of Eston Nab, slopes only suitable for woods.

It was Easter weekend and William had come to say goodbye to his parents at Stokesley and his friends and patrons in Cleveland.

~~~

'Tuesday April 5th …William Stevens junior who leaves his Father tomorrow to go to the East Indies as Deputy Engineer to the Company.'

On 7th January 1764, William Stevens aged 21 was appointed an Ensign in the Madras Engineers.

In India, William Stevens took part in a siege, then was sent to find a navigable channel between India and Sri Lanka. He fought with the Army, surveyed coasts and built defences. He was promoted: 'a most deserving young man'. In 1772 he surveyed Coringa Bay as a possible shelter for Company ships.

In 1778, William Stevens used 'an astronomical brass quadrant', on top of the Chief Engineer's house, to calculate the latitude of Madras: 13° 4' 54"N. It was an excellent result at the time. The modern true latitude is 13° 8'N.

In the clever William Stevens, born a poor boy, we have another great surveyor from near Great Ayton.

As Major Stevens, William was killed at the battle for Pondicherry in 1778, aged only 34.

'Major Stevens, the C.E. went immediately to repair the gallery, and on his return was unfortunately wounded by a cannon ball and died that evening. In him the Society have lost an honest man & the Company a most gallant soldier.'

General Hector Munroe…. 25th October 1778. BSCC

A Monument to William Stevens' memory was erected by Gen. Munroe on the high road at Pottanur, 4 miles west of Pondicherry.[7] *(Ref Cotton 157).*

His mother, being so poor, received a pension from Clive's fund.

~~~

BARTHOLOMEW RUDD
Cleveland Surveyor
1726 – 1808

Would there have been opportunity as a surveyor in Cleveland for James Cook? Men were trying to control the awkward River Tees. Bartholomew Rudd was a Civil Engineer who arranged the surveying and building of embankments, bridges and roads.

Two years older than James Cook, Bartholomew Rudd was a rich enough young man at 32, to have bought Airyholme farm in 1758 from Squire Thomas Skottowe. Mr. Rudd seems to have bought the farm, on the ridge of the moor, as a shooting estate. He and Ralph Jackson often ranged over the farm with their guns, for woodcock and pheasant in season. The Rudds lived up the street from Ralph in Guisborough, near to their friend Mr. Harrison the attorney.

In Cleveland, surveying was being extended to the problems of the Tees valley, which naturally flooded, causing havoc. Bit by bit, Cleveland landowners were attempting to control the river.

The winters of 1765-7 were severe, travel grew difficult, the river froze over. There was still no bridge over the Tees at Stockton. Ralph, riding on 17th December 1765 to Mr. Baker's at Elemore, near Durham, had to ignore Thornaby, and go via Yarm 'not being able to go by Stockton for the great quantity of loose Ice in the River that Freighten[s] the horses in the boat.'

The spring thaw was bound to bring flooding to the salt meadows edging the Tees, and Ralph became worried about his Normanby estate. As early as October he met Mr. Smith and Mr. Rudd there 'to view land adjoining the river to judge what could be done to secure it.'

January 1766 saw Ralph's 30th birthday. There was heavy snow. Mr. & Mrs. Rudd and Ralph played cards at Mr. Harrisons. Everyone waited for the spring. By late March it was time to attend to the river embankments. On Thursday 27th, Ralph met Bartholomew Rudd and rode to Normanby batts, to land which John

Appleton rented from Ralph, 'adjoining upon the river, as I intend this Spring to make a Mound or Bank under his [Mr. Rudd's] direction to keep the water off which now overflows and damages me much, we found the water high, and rough from the strong north west wind.' Mr. Rudd being a gentleman engineer, Frances Dryden was appointed actual surveyor of the work who, with some workmen, set out the sea bank. The gentlemen together 'fixed upon a plan for throwing down a slope and sodding it to prevent the river's washing away the land'. Men began work on 'the first great slope at the west end of Normanby cliff.'. The water had to get out if it flowed over, so they had to build a brick sluice.

Jeffrey Jackson, chief Mate of the *Pitt,* East Indiaman, was visiting the Wilsons; he and Ralph 'went upon the water in a coble an hour from Appleton batts on Tuesday 24th June', to study the flow of the river.

Soon that year's work was complete, and they all hoped for a secure winter along the Tees.

It was a very wet summer, the land lay sodden. Ralph had another problem at Normanby for Mr. Rudd. On his western boundary formed by Spencer Beck, he found the boundary had been shifted, the beck* channel moved, and a wharehouse built over the old watercourse. On 20th June, Ralph had to attend the half-year pay at Boulby alum works, taking with him 'a cold mutton pye' as usual, which was eaten by Rev. & Mrs. Oldfield, Mr. Easterby, Mr. Sanderson, Mr. Harrison and happily Ralph himself. Duty done, next morning found Mr. Harrison, Ralph, Mr. Smith and Bartholomew Rudd taking a coble from Normanby Batts, rowing up to Sampher Batts 'an island in the River opposite to Middlesburgh enclosed 3 years ago by Mr. Jonathan Davison (now Collector of Stockton customs, Mr. Rudd and Francis Dryden were the engineers), we called at Cargo (or Cauldgate) Fleet on our return ...' Their expedition was to look at Spencer Beck boundaries; who was the transgressor? *beck = stream*

The weather improved. Jeffrey Jackson, Ralph, and George's girls Pally and Kitty Jackson, now 16 and 14, set off for a picnic on Normanby Batts, 'we went upon the water in a coble', he says lightheartedly; it was a pleasantly tame outing for a sailor like Jeffrey Jackson, who had been in the Pacific. The whole family was in holiday mood. Two days later they all went to the seaside at Redcar, went on the sea in a coble and 'dined upon fish'. There was romance in the air. Dolly Jackson arrived back from London. It is just possible that Dolly had known Jeffrey Jackson since 1755. For tucked in the corner of a page of Ralph's diary that year, after recording a letter from Dolly about the girls being at an Assembly Rooms ball, he had added: 'JJ danced'. Now it was marriage.

On 19th July, Mrs. Rudd had 'a boy child (2nd) her first a girl dyed'. Five days later Ralph rode to Normanby Batts with Mr. Rudd who brought his plane table and 'took a plan of the old watercourse at Spencer Beck near Cauldgate Fleet which Mr. Robinson had stopped up, and of the new channel.' Ralph was determined to secure his estate from encroachment, before he went to London for an August visit. He made Robinson move the wharehouse.

Bartholomew Rudd was a surveyor, sportsman and Ralph's friend. Although 9 years older, he deferred to Ralph's interest in woodlands, ' … after breakfast I rode to Ayriholm with Mr. Rudd, after looking over the ground he is preparing for a nursery for Oaks etc. and an orchard, he returned, but I dined at Ayton.' Ralph's London visit brought new woods to Normanby. There he 'sowed 8 bushels of Acorns which I had from Mr. Stow of the Navy Office who procured them out of the county of Sussex'. Wooden ships need timber, commercial woodland was a duty for a country gentleman. Ralph had a family obligation to support the Royal Navy. 'Hearts of oak are our ships, jolly tars are our men, We always are ready … etc.' says the song. But not without trees. Do Ralph's oaks, still stand today? He planted many himself.

The daylight shortened, Normanby estate was ready to face the winter. It proved to be terrible. In January, Ralph's sea bank broke.

Seawater raced across the meadows, in rampaging destruction.

At Boulby Alum Works half-year Pay Day on 19th December, the weather was cold and stormy. Mr. Sanderson did not attend the dinner, it was his son John who ate Ralph's mother's cold mutton pie. Friday 2nd January was 'a most stormy day, the wind began to blow from the north last night', writes Ralph, apprehensively. Next morning at Normanby he found 'two breeches in the Batts, and two in that upon the Sieves, both of which batts are much damaged in other places.' His banks, he saw at once, were built too low, 'but this tide is supposed to have risen about three feet perpendicular water, higher than ever known in the memory of man, the cause of which I account for thus'…and he records the general opinion of men who knew the North Sea:

'the Gales of Wind we had this autumn were from the south and SW especially at Spring Tides, which kept the Sea to the northward (having sometimes had high neap tides) till the latter end of last week, when the wind blew fresh at North West, the Moon changed last Wednesday, the wind blowing a hurricane Thursday night and last Friday (the day being the 3rd after the change the height of the Spring is always expected) proved critical, there was supposed to be about 2 feet of water upon the top of my bank if it had been still water; though my banks were highest upon the Tees except Mr. Turners.'

It had clearly been a Sea Surge.*

Others had suffered too. 'Mr. Wm. Jackson Jnr's bank below Lackenby, is much torn … a break of about 50 yards in the NE end of Mr. Turner's bank, and the sea broke through the bent grass a hundred yards in breadth between West Coatham Town and the Storehouse.'

After breakfast on Tuesday 6th January, the Reverend Oldfield of Easington, a Mr. Easterby and Ralph rode together, they called at Skinningrove and Loftus. Ralph stayed at Boulby, involved with business, while the others went down to Staithes to see the worst.

Ralph says, 'Mr. Wardell told me of the most dismal scenes at Mr. Sanderson's and the generality of the Town of Staithes occasioned by the storm last Friday, Whitby and Scarborough have also suffered immensely.'

That Spring of 1767 saw everyone along the Tees and Cleveland coast repairing their sea defences. The new attitude was 'Improvement'. Man could, and should, manage the landscape to his benefit. And they determined they would.

The 1760s were years of increased land surveying, embankments, new roads, bridges, and the first canals. It was fashionable and could make men wealthy. James Cook could secure his future by land surveying.

George Jackson decided to take part. He would build a canal.

~~~

A Sea Surge moves anti-clockwise in the North Sea, taking only 24 hours to travel from Scotland, down the east coast of England, along the north coast of Holland and Germany, up the west coast of Denmark to reach Norway. It is caused by a strong wind and low pressure, 1 millibar fall in pressure from the norm = 1 centimetre rise in sea level above normal. A deep depression can raise the sea over 6 feet (2 metres). Co-inciding with high spring tides this can be devastating.[8]
These conditions were met on this occasion, and in 1953.
Repeated in 1983, Staithes fishermen were expecting it. Mr. Sanderson's shop was washed away in 1812. In 1991 & 2001, large scale harbour protections were built at Staithes.

STORT NAVIGATION
1766

'Wednesday] 3th August, 1766. We dined with several
Gentlemen at a Club held there [in London], many of
whom were Commisioners of the Stort Navigation
we were very merry'
Ralph Jackson.

James Cook was now skilled enough to become a land surveyor,
should the Newfoundland surveys be completed. There were new
opportunities. Canals were being built. Accurate surveying and
measurement were essential, or the canal water flowed away.

By 1760, river navigation had reached its natural limit. James
Brindley and the Duke of Bridgewater showed the way around the
impasse, by cutting the Worsley canal in 1761, halving the price of
coal in Manchester. Could the same thing be done for London? If so
the Newcastle coal trade could also be cut, halving costs by sea.
North East seamen and London river pilots could find themselves
unemployed. It was George Jackson who took the initiative which
could decimate the North Sea collier fleet.

George Jackson has always been credited with the idea of making
the River Stort navigable, from the River Lea up to Bishop Stortford.
In fact, the idea to make the Stort navigable first came from an
Innkeeper, Mr. Adderly, who formerly kept the Crown at Hockerill, a
fact which George Jackson himself made clear. George Jackson was
the 'Energiser' that is Promoter of the project.

It is said they intended to push the waterway northwards to
connect London to the Wash. This did not happen. If it had, coal
would have arrived more directly in London and to greater profit, and
this may have been why the three Masterman brothers were involved.

Mr. Christopher Masterman, was a wealthy 'crimp' in London,
one of those who financed the purchase and sale of coal. His business
was at Bridewell, above London Bridge, so limited to smaller ships.
The coal trade was already moving downriver to the Pool. The
unofficial coal exchange was at the Dog Tavern, said to be 'a genteel

establishment', until 1762, when it too moved downriver. It was in Christopher Masterman's interest to move with the times. And he knew the area of Bishop's Stortford well. Ralph Jackson notes:

'16th December, 1766. Mr. Baines, a Quaker, nephew to Mr. Chris. Masterman Coal Merchant in London drank tea with us at Guisborough.'

Mr. Baines lived near Bishop's Stortford.

The Masterman brothers were Cleveland men, from Ormesby and Great Ayton, but lived in London. William was a lawyer who kept Chambers at 8 Greys Inn, John was a silversmith in partnership as 'Masterman and Archer'. The three brothers had the money, expertise and position to back a canal project.

August 12 1766 'after dinner my Bro. and Mr. Wm. Masterman and self went to Harlow, near the River Stort (in Essex) where we met Mr. Yeoman their Engineer,' says Ralph.

To build a canal was a vast undertaking.

George Jackson got involved because he had bought a country estate at Roydon next to the River Stort, as an escape from the fevers of London, from which he had suffered too often. There he built a house, though not too grand a house, for his son later pulled it down and re-built it.

The canal was opened three weeks before George Jackson was appointed 2nd Secretary to the Admiralty.

George Jackson writes:*

'Tuesday 24th October, 1766. The first barge came this day to Bishop Stortford with colours flying, drums beating, attended by a band of music.'

The opening was meant to go off with a bang. One week before, on Monday 16th October George went himself to Limehouse and ordered 36 fir poles for flags; two poles were to be set at Mr. Adderly's door as the originator of the scheme. There were to be guns for a 21 gun salute, colours and plenty of malt, they sent to Mr. Baines for 'samples'. A booth was built in North Street for speechmaking and Mr. Plomer Member of Parliament for the County gave an ox for roasting.

On the Friday George took 11 year old Bessy with him to Bishop Stortford to oversee the preparations. On Saturday his two other daughters, sister, Mrs. Ward and Mrs. Fisher came to be present at the opening of the river. Tuesday came, the big festive day, George found that 'some got drunk soon and giving room to fear a riot.' He stuck to the celebrations until early the next morning when he left the Stort 'carrying with me the noise of bells, music, singing, roaring and dancing, all together making such a head ache, that I was more indulged in the quiet of my sister's house than I was ever before sensible of,' he says. He was safe at Woodfordbridge with Dolly, who was probably the sister at the celebrations, we cannot imagine her missing the fun.

There is a nice story told by his grandson about George and the Stort: the story of the old watch. A lock-keeper employed on the Stort Navigation had his house broken into and ransacked. George met him when riding by. 'Here take this watch,' he said, drawing it out of his breeches pocket, 'and I give it to you on the understanding that at your death the next oldest lock-keeper on the river gets it, for it belonged to my grandfather.' Long years later, when the Stort canal was made uneconomical by the newfangled railways, the watch was returned to the family, but was given to Bessy's branch who still had it 100 years ago. It was made by Quare, the inventor of the chronometer in the time of Charles I. George's two grandfathers were George Jackson, Dyer of Thirsk, also of Ellerton Abbey, and William Ward of Guisborough, amply rich.

Today the Stort Navigation has been restored and is open to canal boats. The industrialised River Lea has been cleaned up for the Olympic 2012 site; the Lea passes London water reservoirs, parks and sports fields, then joins the Stort. The Stort is a pretty river. Its 14 miles of countryside, fat white sheep, parkland and farms, are punctuated with old watermills and 15 locks. George Jackson's canal badge, a witty red hand stood over the doorway at Sheering Mill Lock cottage. In later life he changed his name to Sir George Duckett. It would be pleasant to think George was just being witty, being caught red-handed as responsible for the canal. But the hand is the sign of the baronetcy which came to him through marriage.

George Jackson, the Mastermans and the speculators, had risked and won.

The risk for James Cook, a married man with a family, could find himself beached by the Royal Navy on half pay, was real. Would his surveying make him valuable enough to his patrons? And would they continue to help him?

James Cook in 1766 was a ship's Master, working at sea. He was prospering. Yet to rise any higher would be a great leap. However, his patrons too were rising in importance. Commodore Hugh Palliser was now Governor of Newfoundland. Admiral Charles Saunders was about to become First Lord of the Admiralty. And George Jackson was to be promoted from the Navy Board to become 2nd, or Deputy, Secretary to the Admiralty.

GEORGE JACKSON
DEPUTY SECRETARY TO THE ADMIRALTY
1766

'This post brings a letter from My Brother Jackson to
my mother giving her the agreable account of his being
appointed Deputy Secretary to the Admiralty in the
room of Chas.Fearne Esq. Salary of £5000 per an.
Ld. Chatham was his Friend with
Mr. Chas. Saunders 1st Lord of the Admiralty. '
14th Nov. 1766   *Ralph Jackson.*

George Jackson's own patrons were now of a very high order. William Pitt (now Lord Chatham)'s patronage was gained by a family connection to a Mr. Dingley. Admiral Charles Saunder's friendship probably arose through the Navy Office.

It becomes clear that George Jackson was promoted for his efficiency. Years later it would be said, in Parliament, that he was the most honest man in Royal Navy administration.

CHARLES DINGLEY

George Jackson was related to Charles Dingley by the marriage of George's cousin, the younger Esther Spencer, to Robert Dingley in 1760. The family all visited London to pay her her Bride's Visit. She inherited with George some part of the Biddick colliery lease, and with Ralph parts of the ships in Whitby and Scarborough.

As early as 1763, Ralph Jackson says George had met the great man, William Pitt, through the Dingleys:

On 6th November 1763. George Jackson and Mr. Charles Dingley 'visited Mr. Pitt last Wednesday' and 'were mutually pleased.'

Charles Dingley was close to William Pitt having been his secretary. Known as 'Dingle-Dangle' to the Pitt children, he was always loyal to their family. He knew the depths of William Pitt's manic depression, the dire extent of his painful torture by gout. Pitt's whole life was a defiance of his physical state. Partisan is the word for Charles Dingley. His letters to Pitt include such hopes as that their political opponent Fox 'Captain-General of the Gamblers' would, when he reached Naples, 'throw himself into the flames of Vesuvius'. And he describes Townshend as 'a false friend', probably true.

On Monday 14th July, 1766, William Pitt was so ill that he left the Hoods, with whom he had been staying in Harley Street, and accepted Charles Dingley's kind offer of his house at North End on Hampstead Heath where the air was cooler.

By April 1767, Charles Dingley was begging his relative George Jackson for some neighbouring land George owned at North End for, in a phase of manic activity, Pitt had asked the long-suffering Dingley to agree to add 34 bedrooms to his house and to acquire every building that interfered with his view.

It appears that George Jackson agreed. It is doubtful that the 34 bedrooms were ever built. William Pitt, Earl of Chatham, spent much of his time in his own bed, in pain. He even interviewed politicians from his bed. He was happily married, physically brave.

ADMIRAL SIR CHARLES SAUNDERS.

As a young man, Charles Saunders had been around the world with Lord Anson in 1744.

In 1752 he was Commander in Chief of the Newfoundland station, by 1755 as Comptroller of the Navy, he would come in contact with George Jackson. The Admiral, much admired for his conduct at Quebec in 1759 became an MP in 1760, but spent his time in command of the Mediterranean fleet. He and Palliser served at Havana in 1762, indeed they grew such close friends that Admiral Saunders left Palliser a large sum of money in his will. It was probably through his influence that Hugh Palliser was appointed Commodore of the Newfoundland fleet, to which James Cook was attached.

Charles Saunders was a Whig in Parliament. George Jackson, later became a 'Tory' MP. It made no difference. Pitt would not have political contention. He wanted honest ability.

'He was ready to give office to any politician of character', assuring the King of his intention 'to dissolve all factions and to see the best of all parties in employment.'

In August 1765, Pitt appointed Sir Charles Saunders a Lord of the Admiralty. On 16th September, 1766 he was made First Lord, to the dismay of others before him on the list. Within three months he had resigned (due to ill health?) But for George Jackson, those three months were his chance.

On 11th November, 1766 George Jackson transferred to the Admiralty after 23 years at the Navy Board. He was appointed the new Deputy Secretary to Philip Stevens. It seems he took charge of the Navy's Secret Service Budget.

The appointment put George Jackson in a high influence group.

All James Cook's patrons had risen in power. He was personally known to the First Lord of the Admiralty, the 2nd Secretary to the Admiralty, and to Hugh Palliser, now Governor of Newfoundland.

And he was being paid well for his Newfoundland surveying.

ANOTHER TYPE OF SURVEY
NAVY WAGES
1766

On Christmas Day 1766, George Jackson, newly appointed as 2nd Secretary to the Admiralty, wrote to William Pitt, now Earl of Chatham, about a survey he had made for him on the subject of half pay.

The 'expense of adding 1/- to the half-pay of Captains whose present allowance is 4/- a day, and of all Lieutenants unemployed, will amount to £18,633-5s-0d.' George Jackson expressed the opinion that an increase was 'favourable for the Country's sake, for Humanity's sake and your Lordship's sake as Author.' Pitt intended to put this increase to Parliament and, of course, as he was putting it forward himself, he expected Parliament to grant it.

George gave his reason that 'Lieutenants on half pay cannot keep company except of vulgar conversation' so that, when recalled to sea again, they earned the serving officers' contempt for their coarse manners. George's natural sympathy also went out to the 'unhappy and distressed case of widows' whom, he suggested, William Pitt consider for an increase.

George Jackson enclosed a list. It shows that there were:

104 Masters and Commanders on half pay of 4/- a day.
 34   "   "   on sea pay.
138 in Total

790 Lieutenants   on half pay of 2/- or 2/6 a day.
196   "   on sea pay.
994 in Total.

In 1761 James Cook's regular pay as a Master of the 3rd Rate warship *HMS Northmberland* had been £6-6s-0d a 28 day month. He received £50 bonus for mapping the St. Lawrence. For mapping the islands and harbours of Newfoundland he earned the high sum of 10/- a day, the same as captain of a 4th rate warship. This was arranged by Commodore Hugh Palliser. The sloop *Grenville* was only a 6th rate, so meant a drop in pay: 10/- restored the situation.

Commodore Palliser had been frustrated at the attempt to appoint to the Newfoundland survey ship a draughtsman from the Tower, who had never done a land survey or, more importantly, had never been to sea. He forcefully arranged with the Admiralty not only to appoint Master James Cook, but to have Cook's Master's ticket altered by Trinity House to state 'qualified to be Master of any of HM ships up to 4th Rate.'*

To step down to 6th rate pay was for James Cook his usual pattern of behaviour, another step down to sail further.

So we can see that James Cook was lucky, he was sponsored as a Master to earn for his surveying the same money as a Lieutenant and even to have a job at all.

THE ROYAL SOCIETY

While being paid for his surveying skill, James Cook took another step in his personal advancement. He used his sailor's navigating skill to survey the Heavens.

On 5th August, 1766, Master James Cook observed the eclipse of the sun at Newfoundland, adding his figures for working out longitude at the place of observation. He did not yet have the skill to work out the sums, so he sent them to London to have them calculated. This was the basis of the presentation of his work in the Royal Society Philosophical Transactions 1766 LVII 215-6 which put his name into the Society's view as one of those involved in surveying the heavens.

Two years later in 1768, when the Royal Society was seeking an observer for the Transit of Venus, Master Cook was already known to them.

16

SCURVY DOCTORS

One aspect of Captain Cook's fame, is based on his success in defeating the Scurvy. Every sailor knew about Scurvy.

Scurvy is **horrible.**

It is an illness, not a disease. It is caused by lack of Vitamin C. The human body cannot store Vitamin C, we have to be fed it, day after day. We know that now. In Captain Cook's time they did not. So they died.

Scurvy can take as long as six months to appear. Blood plasma levels of Vitamin C fall within a few weeks, long before any symptoms show. The first signs are weakness, fatigue, listlessness, followed by shortness of breath and aching bones, joints and muscles. Then comes a rash, bleeding under the skin, the gums swell, become spongy and bleed, the breath smells foetid. Teeth loosen and fall out, wounds refuse to heal and scars are easily torn apart, gangrene sets in. How could men work a sailing ship in that condition?

Yet Scurvy is easily reversed. Given doses of Vitamin C, in fruit and green vegetables, the blood begins to improve at once. Severe weakness and bleeding stops within 24 hours. Pain and fever disappear in 2 days. After 10 to 12 days, gums and skin heal, although the blotches can linger for months.

Vitamin C is most present in fruit and green vegetables, but fresh meat helps, and milk, and lots of potatoes. Storing food through the winter, or a long voyage, destroys Vitamin C. The emphasis must always be on fresh food. Today the cure of Scurvy is straightforward. That was not understood in the 1700s - the result was awful.

We need to put Captain Cook's success in context, within the knowledge of the time, and alongside the efforts of other men.

Palliser had had success with onions, on his crossings of the Atlantic. Admiral Howe kept the blockading fleet constantly at sea off France in 1755 by fresh supplies of food from England. But the Royal Navy was losing too many men. To police the wide oceans needed a solution to the problem.

Being a thorough man, James Cook probably did what he always did, build on his basic knowledge, and seek-out the best advice. Doctors were taking a detailed interest in Scurvy. The most famous was Dr. James Lind, senior. He was a Scot, like his namesake, but 20 years older.

We are looking at exploration in Medicine.

~~~

DR. JAMES LIND Senior
1716-1794

There were two Drs. James Lind. The elder became an expert in Scurvy. He trained at Edinburgh and became a Royal Navy surgeon serving in the hot Mediterranean, the humid Caribbean, and the cold English Channel. The weather was thought the main cause of illness.

When the earlier war ended in 1748, he gained his MD from Edinburgh University, his thesis being on the sailor's curse, venereal disease or, as he called it, 'The site of Distress of Love'. Dr. Lind then set up a busy practice in Edinburgh and published his famous 'Treatise on the Scurvy' in 1754.

During that war, in which he had been bitterly involved, more Navy men had died of scurvy than had been killed in battle. On one ten week cruise on board *HMS Salisbury* in the autumn of 1746, 80 out of 350 men were prostrated by scurvy, 23% of the crew. Worse had been known. On Lord Anson's incredible voyage around the world in 1740-3, 75% of the crew died of scurvy, a dreadful result. It was a horrifying voyage, a miraculous return. Dr. Lind says it was the publication of the dire account of Lord Anson's voyage which made him think of writing down his own ideas.

Dr. Lind's 'Treatise on Scurvy' was widely and anxiously read throughout Europe. A popular second edition appeared in 1757, a third in 1772 and it was available to sailors like James Cook.

The gist of Dr. Lind's remedies was to eat onions, or oranges and lemons, and green vegetables wherever possible, or drink lemon juice. It was the gist people remembered 14 years later, as the *Endeavour* provisioned in London river. The first thing James Cook did when reaching Madeira was buy onions and issue them to every man on board. Oranges and lemons he took as a 'rob' or marmalade, but it was fresh greens which James Cook became avid about, and which saved his crews.

~~~

Did James Cook know Dr. Lind? Well, Commodore Wilson certainly did.

If we go back ten years, from James Cook's appointment to the *Endeavour,* back to June 1758, when Dr. Lind was newly appointed physician to the Naval Hospital at Haslar, Portsmouth, we find that *Pitt* under William Wilson's command, had sailed that March with Colonel Draper's soldiers, but had left her boatswain John Hodges sick at Portsmouth. This may have been how Dr. Lind learned of the huge East India ship's voyage. Two weeks out, and the *Pitt* was already running into trouble. Captain Wilson entered in his log:

'Notwithstanding we keep the Ventilator going & a windsail down the After hatchway as often as the weather will permit, the number of sick Encreases having now upwards of Forty down. Latt.30°S.' Robert Truelove, the ship's carpenter died, and Simon Webber one of the young Midshipmen. On 29th April they 'lost one man by Fever'. It is said that typhus, a disease of overcrowding and lice, had been brought aboard by the soldiers. Thirty soldiers were to die. Conditions grew ripe for scurvy when they had been denied a vital port of call for fresh supplies.

As they had approached the Cape Verde islands, they had seen, over the point of Port Praya, three ships at anchor, one a two decker. They looked like the French. 'I hoisted the Dutch flag, but they did not show their colours,' says William Wilson. He consulted the officers, who decided that the three ships must be those carrying French troops to India, to threaten Madras. The officers 'thought it our indespensible duty to use all endeavour to get there before them.' They did but at a human cost, four months without fresh greens. It was the end of August before they reached tropical Anjengo on the tip of India. Many ordinary seamen and soldiers had died, but none of the passengers or superior officers. Since when have lice been choosy? Was it less lice and typhus, more an inequality in food leading to Scurvy? (The total death rate for the *Pitt's* famous round trip to China was around the average 30%.)

Scurvy definitely appeared later in that voyage. Three weeks out of Batavia, after their unsatisfactory re-victualling by the Dutch, as they slipped through the clammy air, past the islands of the Java Sea, men were 'waisting', says Captain Wilson, and even seven weeks out, after buying fish and meat at 'Bocton, Celebes' he says, 'Several of our People have symptoms of the Scurvy.' As the ship ploughed on northwards through the rolling Pacific east of th Philippines, 'our People Daily complain of Scorbutick symptoms and some are taken by the flux.' People was the word used for the common sailors. Flux meant dysentry, an unwelcome gift from Batavia.

All the same this was a voyage to marvel about. And William Wilson brought his ship home.

Pitt came up the English Channel, carrying riches from China, to enter the annals of fame among sea-going men, in March 1760.

On 1st April, Ralph Jackson in Guisborough writes excitedly:

'Got a letter from my Brother George with advice of, the Pitt, my Brother Wilson's safe arrival at Portsmouth* ...In company with the Warwick from China to Kinsale, the quickest passage ever before known.'

The news ran through the naval community. Ralph, still a boyish 23, set off for London with his relative Mr. James, arriving on 19th April to surprise his Brother George at the Navy Office, and Captain Wilson and his wife Rachel who were dining there. That afternoon saw them all drinking tea at their cousin Rebecca Manley's (she had married the Rev. Lawrence) and spending an hour at Uncle Joshua's in Whitehall, and Ralph then going on down to Greenwich to surprise his sister Etty, 'none of them knowing of my Journey,' he says, pleased with himself.

The next day, being Sunday, George Jackson, Commodore Wilson, and 'Messrs Hick and Bensley' with Ralph, walked down to Woolwich and strode about the *Pitt* as the great East Indiaman was preparing to unload. They returned to dinner and - 'Dr. Linn of Portsmouth dined with my Brother Wilson and after he had gone, we walked in Greenwich Park.' (Ralph's spelling was still not good.)

Why was Dr. Lind there? Was it partly to report on *Pitt*'s crew, in hospital at Portsmouth? At that date Dr. Lind was studying typhus, which *Pitt's* crew may have had on the outward voyage. But the incidence of Scurvy on such a long trip, must have been of interest to him.

Dr. Lind cannot have been satisfied that day. His message on food was not getting through. Individuals were using lemon juice as a cure for scurvy, Joseph Banks used it this way on *Endeavour.* It would be forty more years before the Royal Navy officially issued lemon juice to the men, to prevent scurvy happening.

Yet it was only eight more years before James Cook proved it possible to defeat scurvy on long voyages: the difference being that he was using Dr. Lind's recommendations on food as a preventative diet, rather than a cure.

In making this leap from cure to prevention, it may be that James Cook's ideas were set upon a foundation much closer to home, on the approach of a surgeon near his home in Cleveland: Dr. Charles Bisset. A man known to many of those James Cook knew, a man who may even have attended the Cook family as their doctor, an experienced man who had written an important 'Treatise on Scurvy.'

~~~

DR. CHARLES BISSET
Surgeon and Surveyor
1717-1791

In 1755 when war again threatened, and just one year after Dr. Lind's Treatise, Dr. Charles Bisset published his own 'Treatise on the Scurvy', dedicating it to Lord Anson and the Royal Navy. There is a strong likelihood his work influenced James Cook.

Charles Bisset was a Scottish doctor who had come to live and practise at Skelton in Cleveland in 1753. That year Mr. Ward was 73, Ralph Jackson aged 19 was still working as an apprentice merchant in the Tyne coal trade. James Cook at 25 was still mate of the Whitby ship *Friendship,* sailing the North Sea with Tyne coal.

Dr. Bisset was 36, an army lieutenant who had retired on half pay at the peace of 1748; he had travelled in Europe and was now ready to settle down. At Skelton he was able to develop both his surgical work and his enquiring intellect. This small farming village, set about a sloping village green, with two pubs, the 'Royal George', and 'The Plough' where a gentlemen's club met, lay next to a deep wooded valley which sheltered the church and Skelton Castle; there the sociable Reverend Lascelles resided and its owner, John Hall-Stevenson, kept a fine library. From Skelton, Dr. Bisset was able to build a lucrative surgical practice, travelling widely throughout Cleveland. Among other things, as Ralph Jackson found out, he was a skilled dentist who could kill a nerve to save a tooth.

Charles Bisset was a remarkably thin man, delicate, clever and brave. He may have contracted malaria in the West Indies, he is described as 'of weakly habit', though he lived to be 75. Mr. Ward, riding home to Guisborough, met him at Willy Childs's,[1] at Brotton one warm day, the 25th July, 1755:

'Drank two tankards of Bombo*, but did
not a[l]ight of horse. Dr. Bisset came
to us with whome went to Skelton
                        * *Bombo was cold rum punch.*

It seems that Charles Bisset was called in at times to treat Elinnor
Jefferson at Staithes. He specialised in skin ulcers, and she suffered
'a breaking out of the thigh' in December 1755. Old Mr. Ward
remarks in November, 1754:
> 'I went to Grange farm from thence to Boulby,
> from thence to Steathes where I met with Mr. Wardell
> and the Skelton doctor at Mr. Jefferson's, and stayed
> there about 2 hours, when we three came away together
> the Doctor to Skelton and Mr. Wardell and I to Boulby. '

So not only was Dr. Bisset known in Cleveland during the two
years before James Cook left his Whitby ship, Charles Bisset was
mixing with the Jeffersons and Mr. Ward during the year before
publication of his Treatise on Scurvy. It would be strange indeed, if
he did not mention his hopeful work to these ship-owning men,
whose cousin and nephew George Jackson was appointed, on 22nd
February that year, Chief Clerk of the Navy Board, the only place
where Dr. Bisset's treatise recommendations could be put into effect.

Charles Bisset was a doubly clever man. He had two areas of
expertise, surgery and surveying, which came from the way his life
had worked out.

In 1740, aged 23, he had been appointed 2nd surgeon of the
Military Hospital in Jamaica, and sailed with Admiral Vernon's
fleet in 1742. There he learned about the diseases prevalent in the
Army and Navy, his comments leave readers in agony for the men.
He spent the year 1745-6 at home in ill health, then joined the 42nd
Highlanders fighting in Flanders, where his bravery and skill, in
surveying trenches and battlements, brought him to the notice of the

Duke of Cumberland who promoted him to the Brigade of Engineers. After the war Charles Bisset published his surveying in 'Theory and Construction of Fortifications' with plans (London 1751), and then headed for Cleveland. He went on to publish throughout his life, books, medical papers, essays and, it is said, a treatise on naval tactics. He was an academic, a practical doctor, a surveyor and a naval surgeon all in one. Old Mr. Ward comments on 9th February 1756, 'Dr. Bisset came to whome gave half a ginny for 2 books he formerly lent me'. Does he mean he was buying the doctor's two published works, the treatise on fortifications and that on the Scurvy? In other words, the Scurvy treatise could have been in Mr. Ward's library and available to George Jackson of the Navy Board as early as 1756. If the Doctor was lending and selling his Scurvy treatise in Cleveland, did James Cook know of it? Had he listened to talk of it, perhaps even read it?

Charles Bisset seems to have been a quiet, professional, independent-minded Scot. In 1762 he published a 344 page 'Essay on the Medical Constitution of Great Britain', which convinced at least one reviewer that Cleveland was not the most unhealthy place to live. In 1766 a collection of research papers earned him an MD from the University of St. Andrews. As late as 1786, when aged 71, his manuscript with the awkward title 'Permanent and Temporary Fortifications and the attack and defence of Temporary Defensive Works' was dedicated to George, Prince of Wales. It shows that Dr. Bisset's interest in surveying did not wane.

In the spring of 1768, when the *Endeavour* voyage was preparing, Charles Bisset was 51, a well-known doctor travelling about Cleveland. Both his experience in land surveying and his work on Scurvy would interest him in James Cook's voyage. The two men had shared the same locality and had people in common, so it is highly probable they knew of each other.

Socially, Charles Bisset was a member of the Saltburn club started in 1762, and meeting on the first Monday of every month. Mr. Wardell became its president and Mr. Sanderson and Ralph Jackson were both attending in May 1766. They respected Dr. Bisset's status, and he theirs. On the afternoon of 8th November, 1762, Ralph Jackson witnessed Charles Bisset's will and, while James Cook was surveying New Zealand aboard the *Endeavour,* on 24th October 1769, Ralph, who had bought the Normanby estate, had his own new will witnessed by three neighbours and the independent gentleman Dr. Bisset.

Professionally, like most doctors, Charles Bisset mixed at all levels of society. The patients he cured of ulcerous scurvy between 1753-55 included he says: 'a young man of 25, living in Guisborough', a 'woman of robust habit, aged 46,' with ulcers on both legs, also 'a woman of lax fibres, aged 35' with an ulcerated ankle, both 'living near Stokesley' and 'John Peart, a labourer, at Broughton' with ulcers on the left side of his face. The 3 year old son of Robert Thompson, the Skelton weaver, he innoculated against the smallpox. A ship's carpenter he cured by a diet of green salad and seawater. But on a dry note he cites as 'miraculous' the case of John Stonehouse, a Skelton shoemaker, whom even one pint of malt ale would cripple with rheumatism, while pure brandy and gin would have no effect, 'even when taken to excess'!

Living in the same landscape, riding the dirt lanes from Skelton, to Stokesley, Broughton and Ingleby, the doctor would pass the door of the house built by James Cook's father in 1755 and, as one Scot nearly always acknowledges another Scot when they 'come down to England', it would be surprising if James Cook's father and Dr. Bisset never spoke, during thirteen years of the doctor riding past Mr. Cook's door. In 1755, the academic doctor and the retired farm steward would have little in common. By 1765, the doctor/surveyor would be interested in the surveying activities in Newfoundland of Mr. Cook's married son. By 1768 Dr. Bisset would be alerted by the proposed voyage across the Pacific, it was a wonderful chance to try out his theories on Scurvy. He wanted to prevent the disease by diet. And it is exactly this leap which James Cook made, of advancing a **cure** by diet, to **prevention** by diet.

So, did James Cook know of Charles Bisset's Treatise, with its full chapter 3 on dietary prevention? If we apply commonsense and probability, then we have to point out that Charles Bisset knew Dr. John Pringle, Fellow (and soon to become President) of the Royal Society which appointed James Cook to the *Endeavour.* Indeed it was in the form of a letter to Dr. John Pringle that James Cook later presented his famous paper on the Health of Seamen which earned him the Copley medal. And Dr. John Pringle certainly knew of the Bisset Treatise on Scurvy.

As young men in the 1730s, Dr. Pringle had practised medicine in Edinburgh, and was a professor lecturing in metaphysics when Charles Bisset was a student. By 1744 the Duke of Cumberland had made Dr. Pringle physician-general to the army in Flanders; he worked on the battlefields throughout that war. It may have been there the two men met. They both retired from the army in 1748. Neither forgot the carnage, nor the appalling diseases which followed. Both put their minds and hearts into improvements in medicine. Dr. Pringle became a spearhead in London, a fashionable Royal Physician with immense wealth and influence. His early outstanding paper for the Royal Society was on Septic and Antiseptic Substances. In 1752 he published a medical classic 'Observations on the Diseases of the Army', and it is in reference to this work, that we learn, from Dr. Bisset's Treatise, that the two men knew each other before 1752. He says on page 69 of the Treatise:

'I made some mention of this to Dr. Pringle previous to the publication of his judicious observations on the Diseases of the Army who I found had before conceived a like opinion.'

In 1762 Charles Bisset dedicated his 'Essay on the Medical Constitution of Great Britain' to Dr. John Pringle. So, both doctors were aware of each other's work.

A TERRIBLE SCOURGE

To us Scurvy is an avoidable illness, to them it was a sure killer. They did not know the cause was an easily-corrected lack of Vitamin C, but they were trying hard to find it.

Some of Dr. Bisset's Treatise makes us laugh, some brings tears. We feel like yelling down the centuries, 'There is no need for you to die!' Some of the Treatise is not for those of a nervous stomach. And much of it finds echoes, in James Cook's approach to health during his voyages. It is time to take a close look at this Treatise on Scurvy.

THE BISSET TREATISE OF 1755[2]

Doctors of Charles Bisset's day thought in terms of the body's juices: blood, saliva, urine, sweat and faeces. They believed the weather made disease. Dr. Bisset was studying the effects of the weather on the human frame. He came to the conclusion that the 'Predisposing cause' of Scurvy was bad weather, while the 'Exciting cause' was a bad diet. In fact he arrived at the right answer from the wrong direction. Taking the symptoms which faced him, he tried to group them to distil their cause and, even if he did mix up symptoms of jaundice and other fevers, this method gave him the correct cure.

Two hundred years before vitamins were 'discovered', Charles Bisset said that the cause of Scurvy was an atrocious diet upon His Majesty's ships and recommended that the Royal Navy should change it. He was, in modern terms, tremendously right. Sadly, in 1755, the experiments were just starting to be official, while the results were not conclusive. There were so many diseases aboard ships, so many things to die from, in the Royal Navy.

As Dr. Bisset describes the sea diet, we can imagine his Scots voice speaking:

'This necessary exciting cause of the Scorbutic Cachexy [*Scurvy*], on board his Majesty's ships of war, consists in the following articles, viz Salted beef and pork; which in the West Indies are sometimes highly tainted; exceeding lean and hard Suffolk cheese, which is served during the greatest part of the passage to Jamaica, or as long as it will keep; butter or oil is served in lieu of it; boiled pease; oatmeal boiled in water to the consistency of hasty-pudding, called burgow, or water-gruel instead of it; flour, which is often weevily in the Torrid Zone, with salted suet, or currants, or raisins in place of suet, which are made into a pudding with water; sometimes salted and dried fish, or stock-fish; very hard and solid biscuit, which in the West Indies is frequently damaged with maggots and weevils; an allowance of a quarter of a pint of rum or brandy, mixed with three-quarters water: the water at sea is commonly more or less putrid and verminous, and the sailors drink of it to excess after salt beef dinners.'

No fruit, no fresh greens are mentioned. No vitamin C, meant the ships of war were floating death traps. On this revolting diet, Scurvy took only 8 weeks to appear. Dr. Bisset warns:

'During the first fortnight from Madeira, with the gun ports all open, except some of the lower ones, and the ship well aired' the men begin to sweat, they become pale and listless and the first symptoms appear .... 7 weeks out from Madeira and the scurvy is rife. Those suffered most who carried forward scurvy from a previous voyage, or those 'of puny constitutions, previous illness, the old, lazy or discontented, provided all these live wholly on the dense, tenacious and salted ship's provisions, and drink nothing but water.'

However, not all on board were equally at risk:

'Adults of clean sound habits, who live at sea chiefly on fresh provisions, and lye well, and rather airy, over a dry deck, are not sensibly affected with any scorbutic taint.'

He means the officers.

He gives us other small insights: Merchant seamen suffered less because, while they worked harder, 'they receive their wages at the end of each voyage and are thereby enabled to buy fresh provisions and liquors at each port.' They often lived ashore on fresh food and so always began a voyage well.

Royal Navy cruises were longer, the men, many of them press-ganged, were kept on board for years to stop them running away; there was a shorter time in port and fresh food was not always available where they anchored. Being strictly confined on board, not only 'sank their spirits' it deprived them of fresh vegetables and recovery time ashore and, says Dr. Bisset firmly indignant: 'Therefore the common practice of turning over sailors, newly arrived from a foreign voyage or long cruize, on board ships that are speedily to be ordered abroad, or on a cruize, except in cases of absolute necessity, is not only inhumane, but highly injurious to the Service.'

It is clear that the problem of Scurvy had to be solved if long voyages of exploration were to be achieved, but Dr. Bisset is saying, it is in the Royal Navy's interest to tackle this problem for **all** voyages.

THE LAND DIET

His first point about the state of the men when they arrived on board, many pressed, already ragged, penniless and not likely to be paid for two years, also leads Charles Bisset to make clear that Scurvy was a landsman's disease too: 'In Cleveland .... scrofulous disorders are also rife in the country', he says.

By giving us details of the diet in Cleveland around 1753-55, not only do we get an intriguing glimpse of what James Cook would have eaten as a farmboy, but we see that meat and bread were the prized food. After visiting a 25 year old Ingelby girl, with a leg ulcer he thought was caused by Scurvy, Dr. Bisset recommended a 'cooling vegetable diet, which her poverty indeed obliged her to observe.' So, the poor ate vegetables. Given a choice, they didn't.

The Cleveland diet 1753-55

FOOD   Heavy, sour, leavened bread
Unfermented flour pudding, dumplings

pease pudding

with: lean cheese

bacon or hung beef

salted and dried fish

Which diet, he says, 'generated more or less of a scurvy every spring in country people and others of low rank in Cleveland'. (In fact poorer people of northern England were still eating this diet during the 1930s.)

DRINK:

Dr. Bisset is more cheerful, when he describes the beer:

Malt Ale: he says was no help to Scurvy. 'The ale of this country, is generally pretty highly coloured, of a dense body, and drank too new ... I find that a pint of Cleveland or Yorkshire ale yields near three ounces of a viscid, ropy extract: which indeed had something of a saccarine taste and appearance, tho' of a very different nature from sugar.' *

* (*See the official experiment with wort of malt on* Endeavour.)

Dr. Bisset adds;

'The oldest people that I know in Cleveland drink very little ale; the men in general drink much of it; they are most commonly outlived by the women, unless these die in child-bed, and are very liable to Rheumatism.'

Small Beer: made from malt but thinner, the Doctor thought no good for Scurvy but London or Edinburgh *Porter*, if old fresh and transparent, was useful 'good for the Gravel [stones] and for labouring people who excersise.'

Small Molasses Beer: 'Is much drank in the houses of farmers and mechanics in Cleveland ... being properly medicated is one of the best drinks in most chronic diseases......if medicated with tar, or by boiling tops, or black spruce, or wormwood, in the water it is made of, it would make an excellent drink for the sailors of his Majesty's Navy; being a good preservative against the Scurvy'. He recommends spruce beer to replace the Navy's malt beer. James Cook, a Cleveland farm boy, would know about making spruce beer.

As a doctor of his day Charles Bisset often talks of the quality of the patient's urine. Urine was important to a medical diagnosis. In Cleveland it was more important for its commercial value. It was collected for use in the Alum Works process, quality was important there too, beer and urine being irrevocably linked. For the alum process, it was said by Colwell writing on alum said:

'the best urine comes from the poor labouring people who drink little strong drink.'

If we dare ask did James Cook sell his urine, the answer must be yes, at least while he was in Staithes, everyone did, and a lowly shop boy would be glad of the money, perhaps to save toward his sea apprenticeship?

To sum up, it may be that James Cook's humble Cleveland childhood in fact provided him with a vegetable-based diet we would now call healthy, and toward which he carried forward no mental objection. Already we can see two plain pieces of logic forming:

1) common sailors are poor, poor people eat vegetables, common sailors can eat vegetables.

2) sailors suffer from Scurvy, Scurvy can be prevented by vegetables, sailors can be prevented from suffering from Scurvy by eating vegetables, and not feel hard done by!

In passing we note that James Cook was over 6 feet tall, which shows he was not stunted in childhood, and must have been reasonably well fed in modern terms. Also, as a farm child he would be brought up to glean the hedgerows as he passed by, raspberries, nettletops, comfrey or dandelion tea in spring, bilberries in July, nuts, blackberries, rosehips, peppermint, sorrel, and sloes to make gin. They are still gleaned today in Cleveland.

Alexander Home describing their second great voyage around the world in *Resolution*[3] says James Cook led by example, and 'as he was not Nice, he commonly Succeded' and the men knew it was 'A great Recommendation to be seen Coming on board with A Handkerchief full of greens.'

Home says scarcely anything came wrong to James Cook that was green. 'It was his practise to Cause great Quantities of Green Stuff to be Boiled Amoungst the pease Soup and wheat'. He did not care what it tasted like, 'But as there was nothing Else to be got they were Obleged to Eat them and it was No Uncommon thing when Swallowing Over these Mess[es] to Curse him heartyly and wish for gods Sake that he Might be Obleged to Eat such Damned Stuff Mixed with his Broth as Long as he Lived.'

DR. BISSET'S RECOMMENDED DIET FOR THE NAVY
In 1755

1.   OATMEAL without husks.
2.   Pepper with BOILED PEASE.
3.   No Suffolk Cheese; BUTTER AND SUGAR instead.
4.   SALT MEAT to be 'well freshened' to open it up.
5.   Made MUSTARD or ONIONS or
         PICKLED CABBAGE with the salt beef or pork.
6.   WATER freshened & PURIFIED (with quick lime).
7.   Molasses SPRUCE BEER, or WATERED spirits.
8.   RICE instead of always dried biscuit.
9.   Each man 2 SUITS OF CLOTHES.
10.   AIRING THE SHIP.
11.   If quick TURNAROUNDS, then EXTRA
         fresh meat and vegetables to be provided.
12.   In bad weather extra RUM.
13.   Ships to the West Indies to arrive in the Autumn.

This diet appears in the Treatise Chapter 3 which is devoted to the **prevention** of Scurvy.

If we compare the actual food taken on *Endeavour,* there are some immediate similarities. They carried 10 bushels of oatmeal and 187 bushels of peas in butts, which they mixed with the portable soup, a method recommended by Dr. Bisset. They took a 'machine for Sweetening Foul water', Spruce beer, 100 lbs of best mustard seed, onions which they replenished at Madeira, and they managed to buy rice in the husk at Rio.

But the Royal Navy worked on written orders, strict amounts per man, limited choice. There was an official system to be satisfied. The Victualling Board controlled the food, the Sick and Hurt Board the men's health, the Navy Board the ships, and the Admiralty the men and their orders. What impresses is the speed of the written orders passing from one to another to get *Endeavour* on her way. Apart from standard food provision, always subject to thieving in the dockyards, fraud by the suppliers (the food was often rotten before the ship loaded), and the purser's 'percentage', there were five items allocated to *Endeavour* for official trial and final report. Victualling and Sick and Hurt Boards applied for Sauerkraut, and Robs of Oranges and Lemons to be put on board for official trial. The Admiralty put forward Dr. McBride's wort of malt cure to be tried under instructions, and ordered a trial of Saloup, that is sassafras (poor man's coffee). It was James Cook himself who asked for portable soup.

Portable dried soup, 1000 lbs of it, arrived on board with strict instructions. It was to be served to all the men, sick or well, on the three meatless (Banyan) days of the week, dissolved either in boiling pease or oatmeal, 'having been found extreamly beneficial in long voyages'. There is no instruction to boil greens in it, but on page 112 of his 1755 Treatise, Dr. Bisset was advising the boiling of greens 'in water-gruel or portable soup' to cure the painful joints and bleeding under the skin of Scurvy. Dr. Bisset also lists all the many greens they could use, including those in the tropics, and says they can be boiled in the broth, and must be also 'for the use of the common seamen'. This is what Captain James Cook did.

Wort of malt, Dr. Bisset thought nothing of, and in fact James Cook needed to use it so little as a cure, they added the malt to the breakfast cereal which was much appreciated by the men. James Cook still felt it had been 'beneficial' to their health.

Robs of oranges and lemons, as a marmalade was pleasant to eat but they did not understand that the valuable Vitamin C was destroyed by boiling. Dr. Lind did not know why lime juice worked, for he recommended boiling it to an extract to preserve it. Dr. Bisset recommended rubbing lime juice on the legs and joints to cure scurvy. (One day in Guisborough, old John Reed wandered across the road to his cousin Mr. Ward's garden to pick blackcurrants to rub on his legs for Scurvy. Had he called in Dr. Bisset?)

So the food was placed on board *Endeavour,* official trials were ordered.

But would the crew eat to order?

Dr. Bisset complains that the husky oatmeal provided by the Navy and boiled up into lumpy 'burgou' was 'indeed only fit for hogs' and was rejected by the seamen. He recommended husk-free finely-ground oatmeal, boiled into a 'flummery' of milky hue. But it was the 'Sour Krout' (pickled cabbage: No.5 in Dr. Bisset's list) which caused the men to turn up their noses on *Endeavour.* Sauerkraut was alien to British sailors. So Captain Cook tried a small ruse, serving it up to the officers' table. He comments: 'The Sour Kroutt, the Men at first would not eat it, until I put it in practice - a method I never once Knew to fail with seamen - and this was to have some of it dressed every day for the Cabin Table..and left it to the Option of the men.' After a week he had to put everyone on a ration. Nothing unusual would go down 'but the moment they see their superiors set a value upon it, it becomes the finest stuff in the world and the inventor an honest fellow,' he comments dryly.

This democracy of diet was the key to his success. Dr. Bisset hammered away at the fact in his Treatise, that the officers did not suffer from Scurvy. 'The Commisioned sea officers are preserved from the Scurvy by fresh meat and Rum Punch; and the petty officers' who lived 'wholly on ship's provisions' had a better chance of escaping the Scurvy 'as they are fitter on arrival, have a little money, can buy food at ports, and have more credit with the purser for sugar and rum'.

James Cook practised equality in food. 'He was,' said Alexander

Home of the later *Resolution* voyage, 'as Careful in providing vegetables for the Messes of the Crews as for his own Table and I do believe that in this Means Consisted his graund Art of preserving his people in Health During so Many of the Longest and Hardest Voyages that was Ever Made'. On *Resolution* it seems he perfected the successful elements of the *Endeavour* voyage.

As for airing the ship, and basic cleanliness, cold baths were enforced on all officers and men, with no exceptions.

Another insight comes from Dr. Bisset's complaint that the marines were usually quartered in the forepart of the gun deck, airless under sail, plunging and lifting, wet, leaky, stinking, unwholesome and, as marines were 'more slothful than sailors', they were he says more disposed to disease. It was the dishonourable behaviour of the marines which William Bligh was later to say caused James Cook's death.

There is one point which makes us think James Cook did know of Charles Bisset's ideas; let us call it 'walking about'. Dr. Bisset felt that in the West Indies the exhalations of plants on shore, absorbed by the pores, 'contributed not a little to prevent and retard the progress of Scurvy'. While Alexander Home says that during the *Resolution* voyage Captain Cook 'would Frequently Order them on shore in partys to walk about the Country and smell the Fresh Earth and Herbage and from His Example and Disposition they were in a Manner Let to Know that it was expected they Woud [line] their Stomach with any green stuff that Could [be go]t if it was even at the Risque of getting the grip [es].'

James Cook on *Endeavour* applied all items chosen for trial in accordance with his orders, but he placed them within a routine based on his own underlying knowledge and ideas. His success came from consistent daily attention to diet. In Dr. Bisset's treatise the word 'Regime' is used for diets applied to cures for scurvy; most people used the word that way. But if the diet was to be brought forward from cure to prevention, why not bring forward its regimented application? That is also what James Cook did. As they

passed Cape Horn all the men were free from Scurvy. Three slight cases appeared just before landfall at Tahiti but were cured.
Prevention worked!
Dr. Bisset's method worked! James Cook's method worked!

In 1768, Dr. Charles Bisset was 51. He continued to live at Skelton for many years. His wife Patience had died after producing twins, who soon died too. He later married a lady related to the Pease family of Darlington, who were Quakers. From the beginning, he prospered. His fortune was such he could lend Ralph Jackson £1200 in 1772. He had two daughters. Margaret Bisset, on 16th August 1785, married at Hinderwell, William Walker, a Thirsk attorney, who at times did business with Ralph Jackson. Patience Bisset married the Rev. Daniel Addison of Thirsk. Her husband became Rector of Knayton. When old, Charles Bisset and his wife Anne went to live at Knayton, where he died in 1791. He left his silver hilted sword to his nephew Lieutenant James Bisset of the Navy, who later became Rear Admiral of the White, together with his two works on Fortifications both 'elegantly bound in red turkey in the Mahogany case made for them,' nestling in velvet.

His restrained memorial stone, stands high on the wall of the parish church at Leake near Knayton, where he is buried in the chancel.

Toward the end of Charles Bisset's life, there was some dispute as to whether, being a military surveyor he could possibly be a doctor; which forced him to write a letter explaining his double career. Mrs. Bisset made it available for his obituary in the Gentleman's Magazine.[4] It says:

'The physician who studies Nature to record her history of diseases, with their symptoms .....His observations are not of less value to posterity than those of the cautious and expert navigator who plans and chalks out the unknown shore.'

Not, we notice, a simple comparison of study in medicine with military surveying, but an evaluation of research in medicine as equal to exploration of new lands. By his adjectives, he appears to mean James Cook. 'Expert navigator' of the 'unknown shore' was most people's idea of Captain Cook, but 'cautious' is a personal evaluation. How did he know that?

On balance, it is reasonable to believe James Cook knew Doctor Bisset's work. Dr. Bisset's published ideas of **prevention,** seem too similar to James Cook's application, to be purely coincidental. Had James Cook also met Dr. Bisset?

Had they talked about Scurvy?

With such attention to the health of his crew, *Endeavour* would set off with a good chance of returning with the results of the Transit of Venus. They could bring home the reports of five official experiments in prevention of Scurvy, set within a regime applied by James Cook. Yet it was the Botanical discoveries of the voyage, an aim added at the last moment, which would overwhelm Europe.

17

THE BOTANISTS

DR. FOTHERGILL

In 1753, the preacher John Wesley caught a terrible cold, which sank to his chest and gave him pneumonia. He decided he had better write the inscription for his tombstone.[1] It included the line: 'Who died of a Consumption in the Fifty-first Year of his Age'. He sent for Dr. Fothergill and lived to be 88.

The Quaker John Fothergill was one of the most popular doctors in London. The son of Yorkshire Quakers, he was sent for by George Jackson in London, both before and after the *Endeavour* voyage.

In 1764 George wrote from London to Ralph Jackson, saying Dolly was ill at his house of a fever ... .in great danger .... attended by Dr. Fothergill.

In May 1771, Ralph himself, visiting London, took ill at George's house in Old Palace Yard. 'I desired my Bro. to send for Doct Fothergill in the evening he ordered a Blister and I went to bed.'

Ralph says 'the blister operated'. He recovered in three days.

For John Wesley, Dr. Fothergill had recommended 'country air, with rest, assess' milk, and riding daily.'

As a Quaker, Dr. Fothergill was attached to the Wapping Quakers to give medical attention to the poor and sick, who were being helped at Wapping Meeting House. He was firmly against the method of paying the coal heavers their wages at public alehouses, such as The Bell.

Dr. Fothergill is known to us now, more as a famous botanist, a Fellow of the Royal Society. He had wonderful botanical gardens at Ham House in Upton, he developed the idea of plant interchange, sending plants all over the world. In 1754 the Royal Society had offered a premium to any Planter willing to try new plants.

To Dr. Fothergill, the 1768 *Endeavour* voyage would be an unmissable opportunity, to find new plants. It was more than likely he had something to do with Joseph Banks going in the first place. They were both botanists, both members of the Royal Society. As was Lord Sandwich who, although he had been 1st Lord of the Admiralty, was at that time Post-Master General. Lord Sandwich could bring his influence to bear at the Admiralty. Dr. Fothergill's acquaintance with George Jackson could provide a route through Royal Navy administration, from the moment the King asked the Navy to provide a ship. The Royal Navy found a way to allow Joseph Banks to join the voyage.

Dr. Fothergill gave him a parting gift.

Joseph Banks notes in his diary on board *Endeavour:*

'23rd [September 1769] ……..We also today made a pye of the North American apples which Dr. Fothergill gave me, which provd very good, if not quite equal to the apple pyes which our friends in England are now eating, good enough to please us who have been so long deprivd of the fruits of our native Country.'

The Royal Society understood that the voyage was to-have a double purpose, Astronomy and Botany.

~~~

JOSEPH BANKS, ESQUIRE
1743 - 1820

This amiable young man of 25 who was to join *Endeavour,* was a rich, upper middle class squire with a country estate in Lincolnshire. As a boy his passion was for fishing, and it would bring him many contacts throughout his life, including that passionate fisherman, his Lincolnshire neighbour, Lord Sandwich.

Joseph left his home at Revesby, aged 9, to attend Harrow School, where he showed not a jot of interest in Greek or Latin, nor any other attributes of a gentleman, apart for country sports. His leaning was for happy play. At 13 his father took him away and sent him to Eton, a savage place, being tamed by the headmaster, Dr. Barnard, where Joseph's strong physique and pleasant manner kept him out of trouble, even though he avoided work. It has been said that one day, when left behind after swimming in the river, walking alone along the river banks, he realised the beauty surrounding him, and was instantly converted to an enquirer into nature. More likely he had a mental shift, a sudden connection of ideas, which turned him to plants, pollination, bugs and butterflies Perhaps at 14 he suddenly understood reproduction? From then on his intellect was applied to botany, his life's work began.

Joseph Banks went up to Oxford at 17. Meeting the mixed bag of brilliant scholars, drunken lecturers, indolent bores, he imported his own tutor in botany. It was common enough for a wealthy student to bring his own tutor, often a clergyman, but Joseph Banks' tutor, Israel Lyons, came from another aspect of 18th century life, the mixing of artisan and academic; where ordinary men still reliant for a living upon silversmithing, ironmongery, engraving, surveying, pursued knowledge for its own sake, with those of high rank. There were many instances, James Cook was one example. In the public view, Captain Cook was serving on Mr. Bank's voyage on the *Endeavour.* Cook was the artisan, Banks the academic.

This social attitude lay also behind the muddle with Alexander

Dalrymple. He appears to have seen himself as the aristocratic academic, directing the voyage. Cook could sail the ship, view the Transit of Venus, and be the artisan. Royal Navy discipline could not allow it. Lord Sandwich knew the Navy Rules. On board His Majesty's ships, the Captain's command was Law.

Joseph Banks did not want to command the ship. He had already sailed as extra-numerary with Constantine Phipps, he would already understand his place on board. Botany was his goal - anywhere!

It was a last minute change of plan for Joseph Banks to join *Endeavour.* As late as April, he was still in correspondence with the naturalist Pennant, who was advising him to take an umbrella, when visiting Lapland.

Banks also had a 'lady', Miss Blosset was expecting him to marry her. He may have seen her as his 'lady of the heart'. Men of property married late and with the head, for social status, land and money. Yet there is strength to the idea that Lord Sandwich's 'lady of the heart' Miss Ray, truly was so, he spent more time with her than with his wife. Clearly Joseph Banks was not urgently seeking matrimony. The *Endeavour* voyage could have fed an irresistible urgency - to escape.

PART III

THE *ENDEAVOUR* VOYAGE

While the *Endeavour* voyage to survey the Transit of Venus turned out to be more than anyone expected, except perhaps Joseph Banks, it was only the beginning of fame for James Cook.

18

CHOSEN!

SHIP + COMMAND + CREW

There were three main ways a ship could be provided.

Firstly, by the Royal Society. Why they did not have the money?

Secondly, by the East India Company, but they were still reeling from the Manila debt. Thirdly, by the King's Navy. So the Royal Society petitioned the young King for help, suggesting £4000. On 5th March 1768, the Admiralty notified the Navy Board that His Majesty would fund the venture, and a proper vessel was to be fitted out. It could be said that, from that date, Alexander Dalrymple's fate was sealed. If the Navy was to provide the ship, they would provide the crew, and Royal Navy rules must prevail. Yet the Royal Society still thought Dalrymple would have its direction. So did he.

He began petitioning for the voyage in the winter of 1766-7. Alexander Dalrymple, through his brother Lord Hailes, had met Adam Smith, who was busy with his own studies at the British Museum. Adam Smith wrote to Lord Shelburne on 12th February, 1767, explaining that Alexander was publishing his discoveries in the South Seas, his interest in discovering a Southern Continent and the terms on which he would take a ship to find it.

'The terms he would ask are, first, the absolute command of the ship with the naming of all the officers

… and secondly, in case he should lose his ship…… before he gets into the South Seas, that the Government will undertake to give him another....

The ship properest for such an expedition, he says, would be an old fifty-gun ship without her guns……but he will go in any ship with a hundred to a thousand tons'

As to 'the ship properest' - compare Lord Sandwich's 1772 letter to Joseph Banks, about him disdaining the Whitby cat *Resolution*:
'the Launceston is a 44 gun ship ... she would cost £8000 to repair ……and could not go to sea with less than 180 men, & could not carry provisions for them for half the time they might chance to be out: if she had her proper masts anchors & cables that crew would not be sufficient to work her, if the masts &c were diminished she would sail no better than a collier, and be unable to ride out a gale of wind….'

A Whitby collier Cat sailed in the North Sea with 16 men, across the Atlantic with about 25. Allowing for the usual one third death rate, 50 crew would be reasonable. (The Navy allowed *Endeavour* at first 70).

CHOOSING THE SHIP

Three ships were considered in 1768. The sloop *Tryall* was rejected within five days. On 21st March the Navy Board wrote to the Admiralty Secretary to say the ship *Rose* would not be able to stow the quantity of provisions required for such a voyage. They suggested instead a Cat-built vessel, which would be roomy enough for the purpose. One of about 350 tons could be bought in the River Thames.

A Cat was hardly Royal Navy trim. They were used as transports, with their owner's crews. A Royal Navy officer would be a shade embarrassed to command a Whitby collier Cat. Where could they find an officer with experience of such a vessel?

Alexander Dalrymple later wrote to Hawksworth*, in connection with choosing the ship 'When I gave as a reason for preferring the Endeavour to the other ship that was smaller *[the Rose?]* that being able to carry another anchor and cable might be of the utmost consequence, a navy Oracle told me that I was much mistaken if I thought I should have just what stores I pleased, that there was an Establishment, although I might be allowed an anchor and cable extraordinary on such a voyage.' Dalrymple had come up against Navy Office bureaucracy. It shows that when the *Earl of Pembroke (Endeavour)* was being chosen in March, he expected to have charge of the ship. It was 3rd April before his hopes were dashed.

THE SHIP CHOSEN

The *Earl of Pembroke* had been sitting idle in the Thames, moored at Mr. Bird's ways. Henry Bird was a shipwright with yards and anchorages along the south bank of the river, from the Rotherhithe bend down to Deptford. His house was near the Deptford Dock. The ship had been built three years earlier in Fishburn's yard at Whitby.

In 1765 Thos. and Rob. Milner had sailed her out of Newcastle on 26th Feb., 4th May, 23rd July, 14th Oct., 29th Nov., loading at 201, 206, 214, 219, 218 chauldrons of coals. Compare other colliers loading that year:

Brotherly Love (Wm. Jefferson)	152
Nautilus (Wm. Bielby)	165
Friends Glory (Wm Milner)	179
Henry & Esther (Rob. Watson)	176

So she was bigger than other Whitby Cats then employed in coal deliveries, more suited to longer voyages. But after three years at sea, in good condition, her sailing qualities known, she was a good buy.

(The ship's owner Thomas Milner of Whitby was paid £2800plus interest of £40-10s.-l1d to his bill of 24th June, 1769.)

On 23rd March, 1768, Deptford officers were told to survey the *Earl of Pembroke,* lying in Mr. Bird's ways. By 29th she had been bought. Within two days she was brought downriver to Deptford and, on 2nd April, docked in the single dock. The very next day, Alexander Dalrymple declined to go on the voyage. Yet he later implied that he chose her. He was certainly giving his opinion on her.

So, is it true James Cook chose her?

Palliser, writing years later, said so. But was Palliser biased? It is true the Royal Navy chose her. Was Palliser saying James Cook helped?

James Cook, a Royal Navy Master, was familiar with the Navy Board surveyors. He was at home living in London. Master Cook was known as an adviser on Whitby Cats. George Jackson knew James Cook's North Sea background in Cats. Master Cook knew the Milners of Whitby who had run her for three years, and her ex-crew would be working on the river, he could find out how she performed. His wife's namesakes,[2] William and Daniel Batts had been shipwrights at Deptford. James Cook was on the official and the unofficial grapevines. It is quite likely he was asked to take a look at *Earl of Pembroke.*

She was named *Endeavour* Bark, on 5th April.

WHO WOULD COMMAND?

The Royal Society had hoped that Captain Campbell would take command. He had served as flag-captain to Sir Edward Hawke, was a well-known scientific sailor, a member of the Royal Society, who had published a paper about Jupiter's moons. He declined to be interested. Maybe it was the comical ship.

Why did James Cook not apply to go as ship's Master? His Master's ticket only allowed him to sail any 4th rate.

The Royal Navy was acting at its best. Competence shines through. From 21st March, Secretary Philip Stevens was signing letters 'same day'.. 'to save time.' Of course there was patronage, as will become clear, but there was also commonsense in doubling up the skills needed. Everyone expected a third of the crew to die. If an essential man died, another must be able to take his place. There would only be one chance to measure the Transit of Venus.

Master Cook had 10 years experience as a surveyor for the Navy. He had presented a paper to the Royal Society on observations of Jupiters moons. He had not applied to the Society to go as Observer, yet was suited as one, should the two Observers die on the outward voyage.

The *Endeavour's* captain should be, at least, double skilled. James Cook had triple skill. He was a Navy Master, a surveyor/astronomer, and a Whitby Cat man. It was inevitable he would be considered for the voyage, even if not chosen. But the ship needed a Leutenant.

On 3rd April, the day after the ship entered Deptford dry dock, the Royal Society met. A letter from the Admiralty informed them that a Cat of 370 tons had been bought to carry their Observers to sea, and asked for instructions, to be given to the Commander after he had arrived in the Latitudes. The Society answered, that the Observers would be two gentlemen versed in the particular science, and instructions would follow.

Alexander Dalrymple being present, the President of the Society informed the meeting that the Royal Society had recommended Alexander Dalrymple to the Admiralty as commander but had been informed that such a posting would be totally repugnant to the rules of the Navy. It was perhaps, unfortunately phrased. That day, Alexander Dalrymple declined to go as Observer unless he could command.

Was it simply a clash of cultures? A mistake in the meaning of the words 'command' and 'direction'? Dalrymple was an East India Company man. In the Company, a captain sailed the ship 'under the direction' of the SupraCargoes, who were still travelling with the ships, to wherever trade lay. In the Royal Navy, a captain commanded the ship, as the King's servant, and followed only Admiralty written orders, as to where he went.

The Royal Navy was clear, their appointed officer commanded. Others were confused. Even after the *Endeavour* returned, her voyage was often expressed in public as being 'under the direction of Mr. Banks'.

Alexander Dalrymple fell between the two different systems.

The second stumbling block was also Royal Navy rules.

The Rules said a ship that size, demanded enough crew to need one, or more, Lieutenants.

Official Regulations said: May 5th, 1766. No persons to pass for Lieutenant until he has served 6 years in the Royal Navy exclusively.

Dalrymple could not qualify.

The Royal Society Resolved to consider a proper person in his place.

JAMES COOK CHOSEN TO COMMAND

On 5th April a routine order to repay Master Cook's vouchers for the *Grenville* went through, but it was the 12th April before the first indication of his involvement. When replying to a letter from Commodore Palliser to the Admiralty saying that in view of:

'Mr. Cook to be employed elsewhere' the Admiralty ordered Palliser to appoint 'in Mr. Cook's absence.'

Between the Royal Navy providing a ship on 5th March and the meeting of the Royal Society on April 3rd, had Palliser interfered?

Kippis writing in 1788 said Sir Edward Hawke had declared 'that he would suffer his right hand to be cut off before he would sign any [brevet][3] commision for Dalrymple'. But the partisan Palliser was Kippis main source of information.

Dalrymple himself wrote in 1773 that he had no 'resentment to, or dissatisfaction with, the worthy and brave old officer *[Hawke]* who was at the head of the Admiralty when the Endeavour was purchased.'

In his memoirs in 1802, he added that Hawke had been 'wrought upon by insinuation that he would be exposed to parliamentary impeachment if he employed any but a Naval Officer.'

Was this Palliser at work, or official legal advice? George Jackson had received his extra appointment as Judge Advocate of the Fleet, on February 19th, 1768, just as the command was being discussed. Official legal advice, surely must have been approved by him. He knew Alexander Dalrymple's East India background but the King had requested a Royal Navy ship.

Sir Charles Saunders, also, may have advised. When he retired as First Lord of the Admiralty in December 1766, he had warmly supported Sir Edward Hawke as his replacement. Hugh Palliser was a friend of Charles Saunders. So was George Jackson; even Ralph Jackson would walk round to Spring Gardens to call socially on Sir Charles.

Charles Saunders had himself been round the world with Lord Anson. A 'Brevet' commision was not unknown, but with a limited budget (which meant limiting the objectives), Navy Regulations, and what was clearly a power group pushing for their own man, Alexander Dalrymple was confronted by Royal Navy refusal. Had he agreed to go as Observer, to give up command of the ship, he might have been on board when the *Endeavour* sailed.

Meanwhile, the *Earl of Pembroke* now *Endeavour* sat in the dock in a heatwave, with her planks drying and gaps yawning open. John Satterly, ship's carpenter, her first crew member, was appointed on 22nd April from the *Prince Edward*. There was urgency to get the ship ready if she was to leave in time. There were mobs and riots taking place in the streets of London, caused by the defiant re-election of John Wilkes as MP, people parading blue cockades, shouting 'Liberty!' There was a seamen's strike.

On 5th May, Master James Cook was appointed by the Admiralty to command the vessel. The Royal Society called him in, and appointed him as a proper person to be 1st Observer. Mr. Green, who had offered in December to go to the South, was appointed 2nd Observer.

On 18th May, *Endeavour's* hull came out of the dry dock and was moved into the huge dock basin. She was ready to receive her masts. Master James Cook knew how to rigg a Whitby Cat. So he and Satterly the carpenter would be fully busy.

That same day, *HMS Dolphin* under Lieutenant Sam Wallis arrived in the Downs anchorage off Kent at the end of her second great voyage around the world.

CHOOSING THE CREW

Sam Wallis was the same age as James Cook, he was 40 that year. He had been a Lieutenant for 20 years, had served under Sir Charles Saunders in the St. Lawrence at Quebec, and commanded the 60 gun *Prince of Orange.* The *Dolphin* had made a circumnavigation in 1765 under Commodore Jack Byron, and discovered little. Sam Wallis took her to unknown parts of the Pacific from 1766-8, discovered islands including Tahiti, and kept his crew free of Scurvy. The voyage was a success. He had sailed home by the north Tongan islands, refreshed at Tinian, one of the Marianas, sailed round north of the Philippines, south to Batavia, refitted at the Cape.

Dolphin had the experienced men to back up Master James Cook.

With typical Royal Navy cruelty, *Dolphin's* key officers and men, after two years away, were posted to *Endeavour.* They had survived the Pacific. Tahiti was within the 'box on the map' where measuring the Transit of Venus was planned. These men knew the way.

Lieut. John Gore had been on *Dolphin* with Byron and Wallis

Molineux,	ship's Master	Wallis
Clerke	Master's Mate	Wallis
Pickersgill	Master's Mate	Wallis
Francis Haite	carpenter's Mate	Byron

Now we begin to see George Jackson's patronage.

Master Cook was appointed 1st Lieutenant on 25th May.

On 26th May, Zachary Hicks was appointed 2nd Lieutenant. Born in Stepney, son of Edward and Thomasine Hicks, he was probably the grandson of Zachary Hicks an East India Company captain in 1719. The Hicks family were friends of William Wilson, who owned a family house at Ripon, where young Zachary Hicks had enlisted in the Royal Navy. A Hicks family lived at South End in Beckenham, and were friends of Aunt Ward, Captain Edward Ward's mother who lived there.

Then there was Richard Pickersgill.

Richard Pickersgill was the nephew of John Lee, George Jackson's Man.

A gentleman's Man was not quite like that fictional fixer, 'Jeeves'. A real Man's Man reflected the interests of his employer, and lived with the family. Thomas Presswick had been Mr. Ward's secretary and household accountant. Harry Pecket supported Mr. Jackson, George and Ralph's father's interest in horse flesh. Long after Mr. Jackson died, Harry would take a horse to London for George, visit Boulby and knock out a horse's wolf tooth for Ralph. John Lee, was George Jackson's Man, living in London at George's house in Old Palace Yard. He escorted George's three girls on journeys north to visit their grandmother and aunts at Ayton.

In the summer of 1763, John Lee was with George and Ralph at Grainge farm. George and Dolly had broken a stay on the spring of the high perch Phaeton sporting carriage. Ralph writes in his diary:

'Friday 1st July 1763 My Brother George, Harry Pecket, John Lee (my Brother's Servant) and myself set out for Whitby before breakfast.' They called at Loftus Grainge and Mr. Wardell's and had dinner at Mr. Pease's in Whitby.

Then there was the appointment of Isaac Manley, a boy who appears to be related to George Jackson's aunt Ann Manley.

George Jackson, it seems, had placed three officers and a boy.

James Cook's promotion to 1st Lieutenant was another matter. Was it pushed by the professionals at the Admiralty; Palliser and George Jackson, both making sure of an expert sailor, once they knew from Lord Sandwich that Mr. Banks wished to go on the voyage? We cannot ignore East India Commodore Sir William James, whose cosy relationship with Lord Sandwich, that year gained him the place of Elder Brother of Trinity House. Yes, it is possible they were simply running out of time to prepare, that the promotion was simply expedient. James Cook had great qualifications, still, it was quite a leap up to 1st Lieutenant. He clearly had Navy backing for the promotion. Was it about a Navy interest-group keeping control? James Cook's support even appears to be political, as well as broad-based and deep.

His Cleveland patronage group must have stood solidly behind him. With their awareness of the details of his sea experience, the length of time they had known him: the 2nd Secretary of the Admiralty, the famous East India Commodore Wilson, James Cook's first patron Thomas Skottowe, the East India men could answer any doubts. We are forced to believe he was their group nominee. They had met and listened to Alexander Dalrymple. They knew his enthusiasm to find the 'Lost' Southern Continent, but the main aim of the voyage was not to wander off looking for it. The main aim was a safe return, with the results of the Transit of Venus.

Looked at another way, most men had to lobby for places on ships. A straightforward man like James Cook would follow the usual pattern by approaching those with influence and asking for their recommendation. It is possible he asked to go as ship's Master, an ambitious but not outrageous request, which fits his personality. But to raise him to 1st Lieutenant, was the result of people pushing hard at the Admiralty, and knowing and using the Navy Rules.

The Royal Society had to be satisfied too. Lord Sandwich as Post-

Master General at the time, was not too far from the ocean, due to the number of Post packet ships sailing all over the known world. His rich young friend Joseph Banks was going on the ship. Lord Sandwich, the Hon. Constantine Phipps, and Joseph Banks were all members of the Royal Society. They made a powerful upper class group. George Jackson knew the *Endeavour* had to stand the best chance of returning. His own position depended on it.

Is it possible Dalrymple was ousted by Lord Sandwich, once he heard that Joseph Banks wanted to go on the voyage? As a Royal Society venture, their member the botanist Joseph Banks, doubled the purpose of their voyage for science. And at his own expense.

Palliser, George Jackson, Sir William James, belonged to the Lord Sandwich influence group. Sir Charles Saunders' politics were slightly different, but he was above all a professional sailor.

In appointing the crew, Lieutenant James Cook now had his own modest influence. He brought with him William Howson, as captain's servant from the *Grenville.*

Once in command, he had to agree each member of the crew.

John Gathrey boatswain, he had no objection to.

Stephen Forwood gunner 'of good testimony'.

Thomas Hardman, Bosun's mate had sailed with Cook in 1767.

Isaac Smith, aged 16, very expert in surveying and maps - was his wife's relation. He had already served in *Grenville* as Able Seaman.

Peter Flower, who would drown at Rio, was practised in navigating unknown coasts, 'a good hardy seaman' who had already served with James Cook for 5 years in Newfoundland.

We have to wonder, were there other political/influence groups placing men on *Endeavour*? The pattern of patronage at that time would suggest so. Even so, Lord Sandwich's group had taken control of the ship. Could anyone else have doubled the value of the voyage by placing Joseph Banks and his entourage on the ship?

19

THE ENDEAVOUR LEAVES
1768

Lieutenant Cook received his final orders from the Admiralty on 30th July. These were in two parts. Firstly the voyage to Tahiti to observe the Transit of Venus. The second part was his secret orders to sail south from Tahiti to 40 degrees then west to discover if possible any southern continent as suggested by Alexander Dalrymple.

James Cook was also carrying the 'Hints' by the Earl of Morton, President of the Royal Society, which included the instructions that, if such a land was discovered, records should be made of its animals, vegetables and minerals. This clause makes clear that the Royal Society was in full support of Joseph Banks and his entourage of botanists and artists.

Joseph Banks was given Alexander Dalrymple's maps of the Pacific to take with him. It was a kind gesture.

Lieutenant Cook joined the *Endeavour* at Gallions Reach on 30th July. The pilot John Blackburne took the ship down the tricky Thames estuary and into the Channel: he may have been Mrs. Cook's stepfather. He left the ship on 7th August.

Endeavour sailed on to Plymouth where the crew were to receive two months wages in advance, and some extra cabin space was being built for Mr Banks.

On 14th August Joseph Banks was still in London happily saying important farewells. It is said he was at the opera when he received the request for him and his party to join the ship. They hurried to Plymouth. The winds were strong and unfavourable for ten days, but on 25th August *Endeavour* set sail and they stood out to sea.

20

'JUNIUS'
1769

On 21st January 1769, the gentlemen of London shook out their newspapers to read in the 'Public Advertiser', the first of a set of vitriolic letters, signed by *'JUNIUS'*. No-one has ever discovered without doubt, who *'Junius'* was. An argument has been made, that it was the pen-name of Alexander Dalrymple. Or was it the agitator John Wilkes? A retort came from *'MODESTUS.'* Who was he?[1]

The Marquis of Granby, commander in chief of the Army, was the prime target. The scholar-soldier William Draper rushed to his defence, protesting in a letter to the newspaper on 26th January. *'Junius'* turned on him with searing ferocity.

'By what accident did it happen that in the midst of all this bustle and these claims for justice to your injured troops, the name of the Manilla ransome was buried in a profound, and since then an uninterrupted silence? Did the Ministers suggest any motive powerful enough to tempt a man of honour to desert and betray his fellow soldiers?'

Had William Draper, he asked, been bought-off by the award of the 'blushing ribbon' of a Knight of the Bath?

Stung and angry, William Draper replied that in September 1768,

Admiral Sir Samuel Cornish and he had visited Lord Shelburne to discuss the Manila ransome claim, which Spain had never paid (His own unpaid share was £25,000).... and had been frankly told that 'their rights must be sacrificed to national convenience.'

The newspapers were sizzling, the readers wide-eyed, William Draper accused *'Junius'* of being a tyrant, and cruel, 'whose assertions are false and scandalous.' All that summer of 1769, readers were avidly talking of the *'Junius'* letters but, on 1st September, William Draper's wife died, and he retired from the fray.

'Junius' had already turned to more agitating matters. In August he addressed the great lawyer Doctor William Blackstone, about the common cause between the people and Mr. Wilkes. The first meetings of the Yorkshire Gentlemen took place that September, about Wilkes and the troubled unbalanced British Constitution. Public order was in doubt, the outcome uncertain. Reason was being challenged by feelings. One gentleman wrote to complain that Sterne's new book 'Sentimental Journey' was 'desultory, unconnected and obscene.' Uneasy readers kept reading.

At the height of the heated exchanges, *'Junius'* attacked the circumstances around the arrest, by civil process, of General Gansell of the Guards, a tacky business which the Ward family would have liked forgotten, but which could be developed by rampant Wilkesites into a point of principle - which ought to prevail, civil or military law? William Draper's last letter had claimed to be 'a word at parting' as he stood 'proud' upon his academic education. Yet now the public believed he had returned to the attack as, suddenly, a new opponent of *'Junius',* appeared, who went by the name of *'Modestus'.*

George Jackson, later, would be rashly accused of being *'Junius'.* It is much more likely that George Jackson was *'Modestus'* writing, not in attack, but in defence of his first cousin, General William Gansell.

According to *'Junius',* a major General of the Army had been arrested by the Sheriff's officers for a considerable debt. Another officer of the Guards 'not then on duty' intervened, neither of those gentleman being 'young officers, nor very young men.' In the scuffle, one officer tried to call out the Guards. Were the forces of the Crown over-riding the common law of the land? It was, said *'Junius'* a crime by the Government administration, against the people!

Readers held their breath. London simmered.

Who would answer?

'MODESTUS' replied.

In steady prose, we can read as follows:

At first and sensibly, he offers detailed facts.

Secondly he explains the procedures of English law and Military law, when the two are in conflict. At the time, George Jackson was Judge Advocate of the Fleet, and had been involved in running courts martial since at least 1757. He had the gravitas and technical knowledge to write the *'Modestus'* letter, as well as access to the true facts, from his cousin General Gansell.

'Modestus' begins by pointing out that the letter from *'Junius'* is full of 'malice, absurdity, barbarity of intention, dullness of stile and composition,' the last point most cutting. He asks why *'Junius'* had not replied to the rebuttal in the Gazette; though the Gazette writer 'could not confirm the facts', so had taken *'Junius'* letter to be true 'but with doubts'. *'Modestus'* lists the false accusations and gives the detailed facts.

With the country deeply uneasy about Wilkes, London boiling to riot, *'Modestus'* makes an obvious attempt to reduce the Gansell incident to a storm in a coffee cup. Two officers sitting in a coffee house, had seen the attempt to arrest General Gansell, one had gone out to demand an explanation, the other had not bothered. There had been an altercation, so the sentry on duty had called his sergeant, a small fracas ended in an arrest.

As to the question, whether military or civil law should prevail, it was a simple matter of rules of evidence. A military trial first, could distort a later civil trial 'for which they are bailed already'. By 'distort' he really means the danger of two opposite verdicts. *'Modestus'* accuses *'Junius'* of putting 'the cart before the horse'. It is a firm plain letter, sensible, very like George Jackson.

Was George Jackson really *'Modestus'*? Look at the first words of his letter:

'Junius ….. you challenge any tool of administration [*the Government*] to defend the conduct of the ministry. I accept of your challenge. I am no tool of Administration but your equal, Junius, perhaps your superior, in everything that may become a man.'

How odd. He accepts the challenge, but is not one of those being challenged. He is of the administration, but not.

A tool and not a tool?

As 2nd Secretary to the Admiralty, George Jackson was subject to the politically appointed First Lord. As also Judge Advocate of the Fleet he was legally independent.

There is one practical point in favour of George Jackson being *'Modestus'*, something he leaves out. Nowhere does he excuse or defend William Gansell's hasty proud behaviour, as that of the natural pride of a General in the Guards when arrested in public. George Jackson would be ashamed of the debt, and he knew his cousin's hasty temper of old. He would defend him, but not for the wrong thing.

The obvious aim of, *'Modestus'* is to calm troubled waters. This purpose, the tool not a tool, the tone, the detailed facts, the ommision, the explanation of the law, all lead to George Jackson being *'Modestus'*.

His grandson George, writing in 1895, says there was no evidence that George Jackson was *'Junius'*, although 'he wrote a lot in the newspapers (the General and Public Advertiser was one)'[2] and …. for some reason of his own under many different signatures.

A hundred years later, the *'Junius'* controversy still intrigued readers. Who could *'Junius'* have been?

In 1850, an exchange of letters appeared in 'Notes and Queries' magazine, putting forward the idea that George Jackson really was *'Junius'*.

P wrote, 'I possess an unpublished letter by Junius to Woodfall [editor of the Gazette] which once belonged to Sir George Jackson.'

W replied, pointing out that George Woodfall 'has recorded the fact that he lent one letter to a Mr. Duppa which was never returned.' W adds that P is illogical, and that George Jackson probably collected the letter for curiosity.

Did he indeed?

Was Mr. Duppa possibly Stephen Dupuy who, in 1763, appears in a list of translators and clerks of the Secret Service branch of the Post Office, the clerks who intercepted mail on behalf of the Government?

There are several indications and facts which link George Jackson with the secret services. The Admiralty set aside large sums for it. In 1764, £1000 was allowed to the Secretary of the Admiralty 'to be applied to such particular and Secret Service as the Board shall order.'

In November 1766, George Jackson was appointed Deputy Secretary to the Admiralty and '£500 impressed to Mr George Jackson Dep. Sec. for Contingencies.' ADM 12. (52).

But on 19th August 1769, George's mother died. He arrived on 26th at Guisborough and Great Ayton, and returned with his daughters to London on 3rd September. The dates do not pre-empt the *Modestus* letters.

Endeavour had sailed off the map, and not been heard of. There was silence, no letters, no sightings by ships. Had she sunk? Then in 1771 a letter arrived from the Cape! The Royal Navy was bringing her home.

21

THE TRANSIT OF VENUS

1769

Venus is always in transit around the sun. In 1761 and 1769 it was due to line up between the sun and the earth. A dark spot against the sun, it would be seen. Here was the chance to survey the sky.

Before Haley died (he of the Comet) he had suggested observing this movement in the heavens. By measuring the angles as Venus passed across the sun's disc, scientists could work out the distance to Venus. With this figure, they already had a calculation called Kepler's 3rd Law, which would then tell them, how far away was the sun from earth.

This would give them the AU, which means Astronomical Unit.

That was their goal.

With the AU, they could then describe the distances to planets and stars and measure the universe. The Transit of Venus gave them a breathtaking chance. It would not happen again until 1874 and 1882.

Preparations had begun to view the phenomenon at all points over the world. Europe would be mostly in darkness. In America it would be visible over the settled areas, and laymen were encouraged to make a smoked glass to protect their eyesight and to take recordings. The East India Company sent orders to seventeen of their ships abroad. There was excitement within scientific circles.

In Britain the 1769 Transit was not expected to be clear enough. In the event it was. The point of the Royal Society sending observers to Norway's Cape, and James Cook to the South Pacific, was to form a web of measurements, a survey from different angles, to increase accuracy. They were taking no chances.

It was the attribute of an educated man to show an interest in science. In Ralph Jackson it was with a touch of wonder, for William Wilson it was a practical tool of navigation, with Thomas Wardell it was sheer enthusiasm.

Ralph had had an early experience of wonder at the heavens. One day in 1756, the 21st May, while in his room high in his master's Newcastle house, he saw a star. He thought it was a kite flying a lantern, a boys' trick. On 26th May it was still passing over Newcastle. It 'now seems to be a Comet Moving west to East, shining brightly to the Naked Eye the size of a Walnut, in less than an hour travelled the breadth of three chimneys,' he records with fascination

On 17th March 1764 Ralph 'sat up till One o'clock in the morning observing an Eclipse of the Moon, t'was near total'.

When William Wilson, came to live at Ayton, the East India Commodore's natural interest in the heavens and navigation, gave Ralph a study companion. He acquired a good reflecting telescope.

On 17th March 1764, Ralph 'sat up till One o'clock in the morning observing an Eclipse of the Moon, 'twas near total.'

On 1st April, a Sunday, 'I rode to Ayton and observed with my Bro. Wilson the Solar Eclipse which was not so great as expected, dined and went to church with them in the afternoon.'

The 1761 Transit of Venus had not been expected to be seen in Britain. Although great efforts were made round the world, the results were not clear. It was widely agreed they could be improved.

In the event, the Transit was seen in Britain. Ralph Jackson says: Saturday 3rd June 1769 he 'observed through my reflecting telescope the Transit of Venus over the Sun's Disc, she came on about four minutes after seven, & went down with the Sun.' This was in the evening.

DR. JAMES LIND jnr

At Hawkhill near Edinburgh, Dr. James Lind the younger observed the Transit of Venus in 1769. He sent an account of his observations to the Royal Society, who printed it in their Transactions. Later he would join Joseph Banks on a visit to explore the Hebrides. Banks also intended to take him on the *Resolution*.

This James Lind was tall, as 'thin as a lath', with a sweet disposition, a love of Eastern wonders gained from an East India trip, a quick hand at conjuring and a fascination with antiquities. He observed the Eclipse of the Moon on 14th December 1769.

There was enthusiasm for astronomy in Cleveland among Ralph Jackson's circle. On 12th September 1769 he dined by appointment at his farm at Loftus Grainge, inviting Rev. Oldfield, Mr. Smith of Marske, Mr. Easterby of Loftus, the lawyer John Harrison, Mr. W. Sanderson and Captain Peacock came to them in the afternoon. At 3 o'clock in the morning, Mr. Wardell called them up 'to see a Comet which now rises to us in the South East, it appeared very plain, and had a long tail (tis said to be 34 degrees).

This was Halley's Comet.

On the other side of the world, James Cook's notes show that for him the transit began at 9 minutes, 21 seconds and 50 mins. In the morning.

Captain Cook's Journal:

'Thursday 1st June 1769. This day I sent Lieutenant Gore in the Long-boat to York Island [off Moorea] with Dr. Monkhouse and Mr. Sporing (a Gentleman belonging to Mr. Banks) to observe the Transit of Venus....Mr. Banks and some of the Natives of this Island went along with them.

Friday 2nd June. Very early this morning Lieutnt. Hicks, Mr. Clerk, Mr. Petersgill* and Mr. Saunders, went away in the Pinnace to the Eastward, with orders to fix upon some convenient situation on this Island (Booarou) and there to observe the Transit of Venus.

Saturday 3rd. This day prov'd favourable to our purpose as we cold wish, not a Clowd...and the Air perfectly clear, so that we had every advantage we could desire in Observing the whole of the passage of the Planet Venus over the Sun's disk: we very distinctly saw an Atmosphere or dusky shade around the body of the Planet which very much disturbed the times of the contacts ...' he adds Dr. Solander, Mr. Green and himself differed 'much more than could be expected' in the timing. Captain Cook is describing the famous "black drop" caused by fuzziness at the rim of Venus, a fault thought to lie in the human eye. *Captain Cook's misspelling of Petersgill's name was a slip. The Wine Vaults next door to his house in Mile End were called Messrs. Petersgill and Curtis.*

Pickersgill describes the Transit and the weather in glowing terms, 'so that if the Observation is not well made, it is intirely owing to the Observers.'

22

THE *ENDEAVOUR* COMES HOME
Summer 1771

It was Mr. Banks' voyage! It was a triumph. The goodhearted 28 year old Joseph Banks, who had funded three years of his own research, travelled thousands of miles around the world, and certainly lost his virginity, if he had taken it, left the ship on 12th July at Deal and raced up to London. He was already rich, now he was feted and would be the talk of Europe but, most important to him, he would dumbfound the circles of scientists, whose admiration for his work he most wanted. Joseph Banks had been a botanist from the age of 14. Now he had brought home more plants, birds and other creatures than any one naturalist had ever seen. He was to remain a scientific observer of nature all his life; that was his life's purpose. But, for the moment, he was young, he was praised, fashionable, idolised, he and the botanist Solander were invited everywhere. They were to receive honorary degrees from Oxford. They were be presented to the King, one week before James Cook as was proper, due to Mr. Banks' social standing. The excitement created in London by this new sensation was intense.

~~~

Meanwhile Lieutenant James Cook anchored the ship and took up

Endeavour's paperwork. He had an earnest desire to see his wife and sons. On that 12th July, he had reported his ship's arrival in the Downs to the Admiralty Secretary, and his intention to come at once to the Admiralty Office with journals and charts and ship's papers. The State and Condition statements for the *Endeavour* showed he had 19 sick men, very little food left, and the Condition of the Bark was Foul. That same day he sent the Admiralty his reports on their Scurvy experiments.

It was a captain's lot to fill-in forms, and more forms, the whole Navy worked on written orders and reports so, next day, he received from the Admiralty instructions to proceed up river to Galleons Reach, and there await further orders. By 18th July the Navy Board were ordered to pay-off *Endeavour's* men at Woolwich. All the officers' journals were to be delivered to the Admiralty. By the last day of July, James Cook was writing from his own home in Mile End, to the father of the two dead Monkhouse brothers, offering his assistance. He was still there happily with his family on 2nd August when he received his letter of approval from the Lords of the Admiralty, saying 'they have great satisfaction in the account you have given them of the good behaviour of your Officers and Men and of the chearfulness and alertness with which they went through the fatigues and dangers of their late voyage.'

The same Admiralty letter also confirmed Richard Pickersgill as ship's Master. His official Warrant was signed next day. James Cook immediately applied for the promotion of Richard Pickersgill, Master, as 'deserving of a Lieut.t's. Commision.' In all he recommended five men for promotion.

As for the young boys, Isaac Smith his wife's relation, and Isaac Manley possibly George Jackson's, he added, 'their behaviour merits the best recommendation,' even though he knew they were both too young for preferment. But what of his own position on the Lieutenants' ladder of promotion?

He visited Lord Sandwich one Sunday morning early in August, Was George Jackson there too? Later that day, sitting in Wills Coffee House in Charing Cross, James Cook wrote to Joseph Banks:

'Your very obliging letter was the first Messenger that conveyed to me Lord Sandwich's intentions. Promotion unsolicited to a man of my station in life must convey a satisfaction to the mind that is better conceived than described.' He adds that Lord Sandwich had renewed his promises to him and showed his approval of the voyage. 'The reputation I may have acquired on this account by which I shall receive promotion calls to my mind the very great assistance I received therein from you,' he tells Mr. Banks, his social superior.[1]

Perhaps Joseph Banks smiled wryly when reading this, when remembering their wrecking on the Great Barrier Reef. He had been warm in his bed when *Endeavour* struck the rock, struggling to the quarterdeck he could hardly keep his feet, the ship's planks were floating away in the moonlight. They were too far off shore, there were not enough boats to save most of the crew. Death, he trembled, now stared them in the face. Yet James Cook and his seamen stayed perfectly cool, though they forgot to swear and, given a hidden stroke of luck - a lump of coral stuck in the hole in the hull – they were able to rescue the ship. Within a few weeks they were again in imminent danger of shipwreck on the reef, and Banks later wrote that the fear of death was bitter. Once more, good seamanship saved them. Joseph Banks owed his life to Lieutenant James Cook, and he knew it.

On 29th August came James Cook's promotion 'to be Commander Scorpion.'

It is at this point we realise that the Admiralty already intended to have a second voyage. *Scorpion* was a normal 'holding' ship, but they made a definite attempt to keep the vital men of *Endeavour's* crew together. *Endeavour,* foul as she was, they demoted to use as a store ship, so a new 'holding' posting was needed to keep the team together. Richard Pickersgill was appointed Lieutenant of the *Scorpion* the same day, 29th. A Warrant on 18th September for Stephen Forwood to be posted to the *Surprize,* was altered that same day by the Admiralty, to send him as gunner to *Scorpion,* and there were others, probably at James Cook's speedy request. It was not possible for a man to get his back pay, until he was posted into another ship. 'Holding ships' were a neat way.

The sloop *Scorpion* was lying at Deptford. With the promotions and pay resolved, and extremely broad orders to make observations and surveys of coasts, it was time for the officers to have home leave. Richard Pickersgill had applied earlier to the Admiralty for leave to go into the country for the recovery of his health. James Cook replied formally as *Scorpion's* Commander that he had no objection, and on 23rd September, the Admiralty Secretary ordered Commander Cook to give Pickersgill leave. By 23rd October, Richard Pickersgill was at Great Ayton staying with Ralph Jackson. Until his Lieutenant came back to the ship, Commander Cook had no official leave, even though he was at Mile End with his family and exceptionally busy.

Richard Pickersgill came originally from West Tanfield; not the Tanfield of Tyne coal, but a small pretty village, along the river Ure, in delightful countryside just north of Ripon in Yorkshire. When these ocean sailors came home from sea after three or more years, they often found their families gone, parents, brothers or sisters dead and no home to return to. It was a combination of politeness, pity, social obligation and interest in their adventures, which made sea-going families invite these sea officers on a round of visits. Of course it was enchanting for the young ladies of the family. And was of the few ways a sailor could meet someone to marry.

On Wednesday 23rd. October, 1771 Ralph Jackson walked out with his gun in the morning. Then 'Sist.Estr.Neice Mary Jackson & … and Mr. Rd. Pickersgill' came.

'Thursday the Twenty Fourth. Mr. Pickersgill (who lately sailed round the World with Capt. Jas. Cook, Messrs Banks, Solander etc. 2nd Voya[ge]) and I went out with our Guns, spent the afternoon at home with Cousn. Foster etc. who are come to stay with me.'

Niger was considered Mr. Banks' first voyage
Endeavour was considered Mr. Banks' second voyage.

Ralph was obliging his brother George, and George's manservant John Lee, Pickersgill's uncle. It may be that Richard Pickersgill had replaced his uncle by escorting Esther Jackson and 17 year old Pally, on their journey north. We can guess Ralph was eager to hear about the whole scientific voyage. We cannot imagine old Mr. Cook at Ayton being less than fully congratulated about the achievement of his son James. Surely Pickersgill would not go to Ayton without calling upon James Cook's father, at least with a letter? William Wilson too would be professionally curious to hear of the Pacific discoveries, and to find out about the new navigation out of the Pacific by the Endeavour Strait.

What did Ralph Jackson make of Pickersgill, described by a colleague as 'a good Officer and astronomer, but liking ye Grog.'?

On the Friday they both breakfasted at Mr. Turner's at Kirkleatham. On Saturday they went shooting and Mr. Consett and three Miss Consetts drank tea. On Sunday the two men walked to the banks of the river before dinner. On Monday while Pickersgill went to dine at Colonel Hale's, Ralph dined at Mr. Harrison's with Mr and Miss Boulby and Mr. Wardell among others, and we can picture him regaling Thomas Wardell with tales of the Pacific and admiration of James Cook, so that Mr. Wardell could retell these to the ailing William Sanderson. Tuesday morning found the two young men shooting again. It seems Ralph thought it was the way to keep his guest happy, and maybe sober; but by Thursday he had worn them both out, 'we were very much fatigued' he says. Next day they switched to greyhound coursing.

Among the locals there was great interest in Mr. Pickersgill; on Saturday they dined at Mr. Smith's at Marske who, with Mr. Wardell, returned to Normanby with them and stayed two days, probably just to listen. Pickersgill had great adventures to tell them.

These Cleveland people were some of the earliest to hear a first hand account. Thomas Wardell in his emotional fashion probably could not wait to get back to Staithes to tell Mr. Sanderson all he had heard of amazing places and of James Cook's authority. Pickersgill was being wined and dined at a socially high level.

By 4th November, the weather had turned stormy, the day was dark, the two men dined at Mr. Marwood's. Storms kept them closeted in the house, though despite severe rain, wet weather, they managed to dine and drink tea at William Wilson's at Ayton and spend an evening at Mr. Consett's. Sunday 10th was Ralph's duty to attend church with his tenants. The drink was running out. Next day he took his eye off his man George Kirtley, leaving him at Guisborough to measure off 40 gallons of gin at Mr. Danby's, whereupon George got drunk, he and the little bay mare fell on their road home and were both lamed. George survived Ralph's anger but, in spite of the kind ministrations of Willy Child, the poor little horse died of her wounds.

One sadness of James Cook's return to great praise, was that his patron Squire Thomas Skottowe had died a few months earlier. Now the Squire's household effects were to be sold, his old Manor house to be let, and Tuesday 12th November was the date fixed for the sale 'Mr. Pickersgill came to me at Ayton, attended Mr. Skottow's Sale', says Ralph, and we wonder if James Cook ended up with a momento of the squire? Old Mr. Skottowe's house now belonged to Captain Nicholas Skottowe, and he agreed that Ralph's sister Esther Jackson could leave her little home on Ayton Green, move in and rent it. Ralph helped her to take a 'Schedule of some Fixtures she is to have the use of in late old Mr. Skottowes House.' The weather was very wet, it continued to rain and rain. Richard Pickersgill must have longed for sun, tropical islands, white sands and bright blue sea.

Sunday was a gloomy bad day, depressing views, and Ralph received a letter in the evening from Yarm, saying there was too much fresh water in the river, and much damage by it at Yarm and elsewhere. This was more like it for two enthusiasts! So the next morning Ralph and Richard Pickersgill rode down to see at Thomas

Appleton's where they met a 'dismal Scene, the shore of the River being covered with dead Cattle, Sheep, Wreck of Houses, & Household furniture timber etc. Robert Jackson sent 8 horses & I attended myself all day,' Ralph says, 'with the assistance to get above high water mark the wreck etc.' For three days he worked in the mud at his tenant Appleton's helping to rescue beasts, goods and vast amounts of timber. He sent a subdued George Kirtley to Yarm to Cousin Foster's with provisions, 'that Town having suffered very melancholy by the late Flood, many Houses were washed in which several Lives were lost; Provisions & furniture were swept away.'

That day, Wednesday 20th November, he writes;
'Mr. Pickersgill went away (for London) on board of a Sloop in the river, he had stayed with me ever since Wednesday 23rd. ulto…... '

Richard Pickersgill's commission as 3rd Lieutenant came through on 29th November and he joined *Scorpion* on 11th December. The *Scorpion* was riding at the Nore an anchorage in the lower Thames.

On December 14th James Cook applied in writing at the Admiralty office:

'Sir,

Having some business to transact in Yorkshire, as well as to see an aged father, please to move My Lords Commissioners of the Admiralty to grant me three weeks leave of absence for that purpose.'

Commander and Mrs. James Cook came north for Christmas. The invitations were in place. On Christmas Eve Ralph went to stay at Ayton. Next day the family went to church in the morning. No doubt the Cook family did too. Standing in the wet churchyard afterwards, we can imagine the gold braid and buttons of the officers, the gentlemen in their velvets and lace, the ladies in silk and wool and furs, the bows and politenesses, the quick words of admiration whispered to old Mr. Cook, the self-contained measured pride in the new hero. Here was a Great Ayton man who had done exceptionally well. We can picture the tall James Cook, dignified and pleased, a bluff William Wilson, the fat and wheezy Augustine Skottowe, the quiet Ralph, and his sisters full of interest and grace. Next day they would have James Cook to themselves to hear from him directly the tale of his adventure. Ralph's journal entry reads:

'Thursday the Twenty Sixth; spent all day at Ayton; this afternoon came Capt. Jas. Cook (& his Wife) whose Father lives in that Town, this Gentleman lately Comanded the King's bark, the Endeavour on her voyage round the World & made many discoverys in the South Seas & in high Southern Latitudes, Mr. Pickersgill (John Lee's Nephew) see Octo.23rd Pa.57. went in the same vessel as Master's Mate; he and his Wife lay'd at Bro. Wilson's.'

During this visit to Cleveland, we know that James Cook visited John Walker of Whitby. We do not know if he visited Mr. Sanderson at Staithes. William Sanderson was ill, his health was rapidly failing. On 13th December Ralph had been down to see him with Mr. Wardell and sat there an hour 'he not being well'. Maybe William Sanderson had mixed feelings about James Cook. He had himself worked hard, fulfilled his public duties as constable, and done his utmost to educate and promote his own sons. William junior had died on the *Royal George,* John had taken over the business, Bob was away at school, Augustine and Isaac sons still at home. Yet the poor farm lad who had worked for him in the shop, was now a celebrated Royal Navy commander, being presented to the King.

The experienced sea-going men of Yorkshire had no doubts about James Cook's worth. He had succeeded beyond anything they could dream of. He had lost many of his crew as fully expected, but he had brought his ship home. What's more, Joseph Banks Esq. the close friend of Constantine Phipps of Mulgrave Castle (whose father held the lordship and was landlord to many at Staithes) had come back alive. What would local reaction have been if James Cook had come home without Banks? Constantine Phipps was a sailor, salty tongued, he would have known the risks, but most likely have boisterously cursed James Cook, demanded the details and, if not satisfied, cut the new Lieutenant Cook out of the Navy, with the help of his friend Lord Sandwich. In Cleveland he would have made a friendly reception almost impossible. James Cook would know all this perfectly well. So would George Jackson.

But, for the moment, James Cook had succeeded. A second voyage was already planned, his core crew kept together, another two ships being chosen.

The coming *Resolution* voyage, would be his personal success which turned James Cook from heroic commander of Mr. Banks' voyage into a hero in his own right.

Ralph Jackson's Journal 1771

Wednesday the Twenty Fifth, being
Christmas-Day I went to Ayton Church in the forenoon.
Thursday the Twenty Sixth; spent all
day at Ayton; this afternoon came Capt.ᵒ Jas Cook (& his
Wife) whose Father lives in that Town, this Gentleman
lately comanded the King's Bark, the Endeavour on
her Voyage round the World & made many discoverys

POLITICS?

The question as to whether James Cook's appointment to command the *Endeavour* was political? Yes. In so far as he clearly belonged to a group led by Lord Sandwich's influence. In so far as his own patrons and friends were Lord Sandwich's group of friends, like George Jackson and Palliser; that was how politics worked then. Admiral Charles Saunders politics were slightly different, yet he too was a friend of George Jackson. When in London, Ralph Jackson would walk along to Saunders' house to call on the Admiral. Palliser and Admiral Saunders had been together in the heat of the battle for Havana, they were close friends, so much so that Charles Saunders left Palliser £5000 in his will. Politics was all a matter of faction, of groups of influence. The Admiralty had their own MPs in Parliament representing coastal towns. The purpose of an MP was to serve the interests of his constituency voters, by bringing them lucrative contracts and pensions. And placing their family members in positions on ships, in the Customs, government offices and sinecure jobs where they need not always turn up. This system got so bad that Lord Anson, and at times Admiral Saunders acted against it. Posting men on dangerous ships for political reasons undermined the efficiency of the Royal Navy. Incompetence at sea was fatal.

Another danger was that as Lord Sandwich rose and fell politically, so did his friends. There is evidence that George Jackson was hedging his bets by mixing with the money men of the Treasury.

We have to ask, what other political groups were placing men on the *Endeavour*? Almost certainly the Treasury and Bankers had a say. So far I would pinpoint 2nd Lieutenant Gore.

There is a lot more research to be done on this point.

Notes and References

ABBREVIATIONS:

BL   British Library.
B/B   Baker/Baker papers. Univ. of Durham.
DNB   Dictionary of National Biography (old version).
RJJ   Ralph Jackson's Journal, Cleveland Archives.
NA   National Archives, Kew, London Office.
NYCRO North Yorkshire County Record Office.
T&WA Tyne & Wear Archives, Newcastle upon Tyne.
WL&PS Whitby Literary and Philosophical Society.

Chapter and Reference Number

Ch. Ref.

1   1   Ralph Jackson's Journals by courtesy of Cleveland Archives, Middlesbrough

2   1   Dr. Bisset 1762 Essay on Medical Constitution of Great Britain BL 1609/5464

3   1   Ralph Ward's Diary 1754-5 Yorkshire Archeological Society Record Series Vol.CXVII (1952) Leeds

     2   Memorial Deed NYCRO Reel 280 3rd July 1759

     3   Mary Ward's will. 1721 Cleveland Archives vol 77/127

     4   Will NYCRO Feb. 1771 MIC.274. 2 vol. p 213

4   1   Administrative Bond: Cleveland D. Probate documents. University of York, Borthwick Institute of Historical Research. 1728 and B/B Index vol.I 1/2

     2   Seaton Manor By-Laws 1704-56 NYCRO ZPA

     3   Wapentake is the later spelling of the Anglo-Saxon administrative area. Weapontake is its meaning so clearer for readers

     4   Church Terrier: Borthwick Institute. R III M.xxiii 3 and MB.S.1741

     5   James (alias Thomas) Appleton RJ Journal page 92 1764

6 Thomas Wardell letter Baker/Bakers papers University of Durham Paleography Department

7 B/B papers letter T. Wardell to G. Baker

8 Church terrier Borthwick Institute. Diocesan Register RIII M 5 XXIII, Borthwick Institute. 1749

9 Dictionary of National Biography (older version)

5 1 DNB and Burlington Magazine 'A Man of Talent' Agostino Carlini 1718-1790. Part 2: Marjorie Trusted

2 'Hogarth Vol.II' Ronald Paulson in Daily Gazette 5th March 1736

3 Will printed in Gentleman's Magazine 1762 page 208. Supplement of Horace Walpole's letters. Vol.1 p.209/10 Feb.1778

4 *Hardwick*. BL L/MAR/B 198/M, 198/N

5 Collinge JM

6 RJJ August 1774
  Scorpion Captain's Log.ADM.51/872-4

6 1 Apprentice Bonds Cleveland Archives

2 NA. E.190 250/5 *Darling* Outwards 1749 Dec. 24th

3 Transports ADM 106/274

4 Protection Certs. (Apprentices) 1740-46 ADM 7/393-4

5 Surtees Society 197 Liddle-Cotesworth letters

6 NYCRO Reel 270/40 18th February 1752

7 R. Weatherill. P 26-30

8 *Endeavour* small Whitby ship. T& WA 541/12 1749

9 NA E190 246/10 Whitby Inward 1746

7 1 *Freelove*: not to be confused with ships sailing same dates: Thomas Canaway of Shields' *Freelove* or Wm. Hill of Whitby's smaller *Freelove*. T&WA 541/12

	2	T&WA. GU/TH Trinity House 111/5, 111/6
	3	NA. E.190 246/10 Whitby Inwards
	4	J. Carmichael 1881 p 63 Newcastle City Libraries
	5	Henry Simpson's Book. WL&PS
	6	Muster Rolls printed by Whitby Literary and Philosophical Society1990, Plus originals
	7	*Three Brothers*: not to be confused with ship sailing same dates: *Three Brothers*: Frederick Baukes, of Frisland.(Dutch)
	8	T&WA, Newcastle. Primage Dues.109/6 1750-1751
	9	WL&PS for Bosun see Whitby ships *Unity* and *Fell*
8	1	B. Pares p.267
	2	University of Durham. Paleography Dept. Baker/Baker papers. Letter TW to GB 8th Sept.1760
	3	*Hopewell*: Muster Rolls
	4	*Swan*. One of Whitby's 'Bird' ships: *Nightingale, Vulture, Lark*, etc.
9	1	*Friendship*: ship shares. T&WA 541/9-12
	2	Spell/knor: a game: golf x hockey. Still played in the Yorkshire Dales
	3	*Experiment T&WA and RJJ*
	4	Letter Cook to Ellerton: Beaglehole p 445 original at Dixson Library M5 Q 141
10	1	Professor Rogers figures p.608 based on Glete
	2	T. Wardell letter: B/B papers 11th March 1756
	3	'Political and Social Letters of a lady of the Eighteenth Century 1721-1771.' Ed. E & D Osborn p.122
11	1	*Solebay* Log. ADM 51/908
	2	Chivecto: Transports ADM 106/274 could mean Chebucto

12	1	Knox. Beaglehole

12 1 Knox. Beaglehole

2 John Hale NYCRO ZFM MIC 1419 typewritten copy. Diary (1890) of Gen. John Hale before Quebec 1759

3 Kipps: bibliography

4 Kitson: bibliography

5 Ellinor Jefferson's death 1757
The weather was bad. Mr. Ward, grieving, but could not get his boots on to ride to Staithes

6 Collville letters to Cleveland: ADM 1/482
25 Oct. 1762 and 30 Dec. 1762

7 Elisabeth Batts. Baptism Register St. John's Wapping. Ref. PB/JNZ x 89/157. Guildhall Library London. Samuel Batts will. National Archives. Probate 11/719

13 1 Log of *Suffolk*. BL East India Dept. L/MAR/B 397/A & 397/D. Battle f.89. and 116v

2 *Suffolk* battle carved on William Wilson's memorial at All Saints church Great Ayton. The 'blob' at the top of the crest is most likely the Elephant and Castle

3 Read herring: red herring is dried smoked herring

4 Log of *Pitt BL* India Dept East.L/MAR/ 525 A-C to I

5 The French Neptune is a famous book of maps which includes the Dauphin Map. BL

6 A bronze copy of the medal showing Hercules holding up the world is at the British Museum

7 *Royal George* Log. BL East India Dept. old 17H NA.11/951 Surgeon 19th Sept. 1769: Morse Vol V

8 Journal to Eliza: Laurence Sterne 1768

9 Eliza left on '*Earl of Chatham*'

14 1 Fry: biography

2 Kempenfelt Richard: 1718-1782. Served in East Indies with Pocock from 1746. Charnock vi p.246

	3	Royal Historical Society Camden 4th Series. Vol.8 1971 'Documents illustrating the British Conquest of Manila 1762-3' ed. NP Cushner. Inc. Orme MS. ADM 1/102 (2) f.53-6, f.63-6
	4	Anderson. F. & McNeill J.P.
	5	Adam Boulby's Whitby ship, Tryton, a transport at Havana was lost. Her captain Henry Gofton died
	6	Ge. Hale letters NA. Chatham papers 17/8-27
15	1	Natral Is. Cook to Graves 1st March 1764
	2	Commercial: ADM 12/52/22 April 1763-1768 1764 Jan.4th. 10/- a day. ADM 12/57
	3	Shallop (chaloupe) French design open boat with one mast
	4	Ship's time is noon to noon. Pm is the day before in civil time. There was one evening where they could have met
	5	Map: WS 1763: BL 45.K.17(11)
	6	Map: JC 1768: Add.MS.7085.f 2
	7	RHS. 4th Series. Vol 8
	8	Sea surge: 'The Defender' Magazine of the RAF Conningsby Spring/Summer 2003 p.28-29
16	1	W. Child grandson: Cleveland Archives. Ward-Jackson Docs. William Ward's will 231. 6th March 1717/8
	2	Charles Bisset: 'A Treatise on the Scurvy 1755. John Rylands Library. (J.10.92/B 38) Captain Cook's Journal App.III part 2 p.1456
	3	A. Home: Beaglehole p.44/45 Captain John Knox: Historical Journal 1769
	4	Gentleman's Magazine Octo. 1791 p.588

17	1	J.Wesley's Autobioraphy
18	1	Fry: autobiography
	2	D. Batts shipwright. Often pronounced Bates. Unable to fix this link.
	3	Royal Society letters. Appendix III to Fry. Europe Magazine Vol 42 p.325 Brevet: Kippis London 1788 p.15/16
19	1	Opera: Kitchin
20	1	Gentleman's Magazine Vol. 34 p.590 Vol 39 p.68-71, 537-8 Notes and Queries 1st Series Vol I (1850)
	2	Modestus GJ Anecdotes
21	1	Petersgill: Land Tax. Metropolitan Archives
22	1	Letter Cook to Banks: Beaglehole p.275

BIBLIOGRAPHY:.

Anderson Fred: Crucible of War 1754-66 pub. Faber & Faber 2000 BL

Beaglehole JG: The Life of Captain James Cook.

A & C Black Ltd London 1974

Black, Professor Jeremy: 'Pitt the Elder' British Library Series.

Charnock John: Biography of the Navy 6 Vols. London. 1794-8

Collinge J M: Office Holders of the Navy Board and Admiralty 1660-1836 pub.1978. Durham University Library.

Cook Captain James: Journal ed. WJL.Wharton, London 1893

Duckett Sir George: 'Duchetiana' BL 9917 H1 and

Anecdotal Reminiscences BL 10825 (i)3

Fordyce: Sailing Directions/Map of the Tyne 1690

Newcastle City Library L.912 T987

Fry HT: Alexander Dalrymple 1737-1808 and the expansion of British Trade, London 1970

Graham J.Geofrey : 'Captain James Cook "Servant and Friend" of Captain John Walker' 1986

Graves John: The History of Cleveland 1808

Hardy's Register of Shipping: BL East India Dept.

Hamilton: History of the Grenadier Guards 1872 8 Vols.

Herring Archbishop: Visitation Returns 1743

Yorkshire Archeological Soceity p 8/9, 56/7,62/3,169/70,190/1

Keay J: East India Company

Kippis Andrew: Life and Times of Captain James Cook. London 1788

Kirkleatham Hospital Register: Cleveland Archives.

Kitchin Professor C (emeritus): Transit of Venus
pub. Astronomy Now June 2004 p.63-7

Kitson Arthur: Captain James Cook, London 1907

Metropolitan Achives London: Land Tax 5808 & 5810 (1781) Petersgill.

McLaren DG: Nutrition and its Disorders 2nd Ed. 1976 pub. Churchill, Livingstone, Edinburgh.

McNeill JP: Atlantic Empires of France and Spain 1700-1763

1985 University of North Carolina

Morse HB:Chronicle of the East India Company Trading to China Vol ii 1740-1760

Namier Sir Lewis: The Structure of Politics at the Accession of George III 2nd Ed. London MacMillan & Co. Ltd. 1957

O'Brian P: Joseph Banks a Life. 1993 pub UK Collins Harville.

Ord JW: History and Antiquities of Cleveland. London 1846

Pares B: A History of Russia pub Methuen London 1962 UP46

Parish Registers: Cleveland Archives.

Puntis Dr. John & Grace Rollaston: Scurvy Sailors and the Yorkshire Navigator. Pub. Yorkshire Medecine/Winter 1999

Rogers Professor NAM: The Command of the Ocean 1649-1815

(2004) Penguin Group Allen Lane.)

Smith Raymond: Sea Coal for London pub. 1961

Young Rev. George: History of Whitby Vol 2 p 850-7 The Life and Voyages of Captain James Cook. London 1836

Victoria County Histories: Middlesbrough Central Library.

Weatherill Richard: The Ancient Port of Whitby and its Shipping pub. 1908

Wilson Ben: Empire of the Deep 2013 Weidenfeld and Nicholson: 2014 Orion

Ships

Merchant ships:
Anne & Elizabeth
Ann
Ann <£ Mar)'
Blessing
Brilliant Star
Britannia
Brotherly Love
Constant Jane
Darling
Dolphin
Earl of Pembroke .
(Endeavour)
Endeavour
Edward
Elizabeth
Esther
Experiment
Fortune
Freelove 1
Freelove 2
Free Mason
Friendship
FriendGlory
Good Intent
Goodwill
Greyhound
Hannah
Herring
Henry & Esther
Henry & Mary
Hopewell 1
Hopewell 2
Hull Merchant
Ingeber Maria
Isabel & Mary
Jane
John
John & Dorothy
John & Jane
Jos. & Samuel
Joseph & Ann (Elizabeth)
Liberty
Loyal
Lyon
Maty
Mary & Jane
Mellnion
Midsummer
Nautilus
Neptune
Noble Hope
Olive Branch
Owners Adventure
Revolution

Richard &Ann
Ridley
Robert & Jane Roberts
Rose
Satisfaction
Sea Adventure
Sea Nymph
Streatlam Castle
Success
Sukey & Nelly
Swan
Trew Briton
Tryall
Thomas & Richard
Three Brothers 1
Three Brothers 2
Three Brothers 3
Three Sisters
Tryton
Unity
William & Jane
William & Mary

Royal Navy Ships
Antelope
Argo
Centurian
Chesterfield
Diana
Diligence
Dolphin
Dragon
Eagle
Elizabeth
Endeavour
Falmouth
Gosport
Grenville
Guernsey
Hampshire
Hunter
Lark
Leostoffe
Medway
Monmouth
Namur
Neptune
Niger
Northumberland
Panther
Pearl
Pembroke
Porcupine
Prince Edward
Prince of Orange

Princess Amelia
Ramilles
Resolution
Richmond
Royal William
Salisbury
Satisfaction
Scorpion
Seaford
Seahorse
Solebay
Squirrel
Stirling Castle
Surprize
Terpsichore
Thylow
Tweed
Zephyr

East India Company Ships
Bridgewater
British King
Bute
Caernarvon
Cuddalore
Drake
Earl of Chatham
Great Britain
Godolphin
Guardian
Houghton
Lord Clive
LondonPacquet
Northumberland
Princess Augusta
Prince George
Pocock
Protector
Stafford
Success
Suffolk
Warren
Warwick
Wincheslsea
York

French ships
Due d'Acquitaine
Compte de Provence
Esperance
Sylphide

Spanish ships
Santissima Trinidada
Philippina

GENERAL INDEX

347

351

ACKNOWLEDGEMENTS

I would like to thank for their patience and help:

British Library East India Dept. staff at London, Euston Road and Blackfriars Road.

Borthwick Institute, University of York.

Captain Cook and Staithes Heritage Centre.

Cleveland Archives and Middlesbrough Central Library.

North Yorkshire County Record Office, Northallerton.

Tyne and Wear Archives, Newcastle upon Tyne.

Victoria and Albert Museum, London, sculpture staff.

Especially: Professor K. Pratt, (emeritus) University of Durham and Jill Renny – for their helpful criticism and support.

Not forgetting the staff of Moorleys Print & Publishing Ltd.

And all the tourists to Staithes, who asked questions which made me search for correct answers: 1982-2010.

Jean Eccleston LL.B is wearing the
Staithes Bonnet, by permission of
the last women of the fishing families
of Staithes who wore it every day. It
is designed to keep fish scales off the
hair, and to stop fish water running
down their necks when carrying huge
baskets of fish on their heads.
Rest in Peace Florries, Eva, Elsie, Edith,
Ruth, Olive, Lizzie, Annie and others.